From the Ruins of Enlightenment

Caspar David Friedrich (1774–1840), *Two Men at the Sea*, 1817. 51 × 66 cm (20 × 25.9 in.). Staatliche Museen zu Berlin, Nationalgalerie.

From the Ruins of Enlightenment

BEETHOVEN AND SCHUBERT
IN THEIR SOLITUDE

Richard Kramer

The University of Chicago Press CHICAGO AND LONDON

The University of Chicago Press, Chicago 60637
The University of Chicago Press, Ltd., London
© 2023 by Richard Kramer
All rights reserved. No part of this book may be used or reproduced in any
manner whatsoever without written permission, except in the case of brief
quotations in critical articles and reviews. For more information, contact
the University of Chicago Press, 1427 E. 60th St., Chicago, IL 60637.
Published 2023
Printed in the United States of America

32 31 30 29 28 27 26 25 24 23   1 2 3 4 5

ISBN-13: 978-0-226-82163-4 (cloth)
ISBN-13: 978-0-226-82164-1 (e-book)
DOI: https://doi.org/10.7208/chicago/9780226821641.001.0001

This book has been supported by the John Daverio Fund of the
American Musicological Society, supported in part by the National
Endowment for the Humanities and the Andrew W. Mellon Foundation.

Library of Congress Cataloging-in-Publication Data

Names: Kramer, Richard, 1938–, author.
Title: From the ruins of Enlightenment : Beethoven and Schubert in their
solitude / Richard Kramer.
Description: Chicago : University of Chicago Press, 2023. |
Includes bibliographical references and index.
Identifiers: LCCN 2022000987 | ISBN 9780226821634 (cloth) |
ISBN 9780226821641 (ebook)
Subjects: LCSH: Beethoven, Ludwig van, 1770–1827—Criticism and
interpretation. | Schubert, Franz, 1797–1828—Criticism and interpretation. |
Music—19th century—History and criticism. | German poetry—
18th century—Musical settings. | Enlightenment—Austria—Vienna.
Classification: LCC ML410.B42 K67 2022 | DDC 780.92/2—dc23
LC record available at https://lccn.loc.gov/2022000987

♾ This paper meets the requirements of ANSI/NISO Z39.48-1992
(Permanence of Paper).

For Lewis Lockwood

Contents

PREAMBLE: 1815 AND BEYOND ∗ *ix*

In the Silence of the Poem

CHAPTER 1
Hölty's Nightingales, and Schubert's ∗ 3

CHAPTER 2
Herder's Hexameters, and Beethoven's ∗ 33

CHAPTER 3
Whose *Meeres Stille*? ∗ 49

Toward a Poetics of Fugue

CHAPTER 4
Gradus ad Parnassum: Beethoven, Schubert, and
the Romance of Counterpoint ∗ 73

CHAPTER 5
Con alcune licenze: On the Largo before
the Fugue in Op. 106 ∗ 96

Sonata and the Claims of Narrative

Beethoven
CHAPTER 6
On a Challenging Moment in the Sonata for Pianoforte
and Violoncello, Op. 102, No. 2 ∗ 121

Schubert

CHAPTER 7

Against the Grain: The Sonata in G (D 894)
and a Hermeneutics of Late Style * *137*

Last Things, New Horizons

CHAPTER 8

Final Beethoven * *161*

CHAPTER 9

Posthumous Schubert * *189*

POSTSCRIPT: . . . AND BEYOND * *218*

*Acknowledgments * 223*
*List of Tables, Examples, and Figures * 227*
*Works Cited * 231*
*Index * 243*

✳ PREAMBLE ✳

1815 and Beyond

Enlightenment as ruin? It may seem a bit coy to invoke an Enlightenment whose identity, as I proposed in the book that precedes this one—"In Search of the Enlightenment Moment," as it goes in the subtitle[1]—could only be intuited from some music whose wit and irony play against the conventions of a Classical style in bold improvisations performed at the edges of linguistic coherence.[2] However one comes to visualize, to hear, this enlightenment moment, in its multifarious flights within and against the reasoned and reasoning culture of the later eighteenth century, the adventure itself was brief, as must be all such moments. For Beethoven and Schubert, the music of these grand figures of the Enlightenment continued to resonate, but now as models, extricated, even deracinated from the vibrant theater of ideas that gave them life. Walter Benjamin's compelling meditation on the work of art in its state of "technological reproduction" has much to tell us about this distancing from origins. He writes of the work of art in "its presence in time and space, its unique existence at the place where it happens to be"; and then: "that which withers in the age of mechanical reproduction is the aura of the work of art."[3] Writing earlier on Baroque

---

1. That earlier book is *Cherubino's Leap: In Search of the Enlightenment Moment* (Chicago: University of Chicago Press, 2016).

2. Is there a grander evocation of Enlightenment esprit than Stacy Schiff's *A Great Improvisation: Franklin, France, and the Birth of America* (New York: Henry Holt, 2006), whose bracing title does justice to the text that it promises? It doesn't tax the imagination to recognize in the founding of the republic from its chaotic origins that same vigorous engagement in the improvisatory act that invigorates the music of those very years.

3. I take these passages from the version of his text that was published in the *Zeitschrift für Sozialforschung* 5/1 (1936), and translated here in *Illuminations*, ed. Hannah Arendt and trans. Harry Zohn (New York: Schocken Books, 1969), 220–21.

Trauerspiel, Benjamin reads its allegorical transformation of the figures and events of the past as a ruin in which the aura of historical authenticity fades away. "Allegories are, in the realm of thought, what ruins are in the realm of things." The concluding lines of his essay now speak to a historical process in which the work itself becomes increasingly distant from its authentic moment, from the aura of its conception: "[The] restructuring of material content into truth content makes the weakening of effect, whereby the attractiveness of earlier charms diminishes decade by decade, into the basis for a rebirth in which all ephemeral beauty completely falls away and the work asserts itself as a ruin."[4] It is this apperception that seems to me to illuminate that moment in 1815 in its vision, distorted in the manner of all historical reimaginings, of a Europe before the Revolution, before its reconfiguration at the Congress of Vienna. This is the year from which these following chapters take their cue. Here, too, there will be no endeavor to fix in the severe language of definitions the historical moment evoked in the music contained within these pages.

For Beethoven, educated among the *Illuminati* in Bonn, drawn to its ideals and caught up in the fever of revolution in the 1790s, there is yet a sense of composing against the Enlightenment, a coming to his own terms with the exemplary music of Mozart and Haydn, of Emanuel Bach and Gluck. By 1815, the immediacy of these iconic figures had grown more remote in the longer perspective of a turbulent history, and even magnified in that distance, while the esprit that defined Enlightenment aesthetics was lost; only a nostalgia for it remained, in tension with the deeper personal explorations of what would come to be called late style. In 1815, Schubert was absorbed in, if not consumed by, poetry. This engagement with the poem drove his music often to the limits of tonal intelligibility, as it would have been understood by his contemporaries. But in another sense, Schubert was composing against the commanding figure of Beethoven: "Secretly, in my heart of hearts, I still hope to be able to make something of myself," he is alleged to have confessed to Josef von Spaun, "but who can do anything after Beethoven?"[5]

---

4. The essay is "The Ruin," excerpted by Benjamin from his doctoral thesis *Origins of the German Trauerspiel*, now in translation in *The Work of Art in the Age of Its Technological Reproducibility, and Other Writings on Media*, ed. Michael W. Jennings, Brigid Doherty, and Thomas Y. Levin; trans. Edmund Jephcott, Rodney Livingstone, Howard Eiland, et al. (Cambridge, MA: Belknap, 2008), 180–86.

5. *Schubert: Memoirs by His Friends*, collected and edited by Otto Erich Deutsch (New York: Macmillan, 1958), 128, translation slightly altered. The passage, which Spaun does not date, is weighed against the complex evidence of the relationship between the two

Those two men who gaze out at the infinite expanse in Caspar David Friedrich's haunting landscape in our frontispiece: they stand together but apart, and we cannot know how alone they are in their thoughts, in their view of that vast, empty landscape of the future—a future anchored in the past, one might infer from their deliberately outmoded apparel.[6] Beethoven and Schubert, too, stood together and apart—together, only in an imaginary poetic sense, as citizens of a Vienna that flourished as a center of European cultural life and then as the seat of the Congress whose complex political machinations would establish, for better and worse, boundaries and alliances that would configure the European community for a full century. In the studies that follow, Schubert and Beethoven, immersed in their work, seem oblivious of the momentous events around them—setting aside those overtly political works that Beethoven composed to mark the occasion.[7] Like the figures in Friedrich's landscape, in its suggestion of some allegorical subtext, so too the figures of Beethoven and Schubert in 1815 would each envision a solitary future, each rooted differently in their sense of the past.

Against this vision of a traumatized Europe coming to terms with the Napoleonic experience, with the remaking of boundaries, of tenuous political alliances, and the attendant anxieties of cultural disturbance, the lens on my old Leica (pretending to see two hundred years back) would narrow its focus, capturing the tendril of the tiniest mountain blossom, its eye-blink shutter freezing the vibrating throat of a nightingale—a modest conceit that means only to suggest something of the ironic discrepancies

---

composers in Maynard Solomon, "Schubert and Beethoven," in *19th-Century Music* 3, no. 1 (November 1979): 114–25.

6. "The two men in capes and berets . . . are wearing the medieval garb that had been revived by German radical students in the wake of the Napoleonic Wars and the ensuing ultraconservative reaction of Metternich and the Congress of Vienna," writes Sabine Rewald, in a note to this painting, noting further that Friedrich was here "deliberately ignoring the 1819 royal decree that forbade this dress." See *The Romantic Vision of Caspar David Friedrich: Paintings and Drawings from the U.S.S.R.*, ed. Sabine Rewald (New York: Metropolitan Museum of Art, New York/Chicago: Art Institute of Chicago, 1990), 74.

7. Those "political" works have undergone a radical reappraisal in the past twenty years. For a good sense of the issues, see Nicholas Mathew, "Beethoven and His Others: Criticism, Difference, and the Composer's Many Voices," *Beethoven Forum* 13, no. 2 (Fall 2006): 148–87, with its nuanced critique of, among other studies, the ideas set forth in Nicholas Cook, "The Other Beethoven: Heroism, the Canon, and the Works of 1813–14," in *19th-Century Music* 27 (2003): 3–24. The brief for a reevaluation of those works composed for or about the events around the Congress of Vienna is set forth in Mathew's impressive *Political Beethoven* (Cambridge: Cambridge University Press, 2013).

that hold in precarious imbalance the inner workings of the artist's mind against the broad brush of historical narratives too often oblivious of such interiorities.

In this Viennese moment of 1815, the camera would find Beethoven, copying out a handful of poems from Herder's *Blumen aus Morgenländischen Dichtern gesammlet* (flowers gathered from poets of the Orient) and composing two of the most touching. This modest project, begun in 1813 but coming to a head in 1815, suggests a turn inward, away from the grand spectacle at which Beethoven was an occasional participant, and a view outward, beyond the cultural boundaries that otherwise defined his work. In its sweep across Vienna, the camera would locate an eighteen-year-old Schubert a few miles away, in the midst of his manic sprint, in this, his most prolific year, through the composition of some 174 settings from the works of thirty-four poets.[8] And of course there were other projects to contend with: two piano sonatas, the String Quartet in G Minor, the Third Symphony, two masses; and from 8 May until 31 December, four operas: two one-acters: *Der vierjährigen Posten* (Körner) and *Fernando* (Stadler); then, Goethe's *Claudine von Villa Bella*, begun on 26 July; and finally, *Die Freunde von Salamanka*, in two acts, on a libretto by Mayrhofer, completed on the final day—31 December!—of this exhausting year. For a few weeks in May, the concentration on the poetry of Ludwig Hölty is intense, unfolding in a sequence of songs that suggest something more ambitious, the music seeming to reverberate within a cluster of nine poems which, in Schubert's ordering, have a story to tell.

A few weeks later, it was a poem of Goethe's that caught Schubert's eye: *Meeres Stille*, the music written out on 20 June in a setting boldly conceived, then radically revised, its boldness somewhat tempered, the very next day. Simultaneously, or nearly so, Beethoven was finishing his work on a very different reading of the poem, and of its sequel, *Glückliche Fahrt*, for orchestra and chorus.[9] When Steiner got around to publishing it in 1822, the work bore an effusive dedication to Goethe, to whom a copy of the score

8. The calculation is drawn from Otto Erich Deutsch, *Franz Schubert: Thematisches Verzeichnis seiner Werke in chronologischer Folge* (Kassel: Bärenreiter, 1978), taking into account more recent adjustments in the dating of a number of songs.

9. The two poems were always published together on a single page, "eng verbundene Gegenstücke," in the words of Erich Trunz, in *Johann Wolfgang von Goethe: Werke, Hamburger Ausgabe in 14 Bänden*, I, Gedichte und Epen 1, ed. Erich Trunz (Munich: C. H. Beck, 1981), 642. I retain the spelling *Meeres Stille* in deference to the spelling in the first editions of the works by both Beethoven and Schubert, and indeed to Goethe's original spelling. A hyphenated version is found as well in the autograph of the Schubert song that was sent to Goethe. The more common spelling is as a single word, unhyphenated.

was sent, together with a provocative epigraph from Homer's *Odyssey*, apparently at the initiation of the print run. There will be more to say about this very copy, and what it might tell of that magnetic appeal that drew Beethoven to Goethe and his works virtually throughout his life. Goethe's appeal to Schubert was skewed rather differently, a generational difference underscored by the advent of the New Romantics and a fresh understanding how, in particular, the expressive valence of harmony could invigorate, if not disturb, the grammar and syntax of the poetic utterance. In a boldly courageous essay, the young Adolph Bernhard Marx turns a review of the publication of Beethoven's *Meeres Stille und glückliche Fahrt* into a platform for a critical examination of this very issue, questioning whether those unspoken ideas built into the silent interstices of a poem such as *Meeres Stille* are compromised by a music that seeks to embody them.

In 1815, the turn away from the grand public genres led Beethoven to a new engagement with the poetic works of such iconic figures as Klopstock, Herder, and Goethe, a project whose difficulties Beethoven was the first to recognize. It was a year that witnessed another turn as well, this to a renewed engagement with fugue, a project beset with self-imposed difficulties. Beethoven's obsession with the problem of fugue, and indeed with the rigors of Fuxian counterpoint, may be traced to his studies with Haydn and Albrechtsberger shortly after his arrival in Vienna in 1792. How this aspect of the compositional spectrum infiltrated the fabric of his later music is explored in a probe into the first movement of the String Quartet in E♭ Major, op. 74 ("Harp"), and, in a later chapter, the Allegretto ma non troppo of the String Quartet in F Minor, op. 95 ("Serioso"), both composed in 1810. For Schubert, on the contrary, fugue seems to have been an obligatory and largely archaic exercise, and it is only in his final weeks, inspired by the last quartets of Beethoven, that Schubert felt impelled to consult the theorist Simon Sechter for instruction.[10] The implications of this decisive turn will continue to generate much speculation toward a music that Schubert did not live to compose.

For Beethoven, the allure of fugue intensifies in the years between 1815 and 1817. The "Allegro fugato" finale of the Sonata for Piano and Cello in D Major, op. 102, no. 2 (1815), is an exercise in the deployment of fugal procedure that will strain the conventions of an earlier practice, even in the extreme technical and intellectual demands that breach the limits of

---

10. See, for one, Christa Landon, "Neue Schubert-Funde: Unbekannte Manuskripte im Archiv des Wiener Männergesang-Vereines," *Österreichische Musikzeitschrift* 24 (1969): 299–323; reprinted in *Christa Landon zum Gedächtnis* (Private printing by Bärenreiter, 1978), esp. 37–39.

the genre beyond the social civilities of earlier duo sonatas. "Con alcune licenze" (with some license), Beethoven might have written here.[11] And indeed these very words are inscribed at the outset of the "Fuga a tre voci," the finale of the Piano Sonata in B♭, op. 106, forcing the boundaries of fugue beyond its conventional limits. But it is the brief and idiosyncratic Largo that precedes it, a fantasy-like excursion into the idea of fugue, a page that Charles Rosen thought "one of the most astonishing in the history of music," that inspires this probe into the reaches of Beethoven's inner workshop.[12] Its three fragments of antique counterpoint are as memorable for their incisive clarity as they are for their evocation of earlier musics, as though in search of a subject for the monumental fugal finale to come. I interrogate these passages both as exemplars of Beethoven's perception of an inherited contrapuntal practice, and as stations in an improvisation that will bring the music to the threshold of the main business of his *Fuga*. Two fascicles of remarkable sketches for this music, now in the William Scheide collection at Princeton University, have much to tell us about the evolution of Beethoven's thinking. How do we accommodate these sketches into our understanding of the work, and what, precisely, can we learn from them?

Back to 1815, and op. 102. "Sonate anfangs August 1815," Beethoven scribbled on the autograph of the D-Major Sonata. Entries for it are to be found in an important sketchbook, also in the Scheide collection at Princeton, which contains as well sketches for the Piano Sonata in A, op. 101, and for the song cycle *An die ferne Geliebte*. These, together with the first of the cello sonatas of op. 102, whose autograph is inscribed "Freje Sonate" (free sonata!), and dated "1815 gegen Ende Juli," constitute what Sieghard Brandenburg recognized as "a turning point toward the style of Beethoven's final years."[13] I've noted the significance of the finale of op. 102, no. 2, as an antecedent to the great fugue in op. 106 that will follow in 1816/1817. But it is the expansive opening theme of its first movement that is the topic of this chapter, and in particular the gapped octave A that provokes the cellist to some serious decision-making at the crux of its opening phrase. When it returns in the recapitulation—rather, at the moment when it ought to

---

11. On this point, see Carl Dahlhaus, "'Von zwei Kulturen der Musik': Die Schlußfuge aus Beethovens Cellosonate opus 102, 2," *Die Musikforschung* 31 (1978): 397–405, esp. 403–4.

12. Charles Rosen, *The Classical Style: Haydn, Mozart, Beethoven* (New York: W. W. Norton, 1971; expanded edition, 1997), 429.

13. Sieghard Brandenburg, in the commentary to Ludwig van Beethoven, *Klaviersonate A-dur Opus 101: Faksimile nach dem Autograph im Besitz des Beethoven-Hauses Bonn* (Munich: G. Henle, 1998), iii (German) and xiii (English).

have returned—a strikingly bold interaction between the keyboard and the cello exaggerates the impact of that original octave, posing a formidable challenge not only for the players who must negotiate this treacherous passage but for the critical mind apprehending the significance of a transformative moment.

As if to enact a swerve away from the sharp angularities, the aphoristic dislocations of the music of Beethoven's last decade: this, it might be argued, is one way to hear Schubert's capacious Sonata in G Major (op. 78), composed in 1826. It was Adorno who brilliantly articulated the antitheses that characterized Schubert's music against the late music of Beethoven. Against the dissociated elements that only the integrity of Beethoven's *Persönlichkeit* could control, Adorno posits the notion of landscape, subjectified in its resident wanderer, and of the "lyrical," concepts newly conceived, and problematized, in the music of Schubert.[14] No music comes closer to exemplifying these qualities than op. 78, in the "molto moderato e cantabile" of its spaciously paced first movement. The ominous inflection within its first page on a deep, pedal-toned dominant on F♯ is set alongside *Schwestergruß*, the somber threnody in F♯ minor that Schubert composed in 1822 on the death of the poet Franz Bruchmann's sister. Here again is that dark tonality at the core of those Hölty settings of 1815. But the point here is to seize the implicit resonance between song and sonata. Poem and song, on the one hand; sonata, on the other: how are they to be reconciled? A conundrum resistant to answers, the asking yet brings us closer to the poetics within Schubert's music.

With the death of Schubert a mere two years after the composition of op. 78 comes the inevitable mythologizing of the life, and the construction of a "late" style. Two final projects enrich this story: the three last piano sonatas, published eleven years after Schubert's death; and the formidable draft, unfinished at Schubert's death, for the opera *Der Graf von Gleichen*. The publication in facsimile of the drafts for the sonatas (1987) and of the fragmentary autograph manuscript of the opera (1988) inspires reflections on the substance and significance of what would become valedictory works and the historiographic weave that was to follow.

---

14. "Damit wird der Anteil des Subjektiven und Objektiven am Lyrischen, das Schuberts Landschaft ausmacht, neu bestimmt," as Adorno puts it in his pathbreaking essay of 1928, first published as Theodor Wiesengrund-Adorno, "Schubert," *Die Musik* 21, no. 1 (1928), 1–12; reprinted in Adorno, *Moments musicaux* (Frankfurt am Main: Suhrkamp, 1964), 18–36. "The subjective and the objective, forming Schubert's landscape, constitute the lyrical in a new way." The translation is by Jonathan Dunsby and Beate Perrey in *19th-Century Music* 29, no. 1 (2005): 3–14, esp. 7.

A primary occupation of the summer of 1827, *Der Graf von Gleichen* was evidently the topic of several conversations with the composer a year later, in the final days before Schubert's death. Fragmentary as much of the opera remained, there are long stretches more fully drafted. The allusions to earlier music—to Beethoven's *Fidelio*, most prominently—are pronounced and significant, extending even to the recycling of two of Schubert's songs: the early *Wonne der Wehmuth*, returning to a Goethe phase in August 1815, and, most enigmatically, *Die Nebensonnen*, from Müller's *Winterreise*. By some lights the most compelling of Schubert's operatic projects, *Der Graf von Gleichen* remained a fragment, and we are left to work through the mysteries hidden in its unfinished condition.

Schubert's last sonatas have from the outset puzzled their earliest students. Robert Schumann, to whom these sonatas were dedicated upon their publication by Diabelli in 1839, was initially skeptical of the "allerletzte" (the very last) with which the sonatas were advertised on the title page. "Whether they were written on the deathbed or not, I cannot say," Schumann wrote, hearing in them a manner that seemed resistant to Diabelli's ascription of ultimate lateness.[15] Those preliminary drafts for the three sonatas, rare specimens among Schubert's surviving manuscripts, offer glimpses of a mind engaged in the fleet spontaneity of creation—in conspicuous contrast to the sketching and drafting, intense and obsessive, all too evident in the prodigious portfolio of workshop papers that Beethoven amassed throughout his life.

It is precisely this intensity, the seizing possession of the compositional challenge evident in the sketches and drafts for the two last quartets, op. 131 in C♯ minor and op. 135 in F major, and the difficult (and still controversial) decision to compose a new finale for the Quartet in B♭, op. 130, replacing the monumental "große Fuge," that will engage us in the chapter given to Beethoven's final months. Finally, it was again Diabelli who, in 1838, published what he claimed to be Beethoven's "letzter musikalischer Gedanke" (his last musical thought): the fragmentary movement of a string quintet, offered in a transcription for piano. The few inauspicious sketches for it that have survived, and the fragment that Diabelli published (of which we have only his transcription), merely complicate the effort to situate the music of these final months within the theorized reach of a late style.

As we shall learn in that final chapter, Schubert, having gained access through Anton Schindler to the manuscripts for *Fidelio* shortly after Beethoven's death, and having scrutinized the maze of alterations that he encountered, was said by Schindler to have questioned the efficacy of all

---

15. For the citation, see chapter 9, footnote 5.

that labor, thinking the first idea to be "just as good as the emendation."[16] And yet there is some evidence, in the scribbled, penciled messiness in a few of Schubert's latest manuscripts, to suggest that the exposure to the graphic evidence of Beethoven's labor was a humbling if not quite transformative experience. And while we are hostage to Schindler's often exaggerated if not demonstrably fabricated accounts of his relationship with Beethoven, there is yet a hint of something genuine in the image of Schubert poring over these *Fidelio* manuscripts. Whatever we might wish to imagine as to the significance of the moment, it is perhaps enough to register this affecting, if inscrutable, meeting of minds.

*

It was in 1815, Beethoven drawn increasingly to the stripped-down eloquence of voice and fugue, to the fractured concision of aphorism that we have come to recognize as the benchmarks of his late style, that Schubert was discovering the luxuriant expanse of a tonal imagination in bold exploration of the poetic. A modest purpose of this book is to read between its lines the ironies of a history that will have placed in propinquity of time and place the coalescing of these two wondrous congeries of music. We are returned to that opening question: whether this moment in 1815 might be understood as a phoenix-like rebirth from an Enlightenment in ruins, its aesthetic sensibilities no longer in play. Engaging the poetry of Hölty and his contemporaries, Schubert does not seek a rapprochement with an outmoded theater of *Empfindsamkeit* foreign to him, but reads beneath the surface of the poem, hearing the deeper harmonies embedded in its darker conceits. For Beethoven, a child of the Enlightenment, to compose Herder in 1815 was rather an act of retrieval, of rediscovery, even if the studied return to a *Volksweise* had more to do with a turn in his own journey into lateness.

Where their trajectories now and then touch, the temptation to attribute influence and its attendant anxieties is intensified. The pursuit of influence is however a perilous conquest, fraught with speculations around the slippery notion of intention. We serve these two projects, Schubert's and Beethoven's, more justly in allowing them autonomy, admiring the singular achievements of two musicians radically different in temperament, in training, in pedigree. In Caspar David Friedrich's desolate landscape, those solitary figures alone in their thoughts may be apprehended as surrogates for

---

16. Schindler's account is given in *Schubert: Memoirs*, 315. The matter is taken up below, in chapter 4.

the human experience, the blank slate of a mind coming to terms with its environment. Alone with their imaginary lovers and demons, in the aching solitude of their music, Beethoven and Schubert create their own worlds, within and against a Viennese culture at once repressive and robust.[17] This is the veiled subtext in the pages that follow.

17. The poetic condition of solitude and Schubert's expression of it in two remarkable songs is the topic of a searching essay by Susan Youens: "The 'Problem of Solitude' and Critique in Song: Schubert's Loneliness," in *Schubert's Late Music: History, Theory, Style*, ed. Lorraine Byrne Bodley and Julian Horton (Cambridge: Cambridge University Press, 2016), 309–30.

In the Silence of the Poem

✳ CHAPTER 1 ✳

Hölty's Nightingales, and Schubert's

Here, then, is Schubert in the spring and summer of 1815, thoroughly absorbed in the composition of lieder. To make one's way through this cataract of song, leafing through Eusebius Mandyczewski's magisterial edition for the old Breitkopf *Gesamtausgabe*, where the songs follow upon one another as in a calendar of their composition, is to be privy to a diary of sorts, an intimate daily record of Schubert's encounter with his poets. He tends to read them in clusters and to compose in spurts: on 27 February, he sets three poems by Goethe, including the remarkable *Nähe des Geliebten* (written out three times), and then *Sängers Morgenlied* by Körner. On 1 March, there are two more by Körner, another two on 12 March, and a few others later in the month and into April. May was an astonishing month: here are settings of three poems by Matthison and three by Schiller. And then Schubert discovers the poetry of Ludwig Hölty: two settings on the 17th, three on the 22nd, one each on the 24th and 25th—with the tempestuous setting of Goethe's *Rastlose Liebe* tossed in on the 19th. On the 26th—a Friday—there are two more by Hölty and four by Körner. Work resumes on Monday: two more poems by Hölty. This hyperactivity continues through a prolific June and July, including a dozen settings of the poetry of Kosegarten. And then comes a remarkable few days in August, returning to the Goethe project: a song on the 18th, five more on the 19th, and a sixth, *Wonne der Wehmuth*, on the 20th, and finally, *Wer kauft Liebesgötter?* on the 21st. Klopstock makes an appearance in September: one setting on the 12th, five more on the 14th, two of them written out twice, and on the 15th, the very grand *Dem Unendlichen*, it, too, written out twice (and then, a decade later, a third time).

All this rote chronicling means only to illuminate the unflagging rhythm

4 CHAPTER ONE

of Schubert's 1815, the voracious reading, one poet after another; the rush of composing, as though the act of reading would metabolize simultaneously into music. There is an exploratory aspect to the journey: Schubert seeking an entry into the poem, finding his voice. And then there's the voyeur's gaze in our own reading, in its quest for the ravishing phrase, for a song that sets itself apart, for a sighting of the inner Schubert, where something in the poem fires the music in the mind toward the outer limits of expression.

In these formative years, Schubert's explorations often seek out the poets of an earlier generation, among them the classicizing *Oden-Dichter* of the 1770s. In the pantheon of Schubert's poets, alongside Goethe and Schiller, to whose poetry Schubert returned throughout much of his life, Ludwig Hölty occupies a special place. Eighteen of his poems were set in 1815, and another thirteen in 1816. But it is the rich vein of Hölty settings composed in May 1815 that suggests, even in the culling of the poems, a concentration that probes beyond a casual reading. In the following listing—shown in table 1.1—the dates are taken from Schubert's autograph manuscripts.

Moving beyond the pastoral domesticity often encountered in Hölty's poetry, these are poems tinged in the darker tones of love and death, decay and beauty. The *Nachtigall* poems are especially poignant.[1] That they touched a raw nerve in Schubert is evident in the breathless outpouring of song with which *An die Nachtigall* springs open, as if to capture the rush implicit in the imperative *Geuß* that sets the poem in motion, establishing the urgency of Hölty's lovesick nightingale. (The song is shown as ex. 1.1; the poem is given in the Appendix.) In case we hadn't gotten the message inscribed in these passionate phrases, Schubert guides us toward a performance: "Unruhig, klagend," he writes, and then "Im Zeitmasse wachsend bis zur Haltung"—restless, complaining; increasing in tempo up to the fermata. Not even an initial tempo here, as though the impetuosity of the music won't allow us to set our internal metronome. The choice of key further charges the atmosphere. F♯ minor is striking not because it holds some arcane tropological significance for Schubert, but because it places the music outside the conventional modes of pathos, to some darker place, refusing G minor and those other, more familiar tones of lament. Schubert seems to want the piercing sharp side, something that gets the music closer to this "schmelzend Ach," capturing the nightingale's "tonreichen Schall," its tone-drenched resonance penetrating to the depths of the soul: "denn

1. In a touching letter to his intimate friend Charlotte von Einem, Hölty writes of his intention to write a number of "Maiengesänge, wenn die Nachtigall wieder im Blütenbusche schlägt" (May songs, when the nightingale once more sings in the blossoming bush). Letter of 6 February 1775, in Ludwig Christoph Heinrich Hölty, *Werke und Briefe,* ed. Uwe Berger (Berlin: Aufbau, 1966), 252–53.

Hölty's Nightingales, and Schubert's 5

TABLE 1.1. Schubert autographs of Hölty settings

		Location[1]		Voss 1804
17 May	*An den Mond*, D 193. Geuss, lieber Mond	*Wsb 74/c*	F minor [A♭ major]	207–8
17 May	*Die Mainacht*, D 194. Wann der silberne Mond	*Wsb 74/c*	D minor	103
22 May	*An die Nachtigall*, D 196 Geuss nicht so laut	*Missing*	F♯ minor	158
22 May	*An die Apfelbäume, wo ich Julien erblickte*, D 197	*2nd half: Pbn 275*	A major	115–16
22 May	*Seufzer*, D 198 Die Nachtigall singt überall	*Pbn 275*	G minor	193–94
25 May	*Auf den Tod einer Nachtigall*, D 201 Sie ist dahin	*Missing* Fragment, in a copy by Ferdinand Schubert	F♯ minor	141
26 May	*Das Traumbild*, D 204A Geliebtes Bild	*Missing* Only the final strophes of the poem, and none of the music, have survived in Schubert's fragmentary autograph.[2]	—	153
29 May	*Der Liebende*, D 207 Beglückt, beglückt	*Wgm 215*	B♭ major	247–48
29 May	*Die Nonne*, D 208 Es liebt' in Welschland irgendwo	Fragment: *Wsb 75/c; Wnb 19487* Revised and completed on 16 June: *Wsb 2065*	A♭ major F minor	41–45

1 Pbn = Paris, Bibliothèque nationale; Wgm = Vienna, Gesellschaft der Musikfreunde; Wnb = Vienna, National Bibliothek; Wsb = Vienna, Wienbibliothek im Rathaus
2 The date is drawn from a copy of the *Jägerlied* (D 204) that occupied the recto of a torn sheet containing strophes 6–9 of the Hölty poem. See Franz Schubert, *Neue Ausgabe sämtlicher Werke*, Serie IV/8, pp. xxxi, 206, 265; and Otto Erich Deutsch, *Franz Schubert: Thematisches Verzeichnis seiner Werke in chronologischer Folge*, p. 137. Like *Jägerlied*, *Das Traumbild* was very likely a brief duet "for 2 voices or 2 horns," each part on its own stave and without a piano accompaniment.

schon durchbebt die Tiefen meiner Seele dein schmelzend Ach." No innocent instrument of a romanticized nature, Hölty's nightingale, a favored singer in his poetry, is rather an invasive Cupid (the god of desire) whose "liebentflammten Lieder"—songs aflame with love—awaken the lovesick poet.

EX. 1.1. Schubert, *An die Nachtigall* (Hölty, rev. Voss), D 196.

Ironically, these words igniting Schubert's feverish phrase are not altogether Hölty's. Titled originally *An eine Nachtigall, die vor meinem Kammerfenster sang* (To a Nightingale That Sang at My Bedroom Window), the poem was left in a fragmentary state, and completed only at Hölty's death (of tuberculosis at age twenty-seven) in 1776 and radically revised by Johann Heinrich Voss, a close friend of Hölty's and the editor of his poems even during his lifetime.[2] Hölty's fragment is shown alongside Voss's revision in the Appendix. In a strophe that Schubert could not have known, Hölty writes:

Sie tönen mir, o liebe Philomele,	O beloved Philomel, your singing
Das Bildniß wach,	awakens in me the image
Das lange schon, in meiner	that has long slumbered
trüben Seele,	
Im Schlummer lag.	in my troubled soul.

2. For a study of Voss's rewriting of Hölty's poetry, see, for one, Wilhelm Michael, *Überlieferung und Reihenfolge der Gedichte Höltys* (Halle: Max Niemeyer, 1909), 29–49.

In the well-traveled version of the Greek myth, the savagely raped and mutilated Philomel, made speechless, is transformed into a nightingale, whose eternal song, if it awakens images of the beloved, will always sing the baleful accents of its tragic story. Naturalists will remind us that it is only the male nightingale who sings. If the poets of the eighteenth century would not have known this, the hint of an inverted gendering is yet suggestive.

Something of this mythic Philomel sings through in Schubert's opening phrases. We're confronted, as we often are in such songs, with the conundrum of agency. The poet and the sleepless lover are indistinguishable. But what is this music that she (or is it he?) sings—these vaulting phrases, bracketed to a slow chromatic turn around C♯ and D? Is it a reverberation, an unconscious echo of what he hears the nightingale sing, or merely an unhinged response inspired by its song? Perhaps we are meant to hear the two as inseparable, the poet becoming the nightingale, the nightingale the poet.

In release of the tonal tensions that crescendo into the fermata, the music of the second quatrain finds composure, and a proper (and moderating) tempo: *mässig*. Here, the nightingale recedes, and then re-emerges in the piano, its fluttering song finally giving out: *abnehmend*, writes Schubert (at least as transmitted in one copy), as though scripting its actual flight away, vanishing into the bush—"entfleuch, entfleuch!"

A few days later, in the midst of this Hölty session, Schubert sketched out a remarkable fragment, unknown to Mandyczewski and indeed to any of us until a copy by Schubert's brother Ferdinand (who, imprudently, gifted away the autograph manuscript in 1855) was rediscovered in 1970, and subsequently published in the *Neue Schubert Ausgabe* in 2002.[3] *Auf den Tod einer Nachtigall* (On the Death of a Nightingale), the song is titled.[4] The music (shown in ex. 1.2) intones its dark threnody again in F♯ minor, its dactyls calling to mind the second strophe, in C♯ minor, of *Der Wanderer* (composed a year later)—"Die Sonne dünkt mich hier so kalt." The similarity is fleeting. Hölty's quatrain, in its complex syntax, at once pleonastic and paratactic, draws forth an extraordinary phrase, embodying the articulations of the poem in a run of harmonic inflections: isolating "die Sängerin" in C♯ minor, as Hölty isolates her in the short four-syllable line, yet enacting the enjambment that presses the phrase toward its anguished "sie ist dahin." The inner-voice E♯ that disturbs C♯ minor seems imperceptibly to

---

3. The discovery owes to P. Reinhard van Hoorickx, in "Two Essays on Schubert," *Revue Belge de Musicologie* 24 (1970): 81–95.

4. Again, the title owes to Voss. Hölty's title is *Elegie auf eine Nachtigall*.

EX. 1.2. Schubert, *Auf den Tod einer Nachtigall* (Hölty, rev. Voss), D 201. Fragment.

* Hölty: Ton

raise the temperature of the phrase, even as it moves away toward a dominant on E. At "sie ist dahin," the dominant is made to flinch, the singer finding an F♮ against E and D♯. The piercing loss is made palpable. (The poem is given in the Appendix.)

Almost a full year later, on 13 May 1816, Schubert returned to this poem, in what the estimable Walther Dürr (the editor of the songs in the *Neue Schubert Ausgabe*) calls a "zweite Bearbeitung"—a second arrangement—suggesting that our fragment in F♯ minor was only a preparatory run-up to something finished—and indeed, Dürr publishes the fragment as an *Anhang* to the later song.[5] In this new setting, now in A minor, the anguish of the poet's lament seems leached away, along with the acuity of F♯ minor, and what remains is a very pretty song quite oblivious of Hölty's inner *Nachtigall*—and oblivious too of Schubert's extraordinary fragment. Do we read this new setting as a pointed refusal of the earlier one, a radical swerve in how the poem is to be read? Or had Schubert merely forgotten the experience of those weeks in 1815 when Hölty's poem elicited a very different response?

The traces of memory, however, find expression at unsuspected moments. Among the impressive sonata movements of these early years, a fragment in F♯ minor (D 571), composed in the summer of 1817, is extreme in its touching intimacy, its obsessive octave C♯s seeming to recall the opening of the song fragment. (Its opening bars are shown in ex. 1.3.) The sonata exhales its narrative in an expansive breadth, as though to release the compression locked into Schubert's reading of Hölty's poem. The intensity of the poem is transformed, the echo of its music still evident. Even the first dissonance in the song, the D♮ against G♯ in its second measure, is made over in the sonata into a gesture with thematic ramifications, embedded first in the shadowy accompaniment at m. 4, and then, pointedly, in the theme at m. 8, the D itself gradually taking over the tonal discourse of the exposition, finally leaning against C♯ to effect the *da capo*.

That these two expressions of Schubert in search of some inner place remained fragments is worth a moment's reflection. Did they touch uncomfortably close to some internal experience? Did Schubert think their intimacies inappropriate for public exposure? One other work in F♯ minor, one that Schubert did indeed finish, must figure here. This is the song *Schwestergruß* (D 762), composed in November 1822, on a poem by Franz Bruchmann. As though remembering the sonata fragment, its barren octave C♯s intone yet another somber threnody, its tolling bells measuring out the poet's grief on the loss of his young sister, Sybille, with whom

---

5. D 399. *Franz Schubert: Neue Ausgabe sämtliche Werke* [hereafter: NSA] IV/10.

EX. 1.3. Schubert, Sonata in F♯ Minor (July 1817), D 571. Fragment.

Schubert was close.[6] (This exceptionally moving work will reveal more of its mystery in chapter 7—and see examples 7.3–4—where it is heard as a gloss of the great Sonata in G Major, D 894.) Here, too, the traces of memory are powerful.

To situate these nightingale songs of May 1815 at the root of some evo-

---

6. The song was evidently composed for performance at a "Schubertiada" (as it was called) planned for 10 November by the two surviving Bruchmann sisters.

lutionary process that would attribute meaning to Schubert's F♯ minor is to suggest, however tentatively, the subtleties, the sensibilities of a mind reaching across genres, gathering within itself the traces that formulate an essence: not a topic, in the commonplace vocabulary of music analysis, but something given less to specificity than to a deeper well of expression.

Against this vertical, so-to-say synchronic hearing of F♯ minor as a thing in itself, I'd like to explore its place and function from another perspective, along a horizontal axis that would return these songs to the immediacy of a Hölty project in May 1815. But a project of what kind? In the chronology of Schubert's autographs—and here, please refer again to table 1.1—a sequence of songs unfolds that only vaguely insinuates poetic continuities and contiguities. Here is Schubert, antennae raised, leafing through Voss's 1804 edition of the Hölty poems, a volume that Voss constructed from a miscellany of earlier sources from which no semblance of an integral poetic narrative could logically be inferred. And so it is suggestive to find in Schubert's sequence a liaison, fragmentary as it may be, of images and allusions that suggest something more. *An den Mond* opens with that tellingly charged imperative: "*Geuß*, lieber Mond," the flood of moonlight gushing forth as will the song of the nightingale. The word that Hölty uses to open *An die Nachtigall* is *Gieß*—from the verb *gießen*, to pour. Voss, rewriting the poem, prefers *Geuß*, an Upper German [= Oberdeutsch] variant of the imperative, and that of course is the word that Schubert saw.[7]

The lunar atmosphere is sustained in *Die Mainacht*: "Wenn der silberne Mond durch die Gesträuche blinkt." And it is here that Hölty's nightingale emerges: "Selig preis ich dich dann, flötende Nachtigall, weil dein Weibchen mit dir wohnet in *einem* Nest (Happily I praise you, nightingale, in your flute-like song, for you share with your partner a *single* nest)," its domestic bliss echoed in the closing lines of *An die Nachtigall*: "Fleuch, Nachtigall, in grüne Finsternisse ins Haingesträuch, und spend' im Nest der treuen Gattin Küsse"—fly off into the green darkness, into the wooded thickets, and in your nest bestow kisses to the faithful spouse.

A grain of narrative suggests itself in the song that follows, Hölty's touching ode to those apple trees under which the poet earlier caught a first glimpse of the beloved. In *An die Apfelbäume, wo ich Julien erblickte*—to the apple trees where I caught sight of Julia—the figurative, allusive world of the nightingale is brought to human dimension. (The song is shown as ex. 1.4; the poem is given in the Appendix.) The play of tenses is subtle:

---

7. This older form, recognized in Adelung's *Grammatisch-kritisches Wörterbuch des hochdeutschen Mundart* (1811), is no longer to be found in Grimm's *Deutsches Wörterbuch*, first published in 1854.

EX. 1.4. Schubert, *An die Apfelbäume, wo ich Julien erblickte* (Hölty), D 197.

(continued)

the here and now of a solemn murmuring and a *Gesangeston*—the voice of song—sounds with a shiver through the treetops that shade the walk where once the blissful frenzy of first love, "bang und wild," seized the heart. If Hölty's language evokes a confusion of anxiety and uncoiled passion, it is the thread of voice, this poetic *Gesangeston*, that insinuates itself in Schubert's song in its first two strophes, and again in the fourth. Whose voice? we might well ask. Coming to the song from *An die Nachtigall*, as the ordering in Schubert's autograph argues, it is difficult to put out of mind *its* opening line: "Geuss nicht so laut der liebentflammten Lieder tonreichen

EX. 1.4. *(continued)*

Schall *vom Blüthenast des Apfelbaums hernieder, o Nachtigall!"*—these love-enflamed songs that spill from the blossoming bough of the apple tree. In the faintly erogenous scenario that Schubert's sequence imposes on these songs, we listen with Hölty's lover for those "liebentflammten Lieder," the voice of the nightingale continuing to sound through this *Gesangeston*, now tempered and domesticated, the F♯ minor of its complaint now modulated to A major, the figure itself hovering unseen behind the poet's language.

Inspired by Hölty's third strophe, the music finds its moment of ecstasy. The shift of tense has a bit of mystery about it, the memory of

that first passionate encounter brought up into the present. The lovers have been long apart. Will they reunite? Hölty's irresolute subjunctive invites the question. Schubert's liquid phrase captures the urgency of this imagined moment in its seductive voicing, its prosody freed from the solemnity—and the A major—of the first strophes. The unexpected, heart-stopping turn to C major at "Engel[s]kuss" gives way to a diction that approaches the freer expression of recitative, while the harmonies beneath move from a touch of G minor through to a remarkable Neapolitan sixth, *ffp*.

That touch of G minor, as it turns out, portends the key of the third song in Schubert's autograph of 22 May.[8] *Seufzer*, it is called, in the Voss *Umdichtung* of a poem that Hölty titled *Die Nachtigall*. (The opening of the song is shown as ex. 1.5; the poem is given in the Appendix.) "Die Nachtigall singt überall," the poem begins—the nightingale sings everywhere—and it is not until its final lines that we learn that its amorous song brings only heartbreak to the poet's forlorn lover. In the original language of Hölty's poem—which again Schubert cannot have known—the complaint of the lover is raw and exposed:

> Mit frohen Sinne
> Hört jedermann
> Den Vogel an.
> Ich, leider, nicht,
> Es bricht, es bricht,
> Trotz allen Fugen,
>
> So Vögel schlugen,
> Vor Minneschmerz
> Mein armes Herz.

In rough translation: "Everyone happily hears the nightingale's song. I, alas, do not. It breaks, it breaks—despite all those fugues that the birds sang—my poor heart breaks with the sorrows of love." Not until its final word does the poem reveal the vulnerable subject of this deeply felt lament, and we can only wonder whether the unmediated language of Hölty's poem would have challenged Schubert to a music rather less constrained than it is by the formal propriety of Voss's retelling, his lonely wanderer a tame surrogate for Hölty's heartbroken lover.

Following hard upon the placid A major of *An die Apfelbäume*, the restless, anxiety-driven G minor of *Seufzer* seems to play out an event with narrative implications, that lost moment *between* the glow of love consummated and the cruel reality of a broken heart. In very different contexts, poetic and musical, Schubert will years later enlist G minor to again shatter the lover's fantasy: there is the explosive *Eifersucht und Stolz* in *Die schöne Müllerin* (1823); and then, in the proposed reordering of the Heine songs, *Der Atlas* (in *Schwanengesang*, 1828), sounding its brutal exclamation point at the

---

8. Only one page of what must originally have been a bifolium has survived. The leaf, containing the final thirteen bars (mm. 16–28) of *An die Apfelbäume* on its recto and *Seufzer* complete on its verso, is now at Paris, Bibliothèque nationale, Ms. 275. The missing leaf would have contained the autograph of *An die Nachtigall* and, on its verso, the first fifteen bars of *An die Apfelbäume*.

EX. 1.5. Schubert, *Seufzer* (Hölty, rev. Voss), D 198.

(continued)

EX. 1.5. (*continued*)

end of a neurotic romance.[9] Here, in Schubert's imaginative configuration of a Hölty script, the loose strands of narrative intertwine and disentangle.

Three days later, Schubert thought to follow *Seufzer* with *Auf den Tod einer Nachtigall*, as though to deepen the lover's sense of alienation with a song less of mourning than of a nostalgia for a music no longer there. From the poet's here and now, a scene is conjured in memory: a perfect evening in May, the lovers, a *Jüngling* and his bride, enraptured by the nightingale's song. And perhaps it was this disjunction in affect, the poignant complaint of the first strophe against the blithe pastoral images of the remaining three strophes, that led Schubert to abandon the song. In the fragment, at the music that would have set the words "der durch Gebüsch," Schubert (if brother Ferdinand's copy is true to the autograph) wrote somewhat enigmatically "2te Str:", from which we might infer a sensitivity to the shift in syntax between the first two strophes: the declamation for "Wenn ich am Bach ... auf Blumen lag" would now serve "Erklangen drein; Es tanzeten . . ." And so it must have occurred to Schubert that the remarkable dissonance, marked *ff*, at "sie ist dahin" would travel badly in the remaining strophes.

To return once more to the prominence of F♯ minor, this cluster of songs at the core of a Hölty project hints at, if it does not quite clinch, the articulative coherence of a narrative that might be construed this way:

- ¶ *An die Nachtigall*, whose "liebentflamten Lieder" awaken the poet's love
- ¶ *An die Apfelbäume*, its third strophe imagining the lovers in conjugal embrace, the nightingale's "Gesangeston" a subliminal presence
- ¶ *Seufzer*, where now the nightingale's song is heard through the bitterness of a love lost
- ¶ *Auf den Tod einer Nachtigall*, the song and its singer now only a distant memory

9. On the poetic significance of G minor in *Der Atlas*, see my *Distant Cycles: Schubert and the Conceiving of Song* (Chicago: University of Chicago Press, 1994), 135–37.

Hölty's Nightingales, and Schubert's 19

But then there are these other songs, on either side of this central tetralogy of nightingales and lovers. The first and last are the most provocative. The group ends with a long and gruesome ballad, *Die Nonne*, that on its face would seem to have nothing at all to do with the core narrative. A lovesick nun, swept away by her bold lover, is cruelly abandoned by him. Fired by revenge, she has him murdered, then disinters his remains, plucks out the heart and tramples on it, and is forever haunted by its eternal moaning. No nightingales here! We are reminded of Herder's *Edward* ballad, another bloodstained tale, which Schubert set at the end of his life. What these ballads share—what most ballads share—is a proclivity to transfigure the quotidian events of human experience into the timelessness of myth and even of its psychopathological extremities. (I think once again of Heine's *Der Atlas*, another mythic and transformative figure who, as metaphorical stand-in for the poetic ego, infiltrates the core narrative even as he stands apart from it.)

If, in these Hölty songs, we feel ourselves in the presence of some linear unfolding amid the fragments of narrative, *Die Nonne* stands apart. That Schubert may have imagined it as an epilogue to this Hölty project is worth pondering. The ballad, telling its own story with a specificity of plot and character, fixes a time and place that cuts across the temporal grain of this central narrative. Following Aristotle's distinction between *diegesis* and *mimesis*, and the more recent refinement of narrative both as the story implicitly behind the text and as the discourse that tells some part of that story, we might recognize the narrating voice in *Die Nonne*—poet as interested, if dispassionate, witness—as distinct from the inner voice, the *ich* that inhabits, mimetically, the immediate poetic experience in the songs that constitute the core narrative of the group. There are two stories here, and two modes in which they are told.

And yet there are traces in Schubert's music that blur these narrative distinctions. In the lyricism of its opening phrases in A♭ major, the music of *Die Nonne* seems to reach back to the first song in the group, to *An den Mond*, whose lithe opening phrases vacillate between F minor and A♭ major, then blossoming out in the A♭ of its middle strophes, at "Enthülle dich." (See ex. 1.6.)

In the face of the sordid events to follow, the lyricism in the opening pages of *Die Nonne* has a faintly hollow ring. As do all good storytellers, this one is constructing a fiction meant to seem real. Eventually, the music will find its ultimate tonic in a grim strophic refrain in F minor to which the final three strophes are sung: actually, a *return* to F minor, if we will hear this song as the closure-inducing final number of a larger group that opened in F minor, with *An den Mond*. I don't mean to suggest that there is a poetic

EX. 1.6A. Schubert, *An den Mond* (Hölty), D 193.

narrative—a meta-narrative, even—that would couple these two framing songs. The sentiment of *An den Mond*, the poet summoning the moon to illuminate those places once enjoyed in the company of his lost beloved, and now to mourn with him, is touchingly human, a cry from the heart. The final strophes of *Die Nonne*, to be sung "mit Grauen [in horror]," offer no reclamation, no redemptive moralizing that might explain how these two songs constitute a beginning and an end. The two exist as a pair only in some abstract alignment, grounded in Schubert's overarching tonal construct.

And yet tonal excursions within *Die Nonne* seem to draw upon the salient relationships and emphases within the group of songs as a whole. In what is perhaps the most prominent instance, the ghastly scene of the murder (strophe 7) is set in the key of F♯ minor, its first couplet punctuated with a half cadence on C♯. The entire passage, marked "wild, schnell," races through several courses of the full chromatic until, at its final couplet, the corpse of our unfortunate Lothario is entombed in a phrase that closes emphatically in F♯ minor on a triad rolled from the deepest F♯ in Schubert's arsenal. This is not the throbbing F♯ minor in which Hölty's lonely nightingales sing to their lost lovers. Or does Schubert intend a grim irony here, the murder of this inconstant lover meant as a commentary on the death-induced grieving that all lovers suffer at the end of the affair?

As it turns out, the tonal focus of this central episode in *Die Nonne* did not come immediately clear to Schubert. In the fragmentary autograph of 29 May, the passage begins in B minor and makes its way to a protracted half cadence in F minor, resolving on a powerful downbeat at the incipit of the following strophe, at "Die Nonne flog, wie Nacht begann." (The two passages are shown in ex. 1.7.) It's the bestial rage of the nun, now quite out of her mind, that the music seeks to capture here. But there is a curious breach at the page turn in this earlier autograph, a symptom perhaps of a moment of indecision, and the music trails off without resolve, without resolution, unfinished.

EX. 1.6B. Schubert, *Die Nonne* (Hölty), D 208. From the autograph of 29 May 1815.

When, eighteen days later, Schubert again takes up the song, it is F♯ minor that is established as the new locus of this central episode. The unhinged flight of the nun is now told in recitative, the music finding its way to the F minor that will ground its concluding strophes.

It is not often that Schubert leaves behind the evidence of such radical

EX. 1.7A. Schubert, *Die Nonne*, D 208. From the fragmentary autograph of 29 May.

EX. 1.7B. Schubert, *Die Nonne*, D 208. From the autograph of the revision of 16 June.

rethinking. Less radically, a revision of its opening bars hints at other issues. In the earlier of its two versions, eight bars of introductory music anticipate the entrance of voice and text in a squared-off fullness of its harmony and texture that adumbrates those first lines of the poem. In the revision, the redundancy of those eight bars is stripped away, replaced with two bars of simple oscillation around E♭, the teller of this tale feeling for the pitch, for a tune with which to begin, as though coaxing the music back from some recess of memory. More immediately, this new figure seems to play upon the oscillating final cadence of *Der Liebende*, the penultimate song in this Hölty group, hinting at some performative connection from the one song

EX. 1.8. Schubert, from the final bars of *Der Liebende* (Hölty), D 207; and the opening bars of *Die Nonne* (16 June).

to the next (as shown in ex. 1.8). The opening bars of *Die Nonne* are now less a beginning than a continuation, caught in mid-phrase.

These tonal and theatrical recalibrations, driven in the first instance by an intention to get the song right, seem no less to probe the interstices *between* texts, where resonances and reverberations suggest fragments of thought that we are at pains to understand. And perhaps it is this fragmentary process of creation that is at play here: Schubert, feeling his way through these Hölty poems, sensing resonances and reverberations, hearing tonal connections, sketching faint narrative threads. I've tried to capture some of this in the sketchy graphing shown in ex. 1.9.

EX. 1.9. Schubert, the Hölty settings of May/June 1815 in a synoptic sketch.

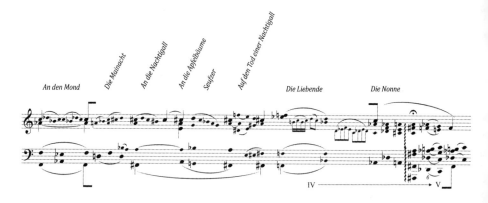

I'm reminded of the title of Elena Ferrante's *A Writer's Journey*. *Frantumaglia*, it is called, an Italian neologism that Ferrante explains as "bits and pieces of uncertain origin which rattle around in your head."[10] "Linear explanations," she writes elsewhere, "are almost always lies." To those of us who too often fall victim to the seductive call of the linear explanation, Ferrante gives us pause. If a faint trace of continuity threads itself through the unfolding of these songs, as it would in any such work, we mustn't, if I grasp Ferrante's point, hold ourselves captive to some a priori linearity of conception, but understand the process even in its fictive sense as a struggle against the condition of *frantumaglia*. This, I confess, is what I hear playing itself out in these Hölty settings: Schubert's music pulling within and against the poetry; the poetry within and against an imposed tonal construct; and finally, within and against an F minor that stakes out the limits of a conventional frame, the remote call of F♯ minor, penetrating an interior space of anguish and desire, of the nightingale lost in its song.

Addendum

If this reading of the Hölty group has merit, it is fair to ask whether, in the copious production of this extraordinary year, other such groupings, the apparently impetuous gatherings of poems culled from a single collection, might now and then display the symptoms of consanguinity or even harbor a tendency toward cycle-making, toward what Dietrich Berke once

---

10. Elena Ferrante, *Frantumaglia: A Writer's Journey*, trans. Ann Goldstein (New York: Europa Editions, 2016). I take her words here from Roger Cohen, "The Violent World of Elena Ferrante," *New York Review of Books* 63, no. 9 (May 26, 2016): 51.

referred to as Schubert's "zyklische Verfahrensweise."[11] Some weeks later, in July 1815, Schubert would embark on a "cycle" of another kind—a *Lieder-spiel*, it has been called—in the setting of some twenty poems by Gotthard Ludwig Kosegarten.[12]

In September, settings of eight poems by Klopstock within a three-day stretch offer occasional glimpses of consanguinity—three of the songs are in the key of A♭ major—even if there is little to suggest meaningful continuities of poem and music. And yet it is tempting to imagine Schubert, in the act of composing, listening for opportunities to shape some larger grouping. The final song in the group, the imposing *Dem Unendlichen*, has a convoluted history that is itself suggestive of a shifting process of thought. The earliest autograph—an "erste Niederschrift," in Deutsch's nomenclature—is dated 15 September 1815, in a manuscript where it is placed between *Die frühen Gräber* (dated 14 September) and *Shilric und Vinvela* (Macpherson [Ossian]). The song was written out a second time, apparently in October 1816, in a clean copy that again includes *Die frühen Gräber*, but now closes with a setting of Klopstock's bardic ode *Hermann und Thusnelda*, an earlier "erste Niederschrift" of which was dated 27 October 1815.[13] This would seem to corroborate the intention on the part of Schubert and his friends to offer for publication eight volumes of songs, each devoted to the works of a different poet, as described by Josef von Spaun in a letter of 17 April 1816 to Goethe: the first two volumes containing settings of Goethe, the third of Schiller, the fourth and fifth of Klopstock, "the 6th of Mathisson, Hölty, Salis, etc., and the 7th and 8th containing songs of Ossian. . . ."[14] While nothing came of the plan, *Dem Unendlichen* clearly lingered in Schubert's mind, for he pulled it from his portfolio somewhere around 1826–1827, writing it out yet a third time, now transposing the opening from F major to G major, and altering the modulation at bar 15 so that the music from here would preserve the harmonic track of the earlier versions to the cadence that would establish the E♭ major of the final strophe.[15]

11. I borrow here from my *Distant Cycles*, 11.

12. See Morten Solvik, "Schubert's Kosegarten Settings of 1815: A Forgotten *Liederspiel*," in *Franz Schubert and His World*, ed. Christopher H. Gibbs and Morten Solvik (Princeton, NJ: Princeton University Press, 2014), 115–56.

13. The manuscript containing this second compilation is now at the Morgan Library, New York, Cary 29–31, accessible digitally through its Music Manuscripts Online. For more on the dating of the manuscript, see NSA, IV/9, 264–65, 287–90.

14. See NSA IV/9, xvi–xvii; the letter from Spaun is given in O. E. Deutsch, *Schubert: Die Dokumente seines Lebens* (Kassel: Bärenreiter, 1964; rev. Wiesbaden: Breitkopf & Härtel, 1996), 41.

15. The late date of the autograph of this third version was deduced by Robert Winter. See his "Paper Studies and the Future of Schubert Research," in *Schubert Studies: Problems*

On the title page of the bifolium on which the song was entered, Schubert wrote "Vier deutsche Gedichte für eine Singstimme mit Begleitung des Pianoforte. Franz Schubert mpia."[16] If Schubert actually had three other songs in view, their identity remains a mystery.[17]

In the end, there is no Klopstock cycle. But what I think we can infer, however cautiously, from these three autographs of *Dem Unendlichen* is that in the very act of writing out, Schubert seems to have been casting about for some entry into a grouping that would make sense, both musically and poetically. We might remind ourselves of the expenditure of mental energy, the expenditure of time that it would take to write out a song in all its detail, with crotchety quill pen and inconsistent ink on costly paper, when the actual differences in the notation of the song were minimal. The very act of writing, of rewriting, itself a kind of performance, would return the music to the front of Schubert's consciousness, imagining it in new contexts, moving beyond an intense initial engagement with the works of the poet to some ex post facto gathering of songs that might induce publication.

Appendix

AN DIE NACHTIGALL	*AN EINE NACHTIGALL, DIE VOR MEINEM KAMMERFENSTER SANG*
Hölty, ed. Voss	Hölty, ms. fragment
Geuß nicht so laut der liebentflammten Lieder Ton reichen Schall Vom Blütenast des Apfelbaums hernieder, O Nachtigall!	Gieß nicht so laut die liebeglühnden Lieder, Zu meiner Qual Vom Blüthenast des Apfelbaums hernieder, O Nachtigall!
Du tönest mir mit deiner süßen Kehle Die Liebe wach; Denn schon durchbebt die Tiefen meiner Seele	Sie tönen mir, o liebe Philomele, Das Bildniß wach, Das lange schon, in meiner trüben Seele,

---

of Style and Chronology, ed. Eva Badura-Skoda and Peter Branscombe (Cambridge: Cambridge University Press, 1982), 242.

16. The manuscript is at the Staatsbibliothek zu Berlin, Preuß. Kulturbesitz, Mus, ms. autogr. Schubert 44. A facsimile of the title page is shown in NSA, IV/9, xxxii.

17. For one hypothesis, see Walther Dürr's preface to NSA, IV/9, xxii.

Dein schmelzend Ach.

Im Schlummer lag.

Dann flieht der Schlaf von
neuem dieses Lager,
Ich starre dann,
Mit nassem Blick, und
todtenbleich und hager
Den Himmel an.

[3 strophes follow, then:]

Fleuch, Nachtigall, in grüne
Finsternisse
Ins Haingesträuch,
Und spend' im Nest der treuen
Gattin Küsse;
Entfleuch, entfleuch!

Fleuch tiefer in die grünen
Finsterniße,
O Sängerin,
Und spend im Nest der treuen Gattin
Küße,
Fleuch hin, fleuch hin!

Do not pour out so loudly the sonorous strains
of passionate love-songs
from the blossom-covered boughs of the apple tree,
O nightingale!

The singing from your sweet throat
awakens love in me;
for already your melting sighs
pierce the depths of my soul.

Then sleep once more shuns this bed,
and I stare,
moist-eyed, drawn and deathly pale,
at the heavens.

Fly away, nightingale, to the green darkness
of the grove's thickets, and in your nest
bestow kisses on your faithful spouse.
Fly off, fly off!

AUF DEN TOD EINER NACHTIGALL*

Hölty, rev. Voss

Sie ist dahin, die Maienlieder tönte,
    Die Sängerin,
Die durch ihr Lied den ganzen
    Hain verschönte,
       Sie ist dahin!
Sie, deren Ton mir in die Seele
    hallte,
       Wenn ich am Bach,
Der durchs Gebüsch im
    Abendgolde wallte,
       Auf Blumen lag!

Sie gurgelte, tief aus der vollen
    Kehle,
       Den Silberschlag:

Der Widerhall in seiner
    Felsenhöhle
       Schlug leis' ihn nach.
Die ländlichen Gesäng' und
    Feldschalmeien
       Erklangen drein;
Es tanzeten die Jungfrau'n ihre
    Reihen
       Im Abendschein.

Auf Moose horcht' ein Jüngling mit
    Entzücken
       Dem holden Laut,
Und schmachtend hing an ihres
    Lieblings Blicken
       Die junge Braut:
Sie drückten sich bei jeder deiner
    Fugen
       Die Hand einmal,

ON THE DEATH OF A NIGHTINGALE

She is gone, the songstress
    who warbled May songs,
who adorned the whole grove
    with her singing.
       She is gone!
She whose notes echoed in my
    soul,
       when I lay among flowers
by the brook that flowed through
    the undergrowth in the golden
    light of evening.

From the depths of her full throat

       she poured forth her silver
       notes;
the echo answered softly

       in the rocky caves.
Rustic melodies and pipers' tunes

       mingled with her song,
as maidens danced

       in the glow of evening.

On the moss, a young lad,
    enchanted, heard
       the lovely sound,
and the young bride hung
    yearningly on
       her lover's glance:
At each of your fugues, they
    squeezed each
       other's hands,

---

*Hölty's original title: *Elegie auf eine Nachtigall*.

Und hörten nicht, wenn deine
    Schwestern schlugen,
        O Nachtigall!

Sie horchten dir, bis dumpf die
    Abendglocke
        Des Dorfes klang,
Und Hesperus, gleich einer
    goldnen Flocke,
        Aus Wolken drang;
Und gingen dann im Wehn der
    Maienkühle
        Der Hütte zu,
Mit einer Brust voll zärtlicher
    Gefühle,
        Voll süßer Ruh.

and did not hear when your
    sisters called,
        O nightingale!

They listened to you until the
    muffled village bells
        sounded in the evening,
and Hesperus emerged from the
    clouds
        like a golden snowflake;
then they went to their cottage

    in the cool May breeze,
their hearts full of tender feeling

    and sweet peace.

AN DIE APFELBÄUME, WO ICH JULIEN ERBLICKTE

Ein heilig Säuseln und ein
    Gesangeston
Durchzittre deine Wipfel, o
    Schattengang,
        Wo bang und wild der
            ersten Liebe
        Selige Taumel mein Herz
            berauschten.

Let solemn murmuring and the
    sound of singing
vibrate through the treetops above
    you, O shaded
        walk, where, fearful and
            impassioned, the blissful
        frenzy of first love seized my
            heart.

Die Abendsonne bebte wie
    lichtes Gold
Durch Purpurblüten, bebte wie
    lichtes Gold
        Um ihres Busens
            Silberschleier;
        Und ich zerfloß in
            Entzückungsschauer.

The evening sun shimmered like
    brilliant gold
through purple blossoms;
    shimmered like brilliant
        gold around the silver veil on
            her breast.
        And I dissolved in a shudder
            of ecstasy.

Nach langer Trennung küsse mit
    Engel[s]kuß
Ein treuer Jüngling hier das
    geliebte Weib,

After long separation let a faithful
    youth
kiss with an angel's kiss his beloved
    wife,

Und schwör' in diesem
  Blütendunkel
Ewige Treue der
  Auserkornen.

and in the darkness of this
  blossom
pledge eternal constancy to
  his chosen one.

Ein Blümchen sprosse, wenn wir
  gestorben sind,
Aus jedem Rasen, welchen ihr
  Fuß berührt,
  Und trag' auf jedem seiner
    Blätter
  Meines verherrlichten
    Mädchens Namen.

May a flower bloom, when we are
  dead,
from every lawn touched by her
  foot.
  And may each of its leaves

  bear the name of my exalted
  love.

SEUFZER

Hölty, ed. Voss
  (1783, 1804)

SIGHS

DIE NACHTIGALL

Hölty (1773)

Die Nachtigall
Singt überall
Auf grünen Reisen
Die besten Weisen,
Daß ringsum Wald
Und Ufer schallt.

The nightingale
sings everywhere
in the green branches
the best tunes,
that sound forth in
wood and stream
  bank.

Die Nachtigall
Singt überall,
Auf grünen Reisen
Die besten Weisen,
Tönt süße Ruh
Den Leuten zu.

Manch junges Paar
Geht dort, wo klar
Das Bächlein
  rauschet,
Und steht, und
  lauschet
Mit frohem Sinn
Der Sängerin.

Many a young couple
goes there, where the
clear brook murmurs,

and stands and listens

happily
to the singer.

Der grüne Wald
Und Busch erschallt
Von ihrer Minne.

Mit frohen Sinne

Hört jederman
Den Vogel an.

Ich höre bang'
Im düstern Gang
Der Nachtigallen
Gesänge schallen;
Denn ach! allein
Irr' ich im Hain.

I hear anxiously
in the dark path
the songs of the
nightingales resound;
for alas, I wander
alone in the grove.

Ich, leider, nicht,
Es bricht, es bricht,
Trotz allen Fugen,
So Vögel schlugen,
Vor Minneschmerz
Mein armes Herz.

✳ CHAPTER 2 ✳

Herder's Hexameters, and Beethoven's

If, in 1815, Schubert was a young composer finding his stride and a voice of his own, Beethoven seems to have been struggling through the symptoms of a mid-life reckoning. The exhausting work toward the revision of *Fidelio*, completed in time for its performance on 23 May 1814, may be said to have marked an emphatic closure, putting to rest the grand heroic enterprise that dominated much of his earlier music. "I assure you that this opera will win for me a martyr's crown," he wrote in exasperation to Georg Treitschke, in the midst of his struggle to salvage, to retool, to re-envision this grand work of 1805.[1] The projects of 1815 seek new directions. The two sonatas for piano and cello, op. 102, in their flashes of intense lyricism, of hymn-like quiescence, in shards of rough-edged counterpoint and fugue, configure that "fragmented landscape" which, for Adorno, was a signature of the late style.

In the midst of his work on the sonatas, in June or July, Beethoven completed an inspired setting for chorus and orchestra of Goethe's *Meeres Stille* and *Glückliche Fahrt*, dedicating the work to the "unsterbliche Goethe" upon its publication by Steiner in 1822, and, as an epigraph on the verso of the title page, had printed a strophe from the eighth canto in Voss's translation (in dactylic hexameters) of Homer's *Odyssey*. The circumstances surrounding the composition, the performance and the publication of this underappreciated work, and the epigraph from Homer will justify its own discussion, to which we shall return in the next chapter.

---

1. Emily Anderson, ed. and trans., *The Letters of Beethoven* (London: Macmillan & Co.; New York: St. Martin's Press, 1961), 455. Ludwig van Beethoven, *Briefwechsel Gesamtausgabe*, ed. Sieghard Brandenburg, 3:20.

Reading in Voss's Homer occupied Beethoven sporadically during these years, captured on occasional pages in the so-called *Tagebuch*, the diary—or better, an exceptionally uncommon commonplace notebook—that Beethoven kept between the years 1812 and 1818, and that has survived today not in Beethoven's hand but in four copies.[2] In one entry from 1815, a telling passage from the *Iliad* is written out, Voss's metrics underscored in penciled prosodic markings. Here is Homer's text, as Voss renders it:

> nun aber erhascht mich das Schicksal
> daß nicht arbeitlos in den Staub ich sinke noch ruhmlos
> Nein erst großes vollendet wovon auch Künftige hören

and in Maynard Solomon's translation:

> But now Fate catches me!
> Let me not sink into the dust unresisting and inglorious,
> But first accomplish great things, of which future generations too
>   shall hear![3]

To read these lines as resonant with Beethoven's sense of his own condition, however theatrical or fantasy driven, is a temptation difficult to resist. The scene in Homer is a memorable one: Hector locked in battle, having wasted his spear against Achilles's shield and knowing now that death was close at hand. It's a traumatic moment, and that alone ought to have been sufficient to have moved Beethoven to set down these lines in admiration of Voss's complex hexameters. Still, to refuse any hint of an autobiographical subtext would seem obdurate.

Such hexameters are to be seen elsewhere in the *Tagebuch*, and indeed on the following page Beethoven is found copying out extracts from several poems contained in Herder's *Blumen aus morgenländischen Dichtern gesammlet*, a remarkable gathering of *Nachdichtungen* (poetic reformulations) drawn from the *Gulistan* (the rose garden) of the thirteenth-century Persian poet Sadi and poems of the Turkish poet Mesihi, active in the sixteenth century. Herder's immediate sources—their degrees of separation

---

2. For an exhaustive description of the sources, see Maynard Solomon, *Beethovens Tagebuch*, ed. Sieghard Brandenburg (Mainz: v. Hase & Koehler, 1990), esp. 6–20. For a translation of Beethoven's text, see Solomon, "Beethoven's Tagebuch of 1812–1818," in *Beethoven Studies 3*, ed. Alan Tyson (Cambridge: Cambridge University Press, 1982), 193–288.

3. *Beethovens Tagebuch*, entry 49, p. 59; the English translation is in "Beethoven's Tagebuch," 232.

from original texts—are shrouded in speculation and inference, but what matters here is the appeal to Beethoven of voices from a distant culture, filtered, as they are, through Herder's poetic sensibility and rigorous metrics.

Related to these pages in the *Tagebuch*, if not in fact removed from the *Tagebuch* itself, is a manuscript in Beethoven's hand now housed with the Stefan Zweig collection at the British Library, a gathered sheet of two leaves, containing five poems from the Herder collection, two of them fitted out with metric markings added in pencil above the text.[4] (Fig. 2.1 shows its first page.)

The first of them is titled *Die laute Klage*, the complaint of the dove giving voice to the sorrow locked silently in the wounded heart of the lover. It must have struck a nerve. With the decision to compose, Beethoven then returns to the poem, here and there entering the letter *R* in large Roman script—a shorthand for "Ritornello," which, in even the earliest sketches for vocal works, is meant merely to signal an instrumental interruption. And at the end of the poem, he scribbles "Es, das erstemal"—E♭ the first time—referring, perhaps, to the cadence in the relative major that will articulate the first couplet. And, as others have noted, Beethoven misread the very last word of the poem—suggestively, for Herder's "den verstummenden Gram" becomes "den verstummenden Sinn": the silenced sense. Here is Herder's poem:

DIE LAUTE KLAGE

Turteltaube, du klagest so laut und raubest dem Armen
        Seinen einzigen Trost, süßen vergessenden Schlaf.
Turteltaub', ich jammre wie du, und berge den Jammer
        Ins verwundete Herz, in die verschloßene Brust.
Ach die hartvertheilende Liebe! Sie gab dir die laute
        Jammerklage zum Trost, mir den verstummenden Gram.[5]

THE LOUD COMPLAINT

Turtle dove, you complain so loudly and rob the poor
        of its single comfort: the sweet sleep of oblivion.
Turtle dove, I too complain, and conceal my complaint
        in a wounded heart, locked in my breast.

---

4. British Library, Zweig MS. 15. See Arthur Searle, *The British Library Stefan Zweig Collection: Catalogue of the Music Manuscripts* (London: British Library, 1999), 16–17, and plate 14.

5. Beethoven: "den verstummenden Sinn."

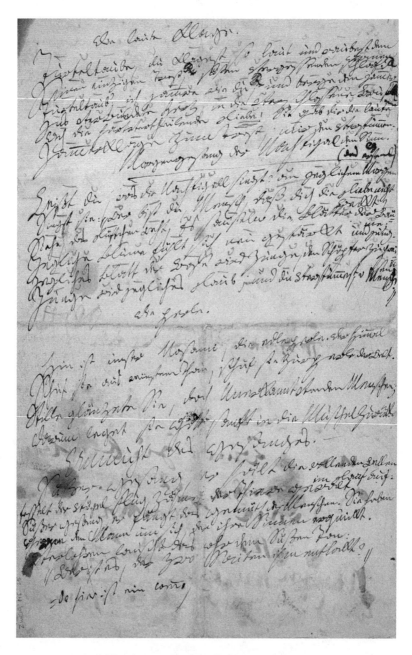

FIGURE 2.1. Beethoven's copies from Herder, *Blumen aus morgenländischen Dichtern gesammlet*. British Library, Stefan Zweig Collection, MS 15, fol. 1r. By kind permission.

Oh, love that harshly divides us! She gave to you the loud
    complaint for comfort, to me only silent sorrow.

Beethoven's music (see ex. 2.1) plays into the ironic reversals of the poet's conceit. If the first two couplets hew dutifully to the metrics of the poem, the third, without violating the prosody, erupts *fortissimo* in a phrase that sings a *Jammerklage* that only the anguished lover in the ventriloquizing voice of the composer could imagine, and that no dove could execute. The halting sighs at the end of the phrase mean to suggest the literal silence of the lover, but in accents that resemble a dove-like throbbing. Here again, the confusion of agency is central to meaning. The complexity of this third couplet, the convolutions of Herder's syntax, deserve a closer look. By the end of the second couplet, the music has settled into a dour F minor, *pianissimo*. The exclamatory "Ach, die hartvertheilende Liebe!" exploding in a diminished seventh shatters the mood, dynamics fluctuating spasmodically with each overwrought word. At "Jammerklage," the music reaches a dissonant threshold, a powerful augmented sixth that refuses the conventional path of resolution (a dominant on C), finding instead an irresolute passing harmony that allows a cadence in A♭ major—only the briefest stop toward a larger cadence in C minor.

Beethoven struggled with the passage. An earlier draft (shown as ex. 2.2) displays ambivalence around this very harmony at "-klage." It's that eternal crux, where music and poem pull against one another. There can be no pause, no harmonic resolution at "-klage," no breath until the comma after "Trost": diction in a face-off with the ironic twist of the language, the finding of comfort (of "Trost") in this "Jammerklage," the stabbing harmony at "Jammerklage" less resolved than liquidated in the fleeting comfort of A♭ major.

On 3 June 1813 (the date entered in his autograph manuscript), Beethoven set Herder's *Der Gesang der Nachtigall*, the first of the poems in this fourth book from the *Blumen aus morgenländischen Dichtern*. The eminent Orientalist Sir William Jones published an English version of the poem in 1772 (reprinted often), which is commonly taken to have been Herder's source. If indeed it was, the extent of Herder's paraphrase is vividly apparent in reading its opening strophe, in strict hexameters, alongside Jones's Englishing of Mesihi. For each of his strophes, Jones offers in a footnote an unrhymed "imitation," a more prosaic, more literal reading. And he follows all this with a rendering of the complete poem in Latin. Here are the opening strophes of Herder's poem, together with its putative source in Jones.

EX. 2.1. Beethoven, *Die laute Klage* (Herder), WoO 135.

DER GESANG DER NACHTIGALL

Höre, die Nachtigall singt: der Frühling ist wieder gekommen!
Wiedergekommen der Frühling, und deckt in jeglichem Garten
Wohllustsitze, bestreut mit den silbernen Blüthen der Mandel.
Jetzt sei fröhlich und froh; er entflieht der blühende Frühling.

Garten und Auen schmücken sich neu zum Feste der Freude;
Blumige Lauben wölben sich, hold zum Hütte der Freundschaft,

Herder's Hexameters, and Beethoven's 39

(continued)

Wer weiß, ob er noch lebt, so lange die Laube nur blühet?
Jetzt sei fröhlich und froh; er entflieht der blühende Frühling.

From *A Turkish Ode of Mesihi* [from Sir William Jones, *Poems, Consisting Chiefly of Translation from the Asiatic Tongues* (1772)]:

Hear how the nightingales on ev'ry spray,
Hail in wild notes the sweet return of May!
The gale, that o'er yon waving almond blows,

EX. 2.1. *(continued)*

The verdant bank with silver blossoms strows;
The smiling season decks each flo'ry glade.
Be gay: too soon the flo'rs of Spring will fade.

Imitation:
Thou hearest the tale of the nightingale "that the vernal season approaches."

EX. 2.2. Beethoven, *Die laute Klage*, from the composing draft.

The Spring has spread a bower of joy in every grove, where the
almond-tree sheds its silver blossoms. Be cheerful; be full of mirth;
for the Spring passes soon away: it will not last.

Against the obscure convolutions of poetic transmission, in its trespassing of cultural and linguistic boundaries, Beethoven's lied is of a simplicity to challenge the sophistications of critical theory. Even the melancholy reminder of the inevitable passing of time, and with it, the ephemeral delights of spring and youth—"er entflieht der blühende Frühling"—with which each strophe ends, is simply transparent in Beethoven's breezy song (shown as ex. 2.3).

Internalized and personified in Schubert's doleful laments, the nightingale's song is here given voice in the trillings and bird-like iterations with which the piano suggests how it might actually sound. The repeated notes in slow syncopations increase in velocity and crescendo to a trill, consistent with Beethoven's depiction of the nightingale in the closing bars of the second movement (Scene at the Brook) of the Sixth Symphony, and true

EX. 2.3. Beethoven, *Der Gesang der Nachtigall* (Herder), WoO 141.

to the single constant aspect in the vast repertory of riffs and figures that constitute the nightingale's song.[6]

Playing against Herder's long hexameters, the rhythmic simplicity of its phrases turning continually around a centered tonic, Beethoven's lied may bring to mind another project that was occupying Beethoven during these years: the composition of those "folk" songs of the British Isles on commission from the publisher George Thomson. We have some 179 of these settings, composed between 1809 and 1820, most of them for piano trio, a richly diverse repertory whose significance for Beethoven's stylistic evolution had until recently been largely undervalued.[7] An entry in the *Tagebuch*, again datable to early 1815, gives a sense of the enterprise: "Die Schottischen Lieder zeigen als ungezwungen die unordentlichste Melodie vermöge die Harmonie behandelt werden kann."[8] (The Scottish songs show how unrestrained the most irregular melody can be treated through harmony.) And on the autograph of the Irish song *Save me from the Grave*, Beethoven wrote "Nb: Voila comme on ne doit pas avoir peur pour l'espression les sons le plus etrangers dans melodie, puisque on trou-

---

6. It will be recalled that Beethoven identified the bird calls (nightingale, quail, cuckoo) in the autograph score of the Sixth Symphony, and added a note to the copyist, who is instructed to retain these identifications in the designated wind parts. See Ludwig van Beethoven, *Sechste Symphonie F-dur Opus 68, Sinfonia pastorale. Faksimile nach dem Autograph* . . . (Bonn: Verlag Beethoven-Haus Bonn, 2000), fol. 67v. Sketches for the passage may be found in Beethoven, *Ein Skizzenbuch zur Pastoralsymphonie Op. 68 und zu den Trios Op. 70, 1 und 2*, transcribed by Dagmar Weise (Bonn: Beethovenhaus Bonn, 1961), II, fols. 23v and 25v.

7. The repertory is carefully studied in Barry Cooper, *Beethoven's Folksong Settings: Chronology, Sources, Style* (Oxford: Clarendon Press [Oxford University Press], 1994).

8. *Beethovens Tagebuch*, entry 34, p. 53. For the English, see "Beethoven's Tagebuch," 227; and Cooper, *Beethoven's Folksong Settings*, 157.

vera surement un harmonie naturell pour cela" (n.b.: Here is how one must not be afraid of the expression of the most strange sounds in the melody, since one will surely find a natural harmony for that), as though to prepare Thomson for the unorthodoxy of an opening harmony constructed around the flat-seventh degree—an Eb triad in first inversion—in bold anticipation of precisely those pitches and that interval in the tune itself.[9]

But of course there is nothing even slightly "unordentlich" about the melody of *Der Gesang der Nachtigall*, none of the challenge to harmonic language that one finds in the most unorthodox of the Thomson settings. Rather, it seems to me that Beethoven is here recalling, if not exactly retrieving, a folk-like idiom famously articulated by Johann Abraham Peter Schulz in the preface to the second edition of his *Lieder im Volkston*, published in 1785, from which the following lines are much to the point:

> In this *Schein des Bekannten*—this illusion of the familiar—lies the whole secret of the folk style [*des Volkstons*]. For only through a striking similarity of the musical with the poetic accent of the lied [*Tone des Liedes*]; through a melody in which the progression never raises itself above the movement of the text, nor sinks below it, which adapts to the declamation and meter of the words like a garment to the body, and which moreover flows on in very singable intervals, in a range adapted to all voices, and in the easiest modulations [*Modulationen*], and finally through the utmost perfection of all the parts to one another, by means of which the melody is given that rounded arch which, in the province of the small, is so indispensable to every work of art, the lied obtains that illusion that is the topic of discussion here: the illusion of the natural (*Ungesuchten*: unsought), the artless, the familiar, in a word, the *Volkston*, by which means it impresses itself so quickly and continuously upon the ear.[10]

In the end, Schulz's idealization of folk song produces a refined and, so to say, civilized simulacrum, this *Schein des Bekannten* purged of those rough edges and idiosyncrasies that otherwise define time and place and *Volk*. If Beethoven's *Gesang der Nachtigall* subscribes superficially to these precepts, its voicing of a *Volkston* is very much of its own time and place. In its stripped-down harmonies, its uncanny control of voicing, its declamatory scansion, Beethoven's *Volkston* has less to do with the recuperation of

9. For more on this song, see Cooper, *Beethoven's Folksong Settings*, 158; and my *Unfinished Music* (Oxford: Oxford University Press, 2008, rev. 2012), 234–35.

10. My translation. Schulz's preface can be found in Max Friedlaender, *Das deutsche Lied im 18. Jahrhundert* (Stuttgart: J. G. Cotta, 1902; repr. Hildesheim: Georg Olms, 1962), vol. 1, part 1, 256–57.

a music of the 1780s than with a quest for a new voice—for voice itself, and further, for the ethics and ethos of Homeric myth and the timeless echo of ancient and remote poetry reduced to pure meter and song.

In the margin at the end of his rough draft of the song, Beethoven scribbled a note to himself: "alle übrigen Verse müßen nur die Exposition des Frühlings enthalten ohne die Nachtigall zu berühren jedoch muß das Ende allzeit dasselbige seyn nemlich: Jetzt sey fröhlich und froh er entflieht der blühende Frühling" (All the remaining verses must contain only the exposition of spring without alluding to the nightingale, and yet every verse must end the same way, namely: Jetzt sey fröhlich [etc.]). But this is to overlook Herder's touching final strophe:

> Hier im reizenden Thal, hier unter blühenden Schönen
> Sang, eine Nachtigall, ich der Rose. Rose der Freude,
> Bist du verblühet einst, so verstummt die Stimme des Dichters.
> Drum sei fröhlich und froh; er entflieht, der blühende Frühling.

> Here in the delightful valley, here under the blossoming beauties
> I, a nightingale, sang to the rose. Rose of joy,
> once you have withered, so too the voice of the poet is silenced.

It will take the adroit performer to find the nuanced tone to convey these plangent lines, of which Beethoven's strophic music seems altogether oblivious: there's not a trace of melancholy in its ecstatic final cadence.

Herder himself made several attempts at the poem, and of particular interest is the final strophe of an earlier draft:

> Singe dein Nachtigall-Lied. (So rufet auch mir
> Philomele.) Singe dir selbst Freuden ins Herz,
> Weise, mässige Freude. Die Rose verblüht,
> Wenn sie verblühet ist, so verstummet auch mein Gesang.
>> Freunde, darum sing' euch jetzt. Er verstummt,
>> Er verstummt, der Ton Philomelens.

> Sing your nightingale's song. (Thus Philomele calls to me as well.)
> Sing of the joy in your heart, wise, moderate joy. The rose withers,
> and when it has withered, my song too is silenced. Friends, it is for this
> reason that I sing to you now. It is silent, Philomele's song is silent.

Constrained, in the published version, by those unforgiving hexameters, the six lines of the draft now compressed into a quatrain, we are left to

46 CHAPTER TWO

TABLE 2.1. Beethoven's copies from Herder, *Blumenlese*

Location of copy	Title of poem	In Herder's Blumenlese	Settings
—	Der Gesang der Nachtigall	Book IV, number 2	WoO 141. Autogr: 3 June 1813
Zweig [MS 15], 1r	Die laute Klage	IV, 6	WoO 135
Zweig, 1r	Morgengesang der Nachtigall	III, 1	
Zweig, 1r	Die Perle	IV, 8	
Zweig, 1r and v	Anmuth des Gesanges	IV, 3	
Zweig, 1v	Macht des Gesanges	IV, 4	
Tagebuch [item] 5	Lerne Schweigen	I, 4	WoO 168/1. Autogr. 24 January 1816
Tagebuch 6	Verschwendete Mühe	I, 26	
Tagebuch 55	Dank des Sterbens	IV, 16	
Tagebuch 56	Müh' und Belohnung	IV, 17	
Tagebuch 57	Das Leben der Menschen	IV, 14	Only lines 21/22, 25/26, 29/30
Tagebuch 58	Trost des Lebens	IV, 15	

unpack "sang, eine Nachtigall, ich der Rose," the conflation of poet and nightingale here bound up in an extreme linguistic knot. Beethoven's blithe song is content to let syntax and meter do its own work.

In her meticulous edition of Beethoven's lieder, published in 1990 for the Beethoven-Haus *Gesamtausgabe*, Helga Lühning suggested that those other poems copied into the *Tagebuch* and on the Zweig leaves, and the unpublished status of the two that were composed, offer the possibility that Beethoven had in mind "eine Art Herder-Zyklus"—a kind of Herder-cycle.[11] If, on its face, the idea has a certain appeal, we might take this as an invitation to consider more closely the conspectus of these poems that Beethoven culled from Herder's *Blumenlese* (see table 2.1).

Setting aside even the broadest view of *Zyklus* as Beethoven might have understood the concept in 1815, perhaps it is enough to imagine these two songs and those other poems as remnants of a project of a different kind. For one, the poems, either in the order in which they appear in Herder's publication, or in the shuffled order in Beethoven's copies, make no pretense to narrative. There is no "story" to be teased out of them, no *personaggi* who might

11. Ludwig van Beethoven, *Werke: Gesamtausgabe* XII/1, *Lieder und Gesänge mit Kla-vierbegleitung*, Kritischer Bericht, ed. Helga Lühning (Munich: G. Henle, 1990), 97.

be understood as protagonists in a lovers' contrivance. And yet these poems have in common an aura that Herder hints at in a preface of 1792:

> It is not however as genuine works of art that I transplant these beautiful children of fantasy and intellect. In my younger years, Sadi was to me a pleasing teacher of morality, often clothing the most beautiful epigrams of the Bible as though in new vestments. I invite you, then, to him as to a teacher of morals among the roses of the most beautiful intimacies, intimacies that one must cultivate with his own heart.[12]

The poem that Beethoven copied out directly after *Die laute Klage* gives poignant expression to these thoughts:

MORGENGESANG DER NACHTIGALL

Weißt du, was die Nachtigall singt? An jeglichem Morgen
     singt sie: "wer bist du, Mensch, daß dich die Liebe nicht
       weckt?
Siehe, das Lüftchen weht, es säuseln die Blätter der Bäume;
     Jegliche Blume fühlt neu sich gestärket und jung.
Jegliches Blatt der Rose wird Zunge, den Schöpfer zu preisen,
     Zunge wird jegliches Laub; und du verstummest, o
       Mensch?"

MORNING SONG OF THE NIGHTINGALE

Do you know what the nightingale sings? Every morning
     She sings: who are you, Man, that love does not
       awaken you?
Look, the breeze blows, rustling the leaves of the trees;
     every flower feels itself newly strengthened and young.
Every petal of the rose becomes a tongue with which to praise the
    creator;
     every leaf a tongue. And you, o Man, are silent?

Here, too, the metric markings, added in pencil (easily visible in the facsimile shown in fig. 2.1 above), run through the entire poem, and Beethoven even

---

12. Johann Gottfried Herder, *Sämtliche Werke*, ed. Bernhard Suphan, XXVI, Poetische Werke 2, ed. Carl Redlich (Berlin: Weidmann, 1882; reprint Hildesheim: Georg Olms, 1968), 309.

took the trouble to furnish, in a note at the bottom of the page, a comma missing after "preisen." Such meticulous attention to scansion and punctuation must clearly have signaled an intent to bring the poem to music. But surely it was more than its hexameters that would have drawn Beethoven to Herder's pensive *Nachdichtung*. In its conceit of a natural world whose beauty speaks to its creator while Man remains loveless and silent, this is a poem that expresses the deep moral sentiment and the apotheosis of nature that threads itself through Beethoven's abiding creative mission. The song of this nightingale penetrates beyond the lover's chamber. Why, in the end, did Beethoven choose not to compose it? We cannot know.

Nor can we know why Beethoven gave up on a larger Herder "Zyklus." If such a project were ever in his sights, the concept would be transfigured a few months later when, in early 1816, Beethoven began to draft *An die ferne Geliebte* on poems by Alois Jeitteles, a true cycle redolent, even to its bird calls, of a sensibility encountered in the Herder songs.

*

Returning to this Viennese moment in 1815, our camera, receding into the distance, would capture a synoptic view of the activity in these two workshops: Beethoven, in C major and minor, laboring over Herder's hexameters; Schubert, a tritone away, finding in F♯ minor the inner nightingale in Hölty's troubled poems. Listening for the intimacies in the music of their nightingales and turtle doves, enmeshed in the dialectics of poem and song, we are witness to that elusive moment at which the sensibilities of Beethoven and Schubert, locked each in their own sensorium, seem to touch— *seem* to touch, because in the end, Schubert reads Hölty as a mirror into his own psychic anxieties, while Beethoven's infatuation with Herder has rather more to do with the structure of his language, in its antique metrics and exotic conceits. How the two come to terms with the same poem— Goethe's inscrutable *Meeres Stille*—is the challenge of the next chapter.

✳ CHAPTER 3 ✳

Whose Meeres Stille?

In and around these few weeks in June during which Schubert was absorbed in his Hölty project, a singular poem by Goethe drew both Beethoven and Schubert into its silent world. The poem is *Meeres Stille*, and it was printed together with a companion piece, *Glückliche Fahrt*, in Schiller's *Musenalmanach* for 1796, and published always as a pair, if not as a single work in two parts.[1] For Beethoven, the relationship of the two poems to one another is at the core of the work, the fearsome mystery of the first dispelled in the exuberant resolution of the second: "und Äolus löset das ängstliche Band" (and Aeolus loosens the fearful knot), as Goethe has it.[2] It has even been suggested that an appreciation of Beethoven's music might well be enhanced by association of its composition and performance with activities during the Congress of Vienna, "in that climate of patriotic celebration and new political hopes, to which Goethe's *Sinngedichte* and Beethoven's jubilant apotheosis are so well attuned."[3] This is to attribute to the composer a political sophistication rather more subtle than is evident in those

---

1. "In allen Ausgaben sind beide Gedichte auf einer Seite zusammengestellt als eng verbundene Gegenstücke im Inhalt, Rhythmus und in der Klangsymbolik," writes Erich Trunz, in *Johann Wolfgang Goethe: Werke. Hamburger Ausgabe in 14 Bänden*. Band I, Gedichte und Epen I, ed. Trunz (Munich: C. H. Beck, 1981), 642. "In all editions both poems are placed together on the page as closely related counterparts in content, rhythm and in the symbolism of tone." Once again (see above, Preamble, note 9), I retain Goethe's spelling of *Meeres Stille* as two words.

2. In Greek mythology, Aeolus is the ruler of the winds, playing a critical role in Book 10 of *The Odyssey*.

3. This, following Frank Schneider, in *Beethoven: Interpretationen seiner Werke*, ed. Albrecht Riethmüller, Carl Dahlhaus, and Alexander L. Ringer (Laaber: Laaber, 1994), 2:182 (in my translation).

other works in which Beethoven overtly courts the public ear. More to our point, when the work was finally published in 1822, it inspired a probing inquiry into the nature of such collaborations between poem and music by the young critic and theorist Adolph Bernhard Marx.

Schubert

But for Schubert, it was *Meeres Stille* alone that captured the imagination. Tellingly, there is no evidence that a setting of *Glückliche Fahrt* ever entered his mind. Schubert in fact set *Meeres Stille* twice, the earlier of the two on 20 June 1815.[4] The second setting, composed the very next day, is the one that is widely known. It was this version that was eventually included in the carefully written presentation copy for Goethe in a collection of sixteen songs sent by his friend Joseph von Spaun to the poet in April 1816.[5] But what, precisely, is the relationship between these two settings? The second of them is less a revision of the first than a rehearing, seeking a music that might come closer to penetrating the anxiety emanating from the *Todesstille* that is the mortifying image central to the poem. (The two settings are shown as ex. 3.1.)

Tiefe Stille herrscht im Wasser,	Deep stillness reigns in the water,
Ohne Regung ruht das Meer,	the sea is calm without motion,
Und bekümmert sieht der Schiffer	and the anxious seaman sees
Glatte Fläche rings umher.	flat expanse all around.
Keine Luft von keiner Seite!	No breath of air from any side!
Todesstille fürchterlich!	Fearful, deathly stillness!
In der ungeheuern Weite	In the monstrous expanse
Reget keine Welle sich.	no ripple stirs.

4. The autograph score of the earlier version, missing its final five bars, is today at Vienna: Wienbibliothek im Rathhaus, MH 16218, and available digitally at the "Schubert Online" site. The text published in Schubert, *Neue Ausgabe sämtlicher Werke*, Lieder, Band 1, Teil b, p. 197, is based on a copy that was evidently prepared for Eusebius Mandyczewski. See Deutsch, *Franz Schubert: Thematisches Verzeichnis*, D 215A. The autograph score of the second version, dated 21 June 1815, is at Vienna: Gesellschaft der Musikfreunde, A 216.

5. The autograph, at the Staatsbibliothek zu Berlin, Preussischer Kulturbesitz, Mus. ms. autogr. 1, is published in facsimile as Franz Schubert, *Sechzehn Goethe-Lieder: Faksimile-Ausgabe nach dem im Besitz der Deutschen Staatsbibliothek Berlin befindlichen Autograph* (Leipzig: Edition Peters, 1978), together with a supplementary study by Peter Hauschild, *Die Goethe-Lieder des jungen Schubert: Beiheft zur Faksimile Ausgabe.*

EX. 3.1A. Schubert, *Meeres Stille* (Goethe). Earlier version, 20 June 1815, D 215A.

EX. 3.1B. Schubert, *Meeres Stille* (Goethe). Published version (op. 3, no. 2), 21 June 1815, D 216.

Strikingly bold in its harmonic trajectory, the earlier setting moves in a sequence of rolled whole-note chords from an initial C major, touching briefly on E major and F major in the singing of its first two lines. Bolder still is the chromatic climb in the next bars, intoning mimetically the increasing anxiety of the seaman, each first-inversion triad inflected by an appoggiatura to the root, and cadencing finally on a dominant on C. A D♭ in the bass, displacing the root, is prolonged for four bars, the flat seventh above it finally read as an augmented sixth folding out to a strong dominant on B♮ at "fürchterlich," answered by E-minor triads in two bars empty of text. The final couplet is then set to music that recapitulates the opening, transforming the E-major triad of its fourth bar into a dominant with a flatted ninth, resolving deceptively to an F-major triad that establishes a true subdominant in C major.

Routine description of this kind cannot hope to convey the impact of the music, in its uncanny succession of harmonies that seem to come out of nowhere. How, one must wonder, did Goethe's meditation on the inscrutable condition of *Stille* play into Schubert's imagination? How to hold suspended the conflict embedded in the poem: the pictorial vista of the vast, silent sea internalized in the human psyche as a portent of catastrophe; the overbearing sense of imponderable quiet at the root of the seaman's disquiet, of an anxiety that senses only the "fearful, deathly stillness." This "ängstlich" that Schubert inscribes at the top of both autographs (and on the *Reinschrift* for Goethe) has perhaps less to do with the actuality of performance than with a state of mind that the composer wishes to share with his players. The seemingly placid surface motion in the keyboard is deceptive. Even its second chord, a diminished triad that introduces F♯ above C in the bass, troubles the aura of motionless calm that emanates from the poetic text.

Returning to the poem a day later, Schubert rethinks and recalibrates. The *Stille* of the poem now saturates the music in every aspect. The rolled chords continue from beginning to end, all appoggiaturas deleted until the final cadence. In the opening bars, the voice barely moves from its initial E. Delayed until m. 8, its tonicization as E major assumes a substance and an authority that it did not have in the earlier setting. And this plays significantly into the closing bars of the song, in its pointed de-emphasis of the final tonic. In the earlier setting, that subdominant on F is followed by an even more powerful augmented sixth with A♭ in the bass, an elaboration of the dominant of the dominant that serves only to strengthen the sense of C major as the true tonic. And the C-major triad that initiates the phrase sung to "In der ungeheuern Weite" in the earlier version is now replaced by E minor in a phrase that shores up E major as a genuine tonic, if not the one that will be left standing at the end. The final phrase enacts a gradual liquidation of E major, approaching C major timidly, through E minor. The two big harmonies that, in the earlier version, indisputably grounded the tonicity of C major through a strong subdominant are here rejected. The final cadence seems a mere formality, an afterthought.

To hear in this later version a playing out of the tension underlying the engagement of these two tonics is to wade into the deeper waters of intertextuality, where music moves beyond the diction of the poem, beyond the illustration of its pictorial surface. These tonal foci can't be assigned material roles. Rather, they suggest a kind of positioning in the mind. The crux of the poem comes at the words "Todesstille fürchterlich," where syntax gives way to bare utterance, and it is precisely here that the harmonies deepen their hold on E major. The first of them, a six-four chord on C♯, implicating F♯ minor, is especially fraught. It's not what we are led to expect, following upon the chromatic descent in the bass. This mordant F♯ minor that never materializes, coincident with "Todes-," has a deeply unsettling, even sinister aura about it—*unheimlich* (uncanny) is the word that comes to mind. And it is this harmonic moment that impels the music toward a powerful dominant in E major.

On paper, the six-four on C♯ has every appearance of an inessential passing harmony between the bass tones D and B. That, however, would be to ignore the articulative, even dramaturgical position of the moment. The singer stops here for an instant, modulating the voice to frame "Todesstille fürchterlich!" The moment is fleeting but significant. And it is in the wake of these grim words that the voice settles on G♯ at "ungeheuern Weite," where E major seems to illuminate the cosmic expanse, setting in perspective the "ängstlichkeit" of this solitary seaman, a mute doppelgänger for the rootless wanderer, the ubiquitous figure in so many of Schubert's works. The seaman, in this reading, is a surrogate whose inner anxieties are acted out in Schubert's edgy tonal divagations.[6]

Much to the point is an appreciation by Heinrich Schenker of a performance of the song by the great Dutch baritone Johannes Messchaert, with whom Schenker performed as pianist in 1899. As Schenker recalled it, Messchaert

> elongat[ed] the notes in so utterly a peaceful way that they sounded like messages emerging from the silence rather than tones issuing from the

---

6. "In his larger forms, Schubert is a wanderer," writes the pianist Alfred Brendel. "He likes to move at the edge of the precipice, and does so with the assurance of a sleepwalker." See his *Music Sounded Out: Essays, Lectures, Interviews, Afterthoughts* (New York: Farrar, Straus & Giroux, 1990), 86.

human breast. Only at the word "ungeheuern" did any tone dare venture into the voice, swelling almost imperceptibly, as far as "ungeheuern Weite," but pulling back immediately. The effect was to render the *Stille* at the end all the more fearful and believable.[7]

In Messchaert's singing, it is this phrase in E major, it alone, that is elevated to song, the return to C major a "pulling back" to the pervasive *Stille* of the poem. We can only imagine that Schubert's "ängstlich" somehow found its way into this performance now lost to memory, and wonder how Schenker might have drawn this state of mind out of his instrument.

Beethoven and A. B. Marx

Schenker's recollection comes at the end of a brief note whose central point is in its admiration of Goethe's expression of the "silence of Nature through silence of language," a quality that the motionless surface and austere harmonies of Schubert's music convey in its own terms. And this returns us to the problem of intertextuality, viewed now from another angle, where the setting of music to poem, however persuasive the coupling, is perceived by its nature to interfere with the linguistic music, its inutterable *Grund-Idee*, inherent in poetry of a certain genre.[8] This is the central thesis in a remarkable critical essay on Beethoven's *Meeres Stille und glückliche Fahrt*, op. 112. Writing in the first volume (1824) of the *Berliner Allgemeine Musikalische Zeitung* [hereafter BAMZ], Adolf Bernhard Marx begins with some reflections on the nature of poetic discourse, his examples drawn from the works of Goethe. He speaks of *dichterischen Pausen*, of the unspoken idea behind the language of the poem, which only those practiced in an art of exegesis supported by "psychology" can intuit.[9] And then comes this penetrating insight:

7. Heinrich Schenker, "Zu Schuberts 'Meeresstille,'" *Der Tonwille* 6 (1923): 41; English, as *Der Tonwille*, ed. William Drabkin (Oxford: Oxford University Press, 2005), 2:35–36. I've altered the translation a bit.

8. In the first instance, Marx spells the term as two words, hyphenated, and I shall retain this spelling even when, later on, Marx writes it as a single word.

9. "Nur eine geübte, durch Psychologie unterstützte Auslegungskunst vermag bisweilen, nur eignes dichterisches Ahnungsvermögen vermag stets, diese *dichterischen Pausen* zu ergänzen." I take the text from *Ludwig van Beethoven: Die Werke im Spiegel seiner Zeit. Gesammelte Konzertberichte und Rezensionen bis 1830*, ed. with introductions by Stefan Kunze (Laaber: Laaber, 1987), 386–94: 386. I am much indebted to Robin Wallace, who graciously shared with me his translation of the Marx essay, and his notes, in advance of its publication as *The Critical Reception of Beethoven's Compositions by His German Contemporaries, Op. 112 to Op. 122*, now available online at the Center for Beethoven Research,

Related to these poems in which we believe to perceive these *dichter-ischen Pausen* are those *veiled* smaller poems of Göthe, whose fundamental idea is not spoken out at all, but is rather only suggested in that which the poem actually says.[10]

The poem that inspires this thought is Goethe's "Über allen Gipfeln." Its final words—"Balde / Ruhest du auch"—induce Marx to identify "the *Idee* of the poem [which is] nowhere precisely uttered," its veiled, unspoken (and inexpressible) mystery [umhüllenden Geheimniß] recognized as the foundational idea of the poem.[11]

This paradoxical "silent concealment, this revelation" that Marx now reads in *Meeres Stille* brings him round finally to Beethoven, "who in the domain of musical art has pressed on so far beyond all previous achievements to the outermost boundaries of ominous portent and of silence!"[12] What follows is an appreciation of the music phrase by phrase, a strategy, it will become clear, that serves only to strengthen Marx's argument as to the incapacity of music—even "very great music by a composer of exceptional capacity," as he puts it—to convey the *Grund-Idee* of a poem such as *Meeres Stille*. "It must be stated," Marx writes, "that the composer did not . . . strengthen the effect of the poem, but rather diminished it. The fault for this, however, lies not with Beethoven, but rather with *the impossibility of setting poems like those indicated above to music in a completely satisfactory manner*"[13] (my emphasis).

And now Marx probes more deeply into the inherent properties of the two arts. "Poetry," he writes, "is the only *incorporeal* [*körperlose*] art." In it

---

Boston University (2020). Here and elsewhere I have differed with Wallace's translation in matters mostly trivial.

10. "Verwandt diesen Gedichten, in denen wir *dichterische Pausen* wahrzunahmen glauben, sind jene *verhüllten* kleineren Gedichte Göthes, deren Grund-Idee gar nicht ausgesprochen, sondern in dem, was das Gedicht *wirklich* sagt, nur angedeutet ist." Kunze, *Die Werke im Spiegel seiner Zeit,* 387.

11. I leave unexamined here Marx's assignment of agency within the poem. That the experience of the poem, the observation of these phenomena that give the poem its extraordinary purchase on the nature of human existence, is to be filtered through the "du" in the poem is a thesis that might be interrogated. For one classic reading of the poem, see Elizabeth M. Wilkinson's close reading, reprinted and most readily accessible in Johann Wolfgang von Goethe, *Werke*, vol. 1, Gedichte und Epen I, ed. Erich Trunz, 555–56.

12. "Und nun ein solcher Funke in Beethovens Brust geworfen, der im Gebiete der Tonkunst so weit über alle bisherigen Leistungen an die äußerste Gränze der Ahnung und des Schweigens vorgedrungen ist!" Kunze, *Die Werke im Spiegel seiner Zeit,* 388.

13. Kunze, *Die Werke im Spiegel seiner Zeit,* 392.

the spirit looks at pure thought and captures it in words, which are not the subject at hand, nor an image of it, but rather the abstract signs that the spirit has chosen for them. For that reason, poetry can seize upon every subject while expressing its thoughts; for, since it has no embodiment or illustration to perform, its powers are not limited by these things, as are those of the other arts. For that reason, the poet's spirit can renounce all outward references and become entirely self-absorbed, concentrating on its own inner activity.[14]

How, then, does music, in its "material" composition as vibrating body, enter the conversation? Marx's obscure formulation, in its convoluted syntax, makes us work for an answer. "But if now the mind stimulates the corporeal, the *Idee* animates the material: this at once spiritual and material stimulation is tone and sound—is made music."[15] And from this it follows that music "can take its place only where both spiritual (or mental) *and* physical capacities, and not merely the first of these, are engaged."

If there is one moment in Beethoven's setting that might have provoked Marx to his pursuit of these impenetrable interactions, it is the setting of the words "in der ungeheuern Weite." (The passage is shown in ex. 3.2.) Here is how Marx first describes the effect:

> . . . the voices press together anxiously for the first time in close harmony, in order to be flung apart in terror at the word "Weite." Here the full orchestra enters for the first time (only trumpets and kettledrums are still silent) with a cry, and the former stillness returns. Only this outcry of terror in the silence gripped by anxiety indicates the sense of the whole, and it frighteningly coincides with the most terrifying feature of the poem. This vast expanse, above which no cry resounds, against which no arm can do battle, beyond which no eye can see—this vast expanse rips apart even the bonds of anxiety.[16]

But now, several pages later, Marx returns to this very passage, hearing it with an ear tuned more keenly to the inner agency of the poem.

14. Wallace, *The Critical Reception, Op. 112 to Op. 122*, 21–22.

15. "Allein nun regt der Geist die Körperlichkeit, die Idee regt die Materie an—diese zugleich geistige *und* körperliche Erregung ist Ton und Klang, wird Musik. . . . Hieraus folgt nun, daß Musik nur da an ihrem Orte sein kann, wo zugleich geistiges und sinnliches Vermögen zur Thätigkeit gelangen, nicht, wo nur das Erstere." Kunze, *Die Werke im Spiegel seiner Zeit*, 392.

16. Kunze, *Die Werke im Spiegel seiner Zeit*, 391.

EX. 3.2. Beethoven, *Meeres Stille [und Glückliche Fahrt]* (Goethe), op. 112, mm. 23–34, in short score, winds and brass omitted.

The poet takes off from the idea of frightful tranquillity at sea, subjects our spirit to the terrors of this loneliness, and abandons it. Everyone who wishes to experience the poem can do so only in this solitude. With Beethoven we are confronted by *a chorus* of people—and the poem disintegrates within itself. Its effect, however, continued to be felt; the poet's idea, destroyed within itself, remained powerful enough that no other structure could arise from it. Apart from some individual beauties, the chorus, on the whole and as a chorus, has no truth.

This notion of "truth," of *Wahrheit*: what, precisely, does Marx have in mind? On the face of it, he means to distinguish the "materiality" of a full chorus, in each of its voice parts, expressing in concert what only the solitary reader, engaging the poem alone with his thoughts, can experience. The chorus, in this reading, cannot engage the poem in its inner *Wahrheit*.

But the conundrum of agency, if that is the issue lurking behind Marx's critique, is a rather more complex thing, one that is in fact central to Goethe's poem. Our own response to this silent, motionless landscape develops only at the appearance in the poem of the solitary seaman, whose apprehensive gaze internalizes what is otherwise a perfectly serene surface. It is not the "ungeheuer Weite" that moves us, but rather the mysterious, unspoken anxiety that it arouses in this figure, dwarfed and isolated in the expanse of the sea.[17] Omit its third line—"Und bekümmert sieht der Schiffer"—and the poem loses its focus, the subjectivity that is internal to its structure. Here, it seems to me, Marx misses what we might take to be the *Wahrheit* of the poem. The decision to set it for chorus and orchestra, mounting the poem on this larger performative stage, may offend certain sensibilities, but it cannot be claimed to violate the textual boundaries of the poem. The chorus, even in its dispersal into an obligatory part-writing, behaves figuratively as a single voice.

Of greater consequence is the articulative, rhetorical extreme to which Beethoven drives that very passage which Marx isolates in his brief against the chorus, the one truly shocking moment in the setting. We cannot hear it without wondering precisely why Beethoven chose to underscore this word, set explosively apart from every other word in the poem, the only *forte* in the midst of a music that moves from *pianissimo* to, eventually, a triple *piano* in the strings. The disposition of its harmony is further unsettling: a dominant that strains the upper and lower limits of the chorus, with a seventh in the bass, sustained for three full bars.

Marx hears it somewhat differently. "That a terrifying scream would tear itself out of the anxiety-driven silence is in itself a beautiful idea." But a closer investigation of the individual voice parts leads Marx to conclude that what we hear is "not natural musical language: the voices have sur-

17. This brings to mind once again those stunning landscapes of Caspar David Friedrich, and in particular, *Der Mönch am Meer* of 1808–1809. On the topic, see the fine discussion of the painting, in the context of Goethe's poem, by Sterling Lambert, in the chapter "The Sea of Eternity," in his *Re-Reading Poetry: Schubert's Multiple Settings of Goethe* (Woodbridge, UK: Boydell Press, 2009), esp. 35–38.

rendered their individuality, their personal truth, and have become the instrument of the composer." And then there is the problem of the reprise of the opening lines of the poem. Can the poet, Marx asks, have sanctioned the return of the opening lines of the poem, following upon that terrifying scream, as we find in Beethoven? "It was perhaps desirable for a rounding off musically, but it illuminates all the more the incompatibility of this poem with music."

At the risk of overstating the obvious, it is here, in the extremity of the passage at "ungeheuern Weite," that Beethoven's setting defeats a central truth inherent in Goethe's poem. Up to this point, the music serves a quasi-narrative function, conveying in a simple diction of tone and rhythm what the poem, in its evocative language, its *dichterischen Pausen*, can only suggest. The poet's inner voice penetrates through the spectral presence of the seaman in silent, if troubled, contemplation. It is this delicate balance of agency that is disrupted at that explosive moment where the music seems to lose its composure. To put it differently, Goethe's "ungeheuern Weite," as poetic figure, is meant less to inspire a painterly vision of the infinite than to suggest something of that "fearful symmetry" (to borrow from Blake's "Tyger"), a deep anxiety that the seaman experiences, and we in sympathy with him. Does Schubert's E-major phrase come closer to the poetic *Grund-Idee*, or does it too, even in the imagined purity of Messchaert's singing of the phrase, traduce the ominous silence, the *dichterische Pause* that for Marx must be sensed in the interstices of language in Goethe's poem?

Consider once more the actual words of that final couplet:

In der ungeheuern Weite
Reget keine Welle sich.

The grammatical point, its principal clause, is its final line: in this infinite expanse, no wave stirs. Beethoven's music does, however, stir, provoking Marx to reflect on the nature of "musikalische Malerei"—musical painting—a much contested topic at the time. "The extent to which Beethoven had been penetrated by a sensory representation [*sinnliche Vorstellung durchdrungen*] is made evident in the depiction of the otherwise insignificant word 'wave,' at which the voices rise in a gentle motion."[18] On first reading, this might seem a simple instance of what is commonly called word painting. But Marx is choosing his words carefully. *Sinnliche Vorstellung* probes beneath the pictorial into the deeper waters of sensibility and

18. Kunze, *Die Werke im Spiegel seiner Zeit*, 389–90.

imagination. The verb is a powerful one: *durchdringen*, meant to convey a process, even a painful one, through which the image penetrates to the sensorium of the artist and triggers the creative act. In a lengthy footnote, Marx pursues this notion of the interiority of the process. The artist, Marx insists,

> does not paint because he wants to, or because it amuses him, or because he has not clearly recognized the *Grund-Idee*, but rather because he must, because the *sinnliche Vorstellung* has penetrated him, has possessed him, and breaks forth overpoweringly.

Finally, Marx asks: "What intention could have moved Beethoven to paint the insignificant word *Welle*?"—and answers: "But he had to, for his soul was filled with the image of the sea, and this pressed forward in its entirety, and to this belonged the image of the wave."[19]

The advantage of Marx's view of the process is that it allows him to move beyond the trivial aspect of "word painting" in search of some deeper explanation of the relationship of music to a poetic *Grund-Idee*. Marx is less concerned about the literalness of the image—of something wave-like—than about the evocation of an "image of the sea" in all its depth and expanse. And yet there is an uncomfortable contradiction here, for even this slightest suggestion of stirring in the music would seem to ignore those final words: "reget *keine* Welle sich."

That Beethoven was entirely conscious of the *appearance* of motion in a performance of the work is made evident in a punctilious instruction scribbled in a copyist's score:

> NB. Bei diesem ersten Tempo hebe der Capellmeister beim Taktgeben die Hand so niedrig als möglich auf—nicht mit dem mindesten Geräusch verbunden sondern mit äußerster Stille—außer beim forte—beim ersten Takt etwas höher, beim 2ten und 3ten schon nachlassend und beim 4ten wieder ganz die unmerklichste Bewegung.[20]

> Nota bene: In giving the beat in this first tempo [that is, in *Meeres Stille*], the Capellmeister raises his hand as little as possible—without even the slightest stirring, motionless in the extreme (except for the forte), some-

---

19. Kunze, *Die Werke im Spiegel seiner Zeit*, 390.

20. For the text, see Beethoven, *Werke: Gesamtausgabe X/2, Werke für Chor und Orchester*, ed. Armin Raab (Munich: G. Henle, 1998), 215. The score is in the possession of the Beethoven-Haus Bonn, and can be studied in its entirety at its digital archive.

what higher at the first bar, less so at the second and third, and once again, at the fourth bar, with imperceptible motion.

The scribbling was done first in pencil, but then gone over in ink. To whom—for whom—was Beethoven writing? While it is clear that this score was the basis—the *Stichvorlage*—for the publication of the work by Steiner in 1822, Beethoven's note, omitted in Steiner's print, makes more sense as a prescription for an actual performance. The first of two performances prior to publication was at a concert for the benefit of the Citizens' Hospital in Vienna, on 25 December 1815. (The second was in May 1820 for Franz Xaver Gebauer's "Concerts spirituels.") The critic for the *Wiener Zeitung* for 6 January 1816 reports that the orchestra was under the direction of "Hr. [Anton] Wranitzky" and that Hr. [Michael] Umlauf was seated "am Clavier."[21] At the bottom of the title page of the copy, Beethoven wrote in red crayon: "H: von Umlauf," leading one scholar to suspect that Beethoven lent the score to Umlauf, who may have been directing the chorus, in preparation for the concert.[22] It was Umlauf, Capellmeister at the Kärntnertortheater, who conducted the first performance of the revised *Fidelio* a year earlier.

But it is the substance of Beethoven's note that invites reflection. His Capellmeister is no longer merely the facilitator who sets the music in motion, the modest servant of the ensemble. Beethoven scripts for him a new role, a stage presence whose every gesture is calculated to convey the expressive sense of the work, even if the clarity of the downbeat may be compromised. Conductor as performer.

Beethoven, Homer, and Goethe

The substantial body of sketches that Beethoven left behind confirms that work on the composition extended from roughly the end of 1814 until July 1815.[23] Publication by the Viennese firm S. A. Steiner & Co. was, however,

---

21. The report is given in Alexander Wheelock Thayer, *Ludwig van Beethovens Leben*, 2nd ed., trans. Hermann Deiters, ed. and augmented by Hugo Riemann (Leipzig: Breitkopf & Härtel, 1911), 3:528.

22. Beethoven, *Werke* X/2, 220.

23. The preponderance of sketches is to be found in the sixteen pages of a manuscript today at the Beethoven-Archiv Bonn (HCB Mh 90) that form a central corpus of what has been described as "the remnants of a homemade sketchbook" that can be dated from roughly December 1814 to February 1815. See Douglas Johnson, Alan Tyson, and Robert Winter, *The Beethoven Sketchbooks: History, Reconstruction, Inventory*, ed. Johnson (Berkeley: University of California Press, 1985), 235–40 (hereafter JTW). A very late entry for

delayed until 1822. Three (and possibly four) states, or impressions, of this first edition of the full score have been distinguished.[24] In the earliest of these, the opus number on the title page was handwritten in ink. In the later impressions, it is printed. Of far greater significance is that on the verso of the title page, but only in these later impressions, are given those lines from Homer's *Odyssey* (cited above, in chapter 2), handsomely engraved in script as an epigraph:[25]

> Alle sterblichen Menschen der Erde nehmen die Sänger
> Billig mit Achtung auf und Ehrfurcht; selber die Muse
> Lehrt sie den hohen Gesang, und waltet über die Sänger.

The text is from Johann Heinrich Voss's much traveled translation, which might be read in English this way:

> All mortal men on this earth fairly hold the bards [the poets, the minstrels, the singers] with esteem and reverence; the Muse herself, holding sway over the bards, teaches them sublime song.

In Robert Fagles's translation from the Greek:

> From all who walk the earth our bards deserve
> esteem and awe, for the Muse herself has taught them
> paths of song. She loves the breed of harpers.[26]

Beethoven wrote out these lines, with the inscription "Homers Odyßee von Voß 8=ter Gesang," on a blank sheet of letter paper today housed at the

---

the work in the "pocket" sketchbook (Staatsbibliothek zu Berlin [currently Cracow, Biblioteka Jagiellónska]) Mus. ms. autogr. Beethoven Mendelssohn-Stiftung 1 can be dated roughly July 1815. JTW, 239 and 342.

24. First identified by Otto Erich Deutsch, in "Beethovens Goethe-Kompositionen," in *Jahrbuch der Sammlung Kippenberg* 8 (Leipzig: Insel, 1930): 125–28.

25. The text of the motto, together with detailed transcriptions of the first edition and its later issues, is given in Deutsch, "Beethovens Goethe-Kompositionen," 125–28. See also Beethoven, *Werke* X/2, 215–24.

26. Homer, *The Odyssey*, trans. Robert Fagles, introduction and notes by Bernard Knox (New York: Penguin Books [Viking Penguin], 1996), 206–7. For another, see Homer, *The Odyssey*, with an English translation by A. T. Murray (Cambridge, MA: Harvard University Press; London: William Heinemann Ltd., 1919), 1:293. Kristina Muxfeldt offers a "fuller context" of the passage in Alexander Pope's translation. See her *Vanishing Sensibilities: Schubert, Beethoven, Schumann* (Oxford: Oxford University Press, 2012), 64–65 and note 31.

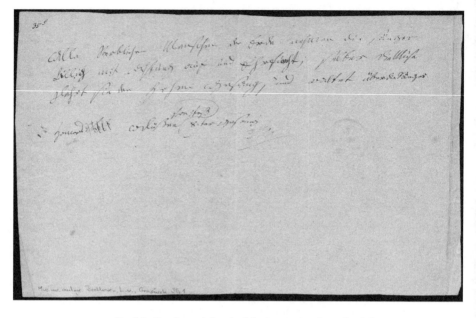

FIGURE 3.1. Draft in Beethoven's hand of the inscription from the *Odyssey* of Homer in the Voss translation. Staatsbibliothek zu Berlin, Mus. ms. autogr. Beethoven Grasnick 35.1. By kind permission.

Staatsbibliothek zu Berlin (see fig. 3.1), conceivably intended for a copyist to make over in cleaner copy for Steiner.[27] It would be worth knowing precisely when Beethoven came to the decision to have these lines inserted in the publication, and what might have provoked him to do so. For one, there is the iconic figure of the poet himself, to whom Beethoven inscribed a lofty dedication on the title page: "In Musik gesetzt und dem Verfasser der Gedichte dem UNSTERBLICHE GOETHE hochachtungsvoll gewidmet"—set to music and dedicated with highest esteem to the author of the poem, the

27. The signature is Beethoven, mus. ep. varia 6 [= Grasnick 35,1]; see Eveline Bartlitz, *Die Beethoven-Sammlung in der Musikabteilung der Deutschen Staatsbibliothek; Verzeichnis* (Berlin: Deutsche Staatsbibliothek, 1970), 199. Presumably, this belonged to the Haslinger collection purchased by Alois Fuchs and later sold to Grasnick. Among the books appropriated by Anton Schindler prior to the auction of Beethoven's estate was a copy of *Homers Odüßee* [sic], übersezt von Johann Heinrich Voß (Hamburg: auf Kosten des Verfassers, 1781), now at the Staatsbibliothek zu Berlin, Beethoven autogr. 40,3. The passages that were marked in some way by Beethoven are given in Albert Leitzmann, *Ludwig van Beethoven: Berichte der Zeitgenossen, Briefe und persönliche Aufzeichnungen* (Leipzig: Insel, 1921), 2:267–72, item 20, and 375–76. See also Maynard Solomon, *Beethovens Tagebuch*, ed. Sieghard Brandenburg (Mainz: v. Hase & Koehler, 1990), 154–55.

immortal Goethe. "I trust," wrote Beethoven to Goethe in the well-known letter of 8 February 1823,

> that you received the dedication to Your Excellency of *Meeres stille* and *Glückliche Fahrt* which I have set to music. On account of their contrasts, they both seemed to me most suitable, even in this regard, to be set to music. How I would love to know whether I had appropriately united my harmony with yours.[28]

While no evidence of a reply has survived, we do have an entry in Goethe's *Tagebuch*, dated 21 May 1822: "Von Bethoven [*sic*] Partitur empfangen."[29] Presumably, this was the Steiner print that is to be found today in the Goethe- und Schiller-Archiv. The date squares with an observation later in the letter to Goethe, a letter whose principal intent was to solicit a subscription from the Weimar court for a handwritten score of the *Missa solemnis*.

> But Your Excellency mustn't think that the dedication of *MeeresStille u.Glückliche Fahrt* is a consequence of this current application on my behalf. The dedication had already taken place in May 1822, and I had not yet thought to offer the Mass in this way until only a few weeks ago.[30]

In the copy of the published work that Beethoven sent (or had Steiner send) to Goethe, the title page leaves blank the space where an opus number would later be printed.[31] Further, the plate number printed at the bottom of the first page of music—S: u: C: 3838—and visible on every other copy of the Steiner print is missing here, suggesting that this copy may well have been the very first impression to have been drawn from the newly struck plates. It will come then as something of a surprise to find that this copy for Goethe does in fact display the Homer epigraph. How, then, do we explain the absence of the Homer epigraph in those other early impressions? Could Beethoven have intended the epigraph, which is very

---

28. For the original, see *Ludwig van Beethoven: Briefwechsel Gesamtausgabe*, ed. Sieghard Brandenburg, V (Munich: G. Henle, 1996), 36. For a different rendering of an English version, see Emily Anderson, trans. and ed., *The Letters of Beethoven* (London: Macmillan & Co; New York: St. Martin's Press, 1961), 997.

29. Frequently cited. See, for one, *"meine Harmonie mit der Ihrigen verbunden": Beethoven und Goethe*, exhibition catalogue, ed. Jochen Golz and Michael Ladenburger (Bonn: Beethoven-Haus; Weimar: Stiftung Weimarer Klassik, 1999), 126.

30. *Briefwechsel* V, 38; Anderson, *Letters*, 998, translation altered.

31. The title page of the copy at the Goethe- und Schiller Archiv may be seen in facsimile in Golz and Ladenburger, *Beethoven und Goethe*, item 65.

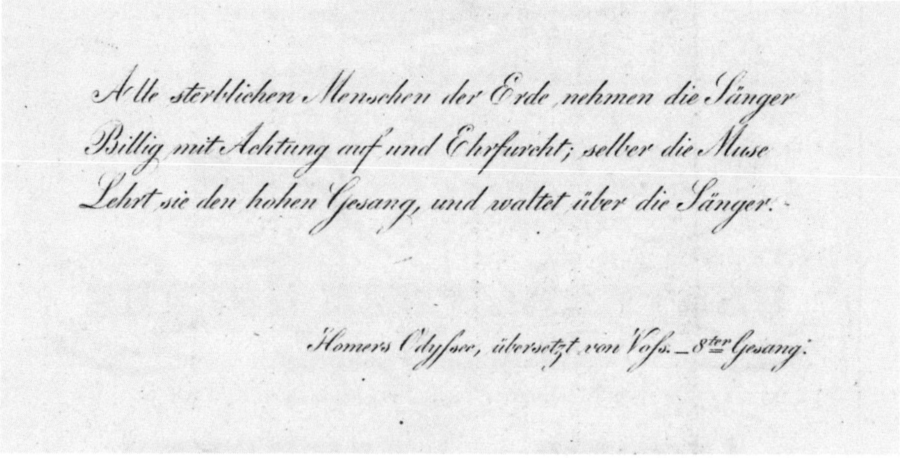

Alle sterblichen Menschen der Erde nehmen die Sänger

Billig mit Achtung auf und Ehrfurcht; selber die Muse

Lehrt sie den hohen Gesang, und waltet über die Sänger.

Homers Odyssee, übersetzt von Voß. — 8ter Gesang.

FIGURE 3.2. The inscription from Homer, on the verso of the title page of the first edition of Beethoven, *Meeres Stille und Glückliche Fahrt*, op. 112. Vienna: S. A. Steiner, 1822.

handsomely engraved on its own plate, as a personal offering to the poet, a *Separatabzug*—a unique impression, made before the general print run? In its text, the Homeric figure of the bard as both poet and singer conjures Beethoven and Goethe as coupled voices in this singular project.[32] Less subtly, Beethoven may simply have wished to impress upon Goethe his own credibility as a discerning and critical reader of this venerable text.

And this brings us back to A. B. Marx. It is precisely this concern that Beethoven expresses to Goethe—"ob ich passend meine Harmonie mit der Ihrigen"—that, from the perspective of a critical dialectic, may be said to have driven Marx to his radical poetics. Beethoven's high regard for Marx's writings is amply documented. In a letter of 19 July 1825 to Adolf Martin Schlesinger, the publisher of the BAMZ, he writes:

> I have received with great pleasure your communication of 24 June together with the Allgemeine Berliner Musikalische Zeitung. Please arrange for it to be sent to me regularly in future. Leafing through its pages, I was struck by several articles that I at once recognized as the

---

32. The inscription, writes Stephen Rumph, "gave Beethoven a chance to insinuate himself into the Olympian company of Goethe and Homer." See his *Beethoven and Napoleon: Political Romanticism in the Late Works* (Berkeley: University of California Press, 2004), 98.

work of the ingenious [*geistreichen*] Herr Marx. I would hope that he will continue to reveal more and more what is noble and true in the sphere of art.[33]

Written more than two years after the letter to Goethe, what is of interest here is the disclosure that Beethoven was already an astute reader of Marx's writings. Which of these could he have known? That very first volume of the BAMZ (1824) contains some of the earliest published writings by Marx. And it was in 1824 that several important essays—on the three last piano sonatas and the Bagatelles, op. 119—appeared in the first volume of the newly created journal *Cäcilia*, published by Schott in Mainz.[34] Marx's account of the newly published Bagatelles opens with this keen insight:

> So günstig die Sonatenform ist, eine Idee musikalisch vollkommen zu entwickeln, so sehr es sich hieraus rechtfertigt, dass der grösste Theil unserer Instrumentalkompositionen—Sonaten, Konzerte, Symphonien—in dieser Form hervorgehen: so wenig eignet sie sich doch für freiere Ergüsse, oder für die Aussprache von Anregungen, welche schon als solche der Aufbewahrung in einer künstlerischen Gattung werth erscheinen.[35]

However favorable is sonata form for the complete musical development of an idea, however much it can be justified from this that the greatest portion of our instrumental compositions—sonatas, concertos, symphonies—arise from this form, sonata form is yet unsuitable for the freer outpouring or for the utterance of impulses which, as such, would indeed seem worthy of preservation as an artistic genre.

Noting the "almost ironically modest" title—*Bagatellen*—Marx continues:

> Die Tonstücke . . . scheinen augenblickliche Anregungen zu sein; niedergeschrieben, wie sie der Moment darbot—ohne höhere Reife abzuwarten, ohne weitere Entwickelung. Allein es sind *Beethovensche* Anre-

---

33. Anderson, *The Letters of Beethoven*, 1222, translation altered. For the original, see Brandenburg, *Briefwechsel* 6:111–13, which contains as well two earlier drafts for the letter, both dated 15 July.

34. Of the BAMZ, Beethoven owned "viele Stücke von mehreren Jahrgängen" of *Cäcilia*, numbers 1–17 and 19–22 (1824–26), as recorded in the "Schätzungsprotokoll" (the appraisal) of 5 May 1827 of Beethoven's estate; see Leitzmann, *Berichte der Zeitgenossen* 2:379–83.

35. I take the text from Kunze, *Beethoven: Die Werke im Spiegel seiner Zeit*, 412.

gungen und man wird voraussetzen dürfen, dass schon der erste Erguss eines solchen Geistes hohe Befriedigung gewähre.[36]

These pieces seem to be instantaneous impulses, written down as the moment offered, without pretenses to greater maturity, without further development. But these are *Beethoven's* impulses and one might be permitted to assume that even the first outpouring of such a mind would ensure great satisfaction.

Grasping this tension between the formal constraints and developmental imperatives of sonata form over against the improvisational impulse, Marx identifies something elemental in the extreme dialectic of Beethoven's late music, and it must have pleased Beethoven to find in Marx a critic with the acuity to recognize what was at play here.

What, then, would Beethoven have made of Marx's probing critique in the *Meeres Stille* essay against the intrusion of a music that would violate the mysteries left to the poetic silences in Goethe's perfect utterance? It is tempting to think that Beethoven, drawn to the figure of the ancient bard whose poetic discourse is inherently musical, would have refused Marx's categorical opposition of the languages of music and poetry. Indeed, the epigraph from Homer, who defines for all later generations the role of *Sänger* as bard, singer and poet in one, would seem a logical rebuttal in response to Marx, even if the actual publication dates of the Steiner print and the Marx essay would suggest the reverse: Marx interrogating Homer. Finally, if these lines from *The Odyssey* would appear to have little bearing on the substance and meaning of Beethoven's *Meeres Stille*, they yet invoke these two iconic figures, Homer and Goethe, whose poetic flights find their way into Beethoven's work in this spring of 1815, and beyond.

Published in late 1821 in a collection of Goethe settings, Schubert's *Meeres Stille* might plausibly have entered into Marx's thinking in 1824. Had it done so, we might then wonder whether Marx would have recognized in it an engagement with the poem at a new level, an *Umdichtung* in which the poem is made over in a music endowed with a harmonic vocabulary, even a poetic sensibility, more closely tuned to Goethe's *dichterischen Pausen* and its underlying *Grund-Idee*. Or would Marx have held firm, hearing Schubert's music as yet another intrusion into the inner

---

36. Kunze, *Beethoven: Die Werke im Spiegel seiner Zeit*, 413. The passages from Marx on opus 119 are given also in Sieghard Brandenburg, ed. *Ludwig van Beethoven: Sechs Bagatellen für Klavier Op. 126. Faksimile der Handschriften und der Originalausgabe*, Teil 2 (Bonn: Beethoven-Haus Bonn, 1984), 59. For another translation of these passages, see Wallace, *The Critical Reception, Op. 112 to Op. 122*, 56.

places of the poem, the purity of whose language is eclipsed in the seductive, sensuous appeal of the music? As did Schubert's contemporaries, and even Goethe himself, we have learned to take pleasure in the agonistic embrace of poem and song.[37] Much to his credit, Marx returns us to the primacy of language. But the argument cannot end there.

37. Goethe's reaction to Schubert's settings of his poetry has been subject to much speculation. Perhaps the most intelligent reading of the evidence is Frederick W. Sternfeld, *Goethe and Music: A List of Parodies and Goethe's Relationship to Music. A List of References* (New York: New York Public Library, 1954), reprinted (New York: Da Capo Press, 1979) with an illuminating introduction by Siegmund Levarie.

Toward a Poetics of Fugue

✴ CHAPTER 4 ✴

Gradus ad Parnassum

Beethoven, Schubert, and the Romance of Counterpoint

But how strange and austere even my first years of study seemed to me—how I felt when I stepped behind the curtain! To think that all melodies (although they had aroused the most heterogeneous and often the most wondrous emotions in me) were based on a single inevitable mathematical law—that instead of trying my wings, I had first to learn to climb around in the unwieldy framework and cage of artistic grammar![1]

Joseph Berlinger's complaint strikes a resonance in us all. It must surely have touched an especially tender nerve in sensibilities closer in time and place to his own. Counterpoint, the most rigorous and, after Fux, the most rigidly codified of the disciplines that might be understood to constitute a *Kunstgrammatik*, had developed an ideology of its own, dissociated from the main lines of musical discourse, encouraging the view of itself as a palliative to the vicissitudes of style.

---

1. "Aber wie fremd und herbe kamen mir gleich die ersten Lehrjahren an!... Daß alle Melodieen (hatten sie auch die heterogensten und oft die wunderbarsten Empfindungen in mir erzeugt), alle sich nun auf einem einzigen, zwingenden mathematischen Gesetze gründeten! Daß ich, statt frei zu fliegen, erst lernen mußte, in dem unbehülflichen Gerüst und Käfig der Kunstgrammatik herumzuklettern!" Wilhelm Heinrich Wackenroder, "Das merkwürdige musikalische Leben des Tonkünstlers Joseph Berlinger," *Herzensergiessungen eines kunstliebenden Klosterbruders* (Berlin: Johann Friedrich Unger, 1797); repr. Wackenroder, *Werke und Briefe*, ed. Wilhelm Heinrich and Gerda Heinrich (Munich: Hanser, 1984), 240; trans. Oliver Strunk, *Source Readings in Music History*, rev. ed., ed. Leo Treitler (New York: W. W. Norton, 1998), 1068.

1

Fux's *Gradus ad Parnassum* promulgated this dissociation, for while it purports to transmit and sustain one certain style—perhaps best characterized as an idealization of Palestrina's music—it has in fact been construed as a set of lessons toward an abstraction.[2] From its publication in 1725, Fux's *manuductio* served to establish a foundational platform in the discipline of music theory. In spite of its modest pretensions, the work propounded nothing less than a systematic exposition of technique, from the control of the barest elements of music to the most elaborate fugue. Embedded in Fux's rigorous curriculum, an *idea* of counterpoint is nurtured; it would be no longer possible to theorize about music without apprehending its position in a *Kunstgrammatik*.

Counterpoint as abstraction is central as well to later theorizing about the classical repertory of tonal music. Central to Heinrich Schenker's work, from *Kontrapunkt* (1910–1922) through *Der freie Satz* (1935), is an endeavor to project the implications of Fuxian counterpoint upon the unfoldings of tonal motion on the largest scale. Even the earliest of his theoretical works, the *Beitrag zur Ornamentik* (1904, rev. 1908), is essentially an argument that surface embellishment is a function of the elemental process of diminution, a process historically and theoretically bound in with counterpoint.[3] For Schenker, the power of counterpoint is a given, an immutable inner law that controls the most remote tonal relations as it does the surface of the work and is the one indispensable index of its coherence.[4] Whether one is prepared to follow Schenker in the breathtaking leap from the local diminutions that enliven the surface of the work to those that govern its

---

2. Palestrina is the spirit behind Master Aloysius in Fux's dialogue. See the preface to *Gradus ad Parnassum*, accessible to English readers in *The Study of Counterpoint: From Johann Joseph Fux's* Gradus ad Parnassum, trans. and ed. Alfred Mann (rev. ed. New York: W. W. Norton, 1965), 18. Fux's promulgation of an idealized Palestrina was just one aspect of a much broader campaign; see below, note 57.

3. In English as "A Contribution to the Study of Ornamentation," trans. Hedi Siegel, *Music Forum* 4 (1976): 1–139.

4. "All diminution must be secured firmly to the total work by means which are precisely demonstrable and organically verified by the inner necessities of voice-leading." See Heinrich Schenker, *Free Composition*, trans. Ernst Oster (New York: Longman, 1979), 98. It is perhaps not well known that in 1922, thirteen years before its publication, *Der freie Satz* was advertised as "Band II[3] Kontrapunkt Fortsetzung . . . (In Vorbereitung)"—that is, part 3 (continuation) of the second volume (*Kontrapunkt*) of the project *Neue Musikalische Theorien und Phantasien*. And see *Free Composition*, xii and xvi. See also *Counterpoint: A Translation of* Kontrapunkt *by Heinrich Schenker*, trans. John Rothgeb and Jürgen Thym, ed. John Rothgeb, 2 vols. (New York: Schirmer Books, 1987).

more distant reaches, the idea of counterpoint as a *Grundgesetz*, a foundational law, invisibly controlling the eccentricities of the work is a concept with powerful implications for a repertory that is no longer explicitly contrapuntal.[5]

Schenker's perception of contrapuntal control as a theoretical determinant in the reading of the repertory is a powerful, and provocative, reaffirmation of the preeminent position that the teaching of counterpoint held in the making of the repertory as well. Here, too, as in Schenkerian theory, there is a paradoxical aspect in the extent to which the teaching of composition in the later decades of the eighteenth century was very nearly synonymous with the teaching of counterpoint. Albrechtsberger's *Gründliche Anweisung zur Composition* (Leipzig, 1790) is essentially a counterpoint text. Kirnberger's *Die Kunst des reinen Satzes in der Musik* (Berlin, 1771–1779) lays out a program that is theoretically more ambitious, but its main argument is in the preparation for the encounter with fugue through a control of harmonic theory.[6] Even its title sets off complex signals. The elaborate essay "Satz; Setzkunst" in Georg Sulzer's *Allgemeine Theorie der schönen Künste* does not so much define the thing as pursue a dialectic that any post-Kantian reflection on the concept must engage. At the same time, the Sulzer essay isolates a more restricted meaning, where "Setzkunst" refers to the mechanical, rule-defining essence true to all composition: "Taken in this narrow sense, *Satz* is to music what grammar is to speech."[7] Pushing the analogy with language a step further, Johann Nikolaus Forkel speaks of

5. Recent allegations, intense and widely disseminated, against Schenker's repugnant views of race and ethnicity, against his vulnerable posture in the catastrophic political developments in Austria in the 1920s and 1930s, only complicate a dispassionate coming to terms with his foundational contributions to an understanding of the music of the eighteenth and nineteenth centuries. "How to reconcile these two aspects of the phenomenon of Schenker: the enduring achievement of his magisterial work over against the all-too-human vituperations of a crusader engaged in a life-and-death struggle to salvage a musical culture that he believed to be vanishing from the face of the earth. Can we fully know the one without the other?" I wrote these lines in exasperated conclusion to a review of *Heinrich Schenker: Selected Correspondence*, ed. Ian Bent, David Bretherton, and William Drabkin (Woodbridge, UK: Boydell Press, 2014); for the full review, see *Music Theory Spectrum* 40, no. 2 (2018): 357–60.

6. A clarification of the complicated publication history of *Die Kunst des reinen Satzes* is given in the preface to the translation of Kirnberger's text, *The Art of Strict Musical Composition*, trans. David Beach and Jürgen Thym (New Haven, CT: Yale University Press, 1982), esp. xi, xii, and xviii.

7. "In diesem eingeschränkten Sinn genommen, ist der Satz für die Musik, was die Grammatik für die Sprache ist." *Allgemeine Theorie der schönen Künste*, ed. Georg Sulzer (Leipzig: Weidmann, 1771–1774; neue vermehrte 2. Auflage . . . 1792–1794; repr. Hildesheim, Georg Olms, 1967–1970), 4:224–25. Beach, *Strict Musical Composition*, xi,

harmony as "a logic in music, for it stands to melody in roughly the same relationship as, in language, logic is to expression; it directs and determines a melodic *Satz* in such a way that it appears to become a genuine truth for the senses."[8]

Implicit in all this is a perception about the interaction of harmony and counterpoint. Counterpoint is the limiting case, explicit and temporal, where the deeper laws that constitute a theory of harmony are timeless. But the rules of Fuxian counterpoint do not proceed from a theory of harmony. In some sense a reaction to this evident dissociation of counterpoint from the other parameters of music, Kirnberger's *Gedanken über die verschiedenen Lehrarten in der Komposition, als Vorbereitung zur Fugenkenntniß* (1782), a gloss on the *Gradus*, endeavors to reconcile Fux with the more refined definition of dissonance that emanates from harmonic theory.[9] But it is precisely this tension between a rigorous linear model and the powerful implications of root theory that invigorates the boldest actions in the tonal repertory. Where such tension generates contradiction and enigma, Schenker is at his most profound, driven to the extreme insight, the gnomic utterance, the obscure abstraction.

The austere rigor of Fuxian counterpoint is absorbed more readily into certain aesthetics than others. Both Haydn and Mozart seem intuitively to have grasped the significance of the *Gradus* for the deepening of their own music, and were quick to insist upon its fundamental place in the curriculum of study for their students.[10] The student to have profited most from their insight and diligence was, of course, Beethoven.

---

clarifies Kirnberger's role in the writing of the music articles for Sulzer's encyclopedia, and Sulzer's role in the formulation of the ideas in Kirnberger's *Kunst*.

8. "Mann kann in dieser Rücksicht die Harmonie eine Logik der Musik nennen, weil sie gegen Melodie ungefähr in eben dem Verhältniß steht, als in der Sprache die Logik gegen den Ausdruck, nemlich sie berichtigt und bestimmt einen melodischen Satz so, daß er für die Empfindung eine wirklich Wahrheit zu werden scheint." Johann Nikolaus Forkel, *Allgemeine Geschichte der Musik*, I (Leipzig: Schwickert, 1788; repr. Graz: Akademische Druck-u. Verlagsanstalt, 1967), 24.

9. Johann Philipp Kirnberger, *Gedanken über die verschiedenen Lehrarten in der Komposition, als Vorbereitung zur Fugenkenntniß* (Berlin: Decker, 1782; repr. Hildesheim: Olms, 1974).

10. The transmission of the *Gradus* in the eighteenth century is described in Alfred Mann's preface to *Gradus ad Parnassum*, in Johann Joseph Fux, *Sämtliche Werke*, series VII, vol. 1 (Kassel: Bärenreiter, 1967), xiv–xix. See also Alfred Mann, "Haydn as Student and Critic of Fux," in *Studies in Eighteenth-Century Music: A Tribute to Karl Geiringer on His Seventieth Birthday*, ed. H. C. Robbins Landon (London: George Allen & Unwin, 1970), 323–32; and Wolfgang Amadeus Mozart, *Neue Ausgabe sämtliche Werke*, series X, vol. 1: *Thomas Attwoods Theorie- und Kompositionsstudien bei Mozart* (Kassel: Bärenreiter, 1965), esp. x–xi.

2

For Beethoven, the study of counterpoint was a challenge with metaphysical overtones. His obsession with it was lifelong. If it may have been difficult for Beethoven to see how the irreducible precepts of Fuxian doctrine could be made to respond to the continually shifting accents of his own language, there seems never to have been any doubt that the continued study of counterpoint would remain central to the enterprise. This sense of obsession comes through in the remarkable fantasy—a "romantische Lebensbeschreibung," Beethoven calls it—on the life of Tobias Haslinger, sent along to accompany a pair of canons contributed to *Caecilia*, the newly founded journal of the publishing firm B. Schott's Söhne.[11] The narrative is worth having in full:

11. The text is an appendix to a letter of 22 January 1825. See Ludwig van Beethoven, *Briefwechsel Gesamtausgabe*, ed. Sieghard Brandenburg, vol. 6 (Munich: G. Henle, 1996), 9–13; *The Letters of Beethoven*, trans. and ed. Emily Anderson (London: Macmillan, 1961), 1167–69. For another translation of just this portion of the letter, with commentary, see *Thayer's Life of Beethoven*, rev. and ed. Elliot Forbes (Princeton, NJ: Princeton University Press, 1967), 934–35. The canons were titled "Auf einen, welcher Hoffmann geheißen" (WoO 180) and "Auf einen, welcher Schwenke geheißen" (WoO 187). The Hoffmann canon was sketched in a conversation book of March 1820, in the vicinity of these suggestive lines: "In den Phantasiestücken von Hofmann, ist viel von Ihnen die Rede." On the facing page, Beethoven wrote "Hofmann–Du bist kein Hof–mann," which comes close to the text of the canon. See *Ludwig van Beethovens Konversationshefte* 1, ed. Karl-Heinz Köhler and Grita Herre in collaboration with Günter Brosche (Leipzig: Deutscher Verlag für Musik, 1972), 318.

The identity of the Hoffmann in the canon has been the subject of much speculation. The arguments are reviewed in Thayer-Forbes, *Thayer's Life of Beethoven*, 759; and Dorfmüller, Gertsch, and Ronge, *Ludwig van Beethoven: Thematisch-bibliographisches Werkverzeichnis*, vol. 2 (Munich: Henle, 2014), 498–500. And see *Beethovens sämtliche Kanons. Notentext mit Kommentar*, ed. Rudolf Klein (Vienna: Doblinger, 1970), 28. The canons were sent, in Beethoven's words, "als Beilage einer Romantischen Lebensbeschreibung," and one might wish to think that the figures of Schwenke, prototype of the old-fashioned North German Kapellmeister, and E. T. A. Hoffmann, whose "romantische Lebensbeschreibungen" were the fanciful models for Beethoven's, were intentionally invoked to gloss the narrative. The publication of the text, in *Caecilia* 1 (April 1825), 206, with some slight differences in detail from the text in the letter to Schott, caused Beethoven some embarrassment. See the letter of 13 August 1825 (*Briefwechsel* 6:132–33; Anderson, *Letters*, 1232–33). Karl Holz announced its appearance in a conversation book on a page that must date from late July; see *Konversationshefte* (Leipzig, 1981), 8:19. But Schott was certainly within the bounds of propriety to read as Beethoven's intent, in the letter of 22 January, that the canons and the biography were both a part of the same story—even that their meanings were mutually dependent.

Part One. Tobias appears as the apprentice of the famous Kapellmeister Fux, who is firm in his saddle—and he is holding the ladder to the latter's *Gradus ad Parnassum*. Then, as he feels inclined to indulge in practical jokes, Tobias, by rattling and shaking the ladder, makes many a person who has already climbed rather high up suddenly break his neck and so forth. He then says goodbye to this earth of ours but again comes to light in Albrechtsberger's time. Part Two. Fux's *nota cambiata*, which has now appeared, is soon discussed with A[lbrechtsberger], the appoggiaturas are meticulously analyzed, the art of creating musical skeletons is dealt with exhaustively and so forth. Tobias then envelops himself like a caterpillar, undergoes another evolution and reappears in this world for the third time. Part Three. The scarcely grown wings now enable him to fly to the little *Paternostergasse* and he becomes the *Kapellmeister* of the little *Paternostergasse*. Having passed through the school of appoggiaturas all that he retains are the bills of exchange [Wechseln]. Thus he causes all sorts of problems for that friend of his youth, and becomes a member of several domestic learned/empty [geleerten] societies.[12]

Whatever its relevance to a life of Haslinger, the three stations of the narrative reflect an aspect of Beethoven's life with uncanny accuracy.[13] The studies with Haydn were essentially studies with Fux.[14] For despite all that one might wish to wring out of those points upon which Haydn would disagree with Fux, they are differences of detail and degree, and not of fundamental ideology. The studies with Albrechtsberger, following directly upon Haydn's departure for London in early 1794, must have seemed to Beethoven as if he had been shown the path to himself.

12. The translation comes largely from Anderson. My reading of "und so schafft er seinen Jugendfreund" differs from hers. This puzzling phrase, edited out in the *Caecilia* version, is explained in *Briefwechsel* 6:13, note 17.

13. The document and Beethoven's motives are discussed in Max Unger, *Ludwig van Beethoven und seine Verleger S. A. Steiner und Tobias Haslinger in Wien, Ad. Mart. Schlesinger in Berlin* (Berlin: Schlesinger, Robt. Lienau, 1921), 18–21. Unger believed that Castelli may have helped Beethoven with the *Lebensbeschreibung*; Castelli is invoked in Beethoven's apology to Haslinger in a letter of 10 August 1825 (Anderson, *Letters*, 1230–31). Maynard Solomon reads the sexual subtext in the document; see his "The Dreams of Beethoven," *American Imago* 32 (1975): 113–44; and *Beethoven Essays* (Cambridge, MA: Harvard University Press, 1988), 56–76.

14. See Alfred Mann, "Beethoven's Contrapuntal Studies with Haydn," *Musical Quarterly* 56 (1970): 711–26; repr. in *The Creative World of Beethoven*, ed. Paul Henry Lang (New York: W. W. Norton, 1971), 209–24. See further Alfred Mann, *The Great Composer as Teacher and Student: Theory and Practice of Composition* (New York: Dover Publications, 1994; a corrected repr. of W. W. Norton, 1987), 63–74, 87–141.

Albrechtsberger may not have been a theorist of the first rank, nor a composer worth emulating. But he taught a counterpoint that was responsive to contemporary language. And Albrechtsberger was evidently willing to countenance Beethoven's endeavor to stretch the concept of that language still further. In the profuse workshop papers that document the studies with Albrechtsberger, a quality of dialogue comes through of a kind evidently not encouraged in the studies with Haydn, whose formal tone is evident even in the calligraphy with which Beethoven presented his homework. For Albrechtsberger, Beethoven routinely submitted rough drafts, some of which bear traces of work carried out in situ. Now and again, we catch a hint of Albrechtsberger's pen, poised to catch a solecism in the making.

As is well known, Albrechtsberger distinguished strict Fuxian counterpoint from a vernacular that he called "freie Satz," in which certain deviations ("Licenzen," in Albrechtsberger's lexicon) were permitted within the formal constraints of the species. The limits of Albrechtsberger's tolerance are on display less through any examples of his own than through the complete set of exercises "in freie Satz" in all five species that Beethoven submitted as part of the curriculum.[15] Whether these exercises followed from some model that would have set forth a modus operandi is a matter for speculation. In any case, example 4.1 may stand for the kind of music that this compromised counterpoint elicited in Beethoven.[16] Perhaps it is a reaction to the rigidity of pure fourth species, the most restrictive of the species, that provokes this display of unprepared sevenths. The inner Beethoven moves within it—in the stretching between the outer voices, in the striking address to the subdominant, and in the characteristic resolution of hanging dissonances. It is not an exercise that we can imagine Albrechtsberger having composed.

Haslinger's third incarnation suggests a transfiguration from larva to

15. The distinction between the two is characterized in the chapter "Vom strengen, und freyen Satze überhaupt" in *Gründliche Anweisung*, pp. 17–19, but the exercises that follow are exclusively in strict counterpoint.

16. The studies with Haydn and Albrechtsberger, constituting but one part of the papers on counterpoint and fugue gathered under the rubric Beethoven A 75 in Vienna, Gesellschaft der Musikfreunde, were given in extract by Gustav Nottebohm in the path-breaking *Beethoven's Studien: Beethoven's Unterricht bei J. Haydn, Albrechtsberger und Salieri* (Leipzig: J. Rieter-Biedermann,1873); repr. Niederwalluf bei Wiesbaden: Martin Sändig, 1971), and are now given more fully in a masterful edition of the studies in *Kompositionsstudien bei Joseph Haydn, Johann Georg Albrechtsberger und Antonio Salieri* (Beethoven, *Werke: Gesamtausgabe* XIII/1), 3 vols., ed. Julia Ronge (Munich: G. Henle, 2014). This example is transcribed in Nottebohm, *Beethoven's Studien*, 60 (missing some of Beethoven's figuring), and in Ronge, *Kompositionsstudien*, 1:248. The revisions are all in Beethoven's hand.

EX. 4.1. Beethoven, exercise for Albrechtsberger, fourth species, "freie Satz."

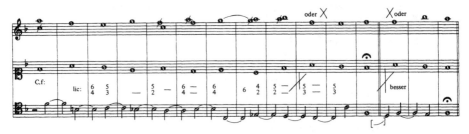

imago. The figure of Tobias, spinning himself caterpillar-like into a cocoon, conjures a phase of dormancy and gestation during which all the outward signs of life are concealed. There is a time of which it might be said that Beethoven's life resembled a kind of cocoon-spinning, a time spent pondering the entire corpus of theoretical and practical writings upon which his own education had been constructed. In the summer of 1809, during the occupation of Vienna by the Napoleonic forces, Beethoven wrote out some 200 pages of extracts from the cardinal texts of theory and practice, from Emanuel Bach and Türk on thorough bass to Fux, Marpurg, Kirnberger, and Albrechtsberger on counterpoint and fugue. It was Nottebohm who first recognized that these papers date from 1809, and that they are categorically distinct from those which Beethoven prepared for Haydn and Albrechtsberger in the early 1790s.[17]

What purpose did these investigations of 1809 mean to serve? The answer to that question, Nottebohm convinced himself, was obvious: they constituted the preparation for the teaching of the Archduke Rudolph, who seems to have been Beethoven's only composition student.[18] But the question will not go away, and indeed Nottebohm asked it several times over in the course of his long, serialized essay on these papers, and its revision for the collection of essays in *Beethoveniana*. That Beethoven pre-

---

17. Nottebohm's study, a meticulous exposé of all the ways in which Seyfried's *Beethoven's Studien* (Vienna: Tobias Haslinger, 1832) misrepresented the lot of counterpoint and fugue papers that Haslinger purchased at the auction of Beethoven's estate, first appeared as "Beethoven's theoretische Studien," serialized in the *Allgemeine Musikalische Zeitung* (neue Folge) 1 (1863), 685; and 2 (1864), 172. It was revised by Nottebohm for publication in *Beethoveniana* (Leipzig: C. F. Peters, 1872), 154–203. An earlier repudiation of Seyfried's book was published by Franz Derckum in *Rheinische Musik-Zeitung* 2 (1852), 572ff, given in translation in Anton Felix Schindler, *Beethoven as I Knew Him*, ed. Donald W. MacArdle, trans. Constance S. Jolly (London and Chapel Hill: University of North Carolina Press, 1966), 468–72.

18. "Es ist nun . . . sehr wahrscheinlich, dass die Auszüge durch den Unterricht des Erzherzogs Rudolf veranlasst wurden." Nottebohm, *Beethoveniana*, 201.

pared so extensively and in such theoretical depth for his lessons with the archduke—who had, in fact, left Vienna on 4 May in anticipation of the invasion—is not a wholly satisfying hypothesis, and one suspects that Nottebohm, disinclined toward equivocation, clung to it in the absence of a more likely one.

Evidence contrary to Nottebohm's view of the matter is contained in the fragmentary draft of a communication that Ludwig Nohl published in 1865. It was in fact Nottebohm who identified the document, on the strength of Nohl's description, as having been written on a leaf torn from a fascicle of the 1809 papers.[19] Its text follows:

> Dear Friends: I have taken the trouble with this simply in order to be able to figure [a bass] correctly and to lead others in this at some future time. As for mistakes, I myself almost never had to learn these things. From childhood on, I had such a tender sensibility that I practiced without knowing that it had to be thus or that it could be otherwise.[20]

To whom might this communication have been addressed? Its text must surely refer to all those extracts that Beethoven was taking so much trouble to cull from the classical texts of theory instruction. Its pedagogical tone and the address in the plural suggest a wider public. Perhaps Beethoven had in mind less a text for publication than a *manuductio* of his own, along the lines of the *Elementarbuch* that Haydn prepared for his students.[21]

An incentive to prepare such a text is not hard to find. For among the

19. Ludwig Nohl, *Briefe Beethovens* (Stuttgart: Cotta, 1865), item 71, p. 76. Nottebohm, *Beethoveniana*, 167–68. Nohl's description appeared two years too late for Nottebohm to have taken account of it in "Beethoven's theoretische Studien."

20. "Lieber Freunde: ich gab mir die Mühe bloß hiermit, um recht beziffern zu können, und dereinst andere anzuführen. Was Fehler angeht, so brauchte ich wegen mir selbst beinahe dieses nie zu lernen, ich hatte von Kindheit an ein solches zartes Gefühl, daß ich ausübte, ohne zu wißen daß es so sein müße oder anders sein könne." The text is taken from a facsimile of the page in Seyfried's *Beethoven's Studien*, plate 3. For slightly different translations, see Anderson, *Letters*, 38; and Donald W. MacArdle and Ludwig Misch, *New Beethoven Letters* (Norman: University of Oklahoma Press, 1957), 12–13. Neither Anderson, who dates the letter "c. 1799," nor MacArdle and Misch, who date it "about 1794," knew Nottebohm's airtight argument for dating it 1809.

21. See Alfred Mann, "Haydn's Elementarbuch: A Document of Classic Counterpoint Instruction," *Music Forum* 3 (1973): 197–237. Nottebohm, as Mann (200) reminds us, took it as assumed that Beethoven, too, used an *Elementarbuch*—a manual distilled from Fux's *Gradus ad Parnassum*—prepared by Haydn for his pupils. But Beethoven's copy did not survive, and Nottebohm reconstructed its text from two unnamed sources, one of which was surely the so-called Magnus copy, the fragment published by Mann in *Music Forum*; see Nottebohm, *Beethoven's Studien*, 21–25.

other traumatic events that mark Beethoven's 1809, the passing from the scene of both Albrechtsberger on 7 March and Haydn on 31 May cannot have failed to have touched him deeply.[22] One may imagine that a sense of loss and of impending isolation, reinforced in other aspects of his life at this time, might have been tempered by a balancing sense of liberation, for here were the two eminent witnesses who could attest to Beethoven's willful encounter with the impediments of the Fuxian discipline. Beyond all that, their deaths might well have led him, finally, to reassess his own equivocal position in the self-imposed obligation to carry forth the tradition. Waldstein's prophetic words—"durch ununterbrochenen Fleiß erhalten Sie: *Mozart's Geist aus Haydns Händen*"—must now and again have reverberated in Beethoven's mind during these fitful months.[23] The sense of mission comes through plainly in a letter of 26 July to Breitkopf & Härtel:

> I had begun to have a little singing party at my rooms every week—but that accursed war put a stop to everything. With this in view and in any case for many other reasons I should be delighted if you would send me by degree most of the scores which you possess, such as, for instance, Mozart's Requiem and so forth, Haydn's Masses, in short, all the scores you have, I mean, those of Haydn, Mozart, Johann Sebastian Bach, Emanuel Bach and so forth—I have only a few samples of Emanuel Bach's compositions for the keyboard, and yet some of them should certainly be in the possession of every true artist, not only for the sake of real enjoyment but also for the purpose of study.[24]

In among the fascicles with the theoretical abstracts from 1809 are some pages that bear witness to the enterprise, showing passages transcribed from works by Sebastian Bach, Handel, and Mozart.

Less altruistic motives were surely at work here as well. The *Akademie* of 22 December 1808, that monumental retrospective of the works of Beethoven's "heroic phase" (as Alan Tyson memorably named it[25]), gave palpable evidence of the exhaustion of a style. Whether consciously or not,

---

22. And, as Maynard Solomon proposes, the death of his physician, Johann Schmidt, on 19 February will have contributed to the gloom; see his *Beethoven* (New York: Schirmer Books, rev. ed., 1998), 195.

23. Max Braubach, ed., *Die Stammbücher Beethovens und der Babette Koch* (Bonn: Verlag des Beethovenhauses, 1970), 19. "With the help of unceasing diligence you will receive the spirit of Mozart from the hands of Haydn," in Lewis Lockwood's translation. See his *Beethoven: The Music and the Life* (New York: W. W. Norton, 2003), 50.

24. *Briefwechsel* 2:71–72; Anderson, *Letters*, 233–36.

25. "Beethoven's 'Heroic Phase,'" *Musical Times* 110 (1969): 139–41.

Beethoven, Schubert, and the Romance of Counterpoint   83

the program summarizes Beethoven's engagement with the grand public genres: symphony (ops. 67 *and* 68), concerto (op. 58), sacred music (movements from the Mass in C, op. 86), an old-fashioned operatic *scena* (op. 65), and finally an orchestral fantasy with solo piano and chorus (op. 80) clearly composed to bring down the curtain at the end of this marathon. The event itself was exhausting as well, a test of endurance to try even Beethoven's most sympathetic admirers.[26]

Nottebohm was the first to dwell upon the silence that followed.[27] The occupation of Vienna put an end to any vital artistic life, and with it, perhaps, the peace of mind to compose. But Beethoven did indeed compose. The String Quartet in E♭, op. 74, is the most important of the works written during these months of political turmoil, and contemporary with Beethoven's intensive theoretical investigations.[28] No other work so eloquently repudiates the ponderous rhetorical accents of the December *Akademie*. Its *Kunstgrammatik* is of another class. From the skewed harmonic rhythm of its opening measures, its narrative unfolds in a language beyond convention—or rather, the signs of convention are consumed in a new poetics. Nearly every event in the first movement is driven in reaction to a premature D♭ that trips the action of the piece at the outset and endows the lyrical principal theme with its special grace. The propensity of D♭ to resolve to C is thwarted at m. 2, and again with increasing ingenuity at each critical bend in the music (see ex. 4.2).

Finally, at mm. 88 and 89, D♭ and C are isolated. Octave whole notes in the viola stare out from the page in some semiotic code—at once the "right" pitches in this fragmented playing out of the theme, and at the same time a memo to the special thematic significance of just these two pitch classes. Harmonic context redefines this D♭ as a minor ninth above its postulated root, C, venting the subdominant bias of the theme (see ex. 4.3).

The descent of D♭ to C sets off a celebration of sorts. The cello sings the

26. "There we sat, in the most bitter cold, from half past six until half past ten, and confirmed for ourselves the maxim that one may easily have too much of a good thing, still more of a powerful one." Johann Friedrich Reichardt's famous account is given in Oliver Strunk, *Source Readings in Music History*, rev. ed., ed. Leo Treitler, 1036–38.

27. Nottebohm drew this inference from the unsettled, distracted picture of entries in a sketchbook—now Staatsbibliothek zu Berlin, Landsberg 5—which Beethoven used between March and October 1809. See Gustav Nottebohm, *Zweite Beethoveniana: Nachgelassene Aufsätze* (Leipzig: C. F. Peters, 1887), 255–75, esp. 263. The sketchbook is now published in facsimile and transcription as *Ein Skizzenbuch aus dem Jahre 1809 (Landsberg 5)*, ed. Clemens Brenneis (Bonn: Beethoven-Haus Bonn, 1992–1993).

28. The sketches for it in Landsberg 5 place its composition in late summer 1809, following the onset of the French occupation. See Brenneis, *Ein Skizzenbuch aus dem Jahre 1809* 2:49.

EX. 4.2. Beethoven, String Quartet in E♭, op. 74, first movement.

EX. 4.3. Beethoven, String Quartet in E♭, op. 74, first movement.

theme at the top of its voice, cutting through an explosion of counterpoint, while the viola, in *stile concitato*, insists upon its portentous C. In the sequel to this ecstatic phrase, the ecstasy is yet more extreme. The cello, attacking its open-string C *fortissimo*, stakes out a sequence of roots beneath the theme that quickens its harmonic pace, spiking the process with a D♭, *sforzando*. It is C major that is celebrated here: not as a remote key at the outer reach of some dramatic unfolding, as it might conventionally have been conceived, but as a thematic event. The key itself has thematic significance.

In its quiet way, the E♭ Quartet signals ahead to later narratives—to the stripped-down voice that sings through *An die ferne Geliebte* and the music beyond—and to a technique in which counterpoint flares in extrinsic battle with fugue, and is subsumed in an elusive part-writing whose integrity is the benchmark of Beethoven's later style.[29] In retrospect, the "romantische Lebensbeschreibung" signifies something about the place of counterpoint in the development of the Romantic composer. And because Beethoven had been taught—by E. T. A. Hoffmann, largely—to understand himself as the pivotal figure in the development of a Romantic music, the fantasy may even be said to stand for the metamorphosis of music itself from a language of grammatical convention to a language of romance.[30]

3

For Schubert, the metaphysics of counterpoint was evidently not at issue. Until 1828, he seems to have been unwilling to bring the counterpoint in his

29. In a thoughtful reevaluation of opus 74, M. Lucy Turner reads the autograph score of its first movement and finale as evidence of Beethoven "renegotiating his relationship to Classical forms and conventions." See her "'So Here I Am, in the Middle Way': The Autograph of the 'Harp' Quartet and the Expressive Domain of Beethoven's Second Maturity," in *The New Beethoven: Evolution, Analysis, Interpretation*, ed. Jeremy Yudkin (Rochester, NY: University of Rochester Press, 2020), 269.

30. The essays in which Hoffmann seizes upon Beethoven's music as the exemplification of the Romantic are the famous reviews of the Fifth Symphony (1810), the Overture to Collin's *Coriolan* (1812), and the music to Goethe's *Egmont* (1813), all published in the *Allgemeine Musikalische Zeitung*, and reprinted in, for one, E. T. A. Hoffmann, *Schriften zur Musik. Nachlese*, ed. and annotated by Friedrich Schnapp (Munich: Winkler, 1963). The review of the Mass in C (1813) anticipates some of the ideas more elaborately developed in the essay "Alte und neue Kirchenmusik" (1814); the two essays were united when all this material was reused (without the music examples) in *Die Serapions-Brüder: Gesammelte Erzählung und Märchen* (1819), repr., with a *Nachwort* by Walter Müller-Seidel and notes by Wulf Segebrecht (Munich: Winkler, 1963), 406–15. For more on the Hoffmann influence, see my "In Search of Palestrina: Beethoven in the Archives," in *Haydn, Mozart, & Beethoven: Studies in the Music of the Classical Period*, ed. Sieghard Brandenburg (Oxford: Oxford University Press, 1998), 283–300.

music up and out of the eighteenth century. Fugue, for Schubert, is inextricably bound in with the archaic genres of liturgical music. But there is a contradiction in this, for the Mass in E♭ (D 950; 1828), when it is not being fugal, is the essence of Schubert. We know now that the fugue at "Cum sancto spiritu" in the Gloria of the A♭ Mass (D 678) is in fact a revision, freshly composed "some time between the autumn of 1826 and the spring of 1827."[31] The motivation for this recomposition has been the topic of further speculation.[32] But whatever Schubert's motives, and granting even the contrapuntal competence of the fugue itself, we must still contend with the question of its integrity in the Mass. When Kurt von Fischer speaks of the fugue as "einen Fremdkörper im Ganzen der As-dur-Messe"—a foreign body in the A♭ Mass as a whole—it is hard not to agree.[33]

Fugue did clearly engage Schubert in his final years. Robert Winter places the new "Cum sancto spiritu" fugue in the A♭ Mass "at the head of an imposing list of contrapuntal tours de force from Schubert's last two years, a period that includes such Handelian homages as 'Mirjams Siegesgesang', the F-Minor Fantasy and the E♭ Mass."[34] If the list is imposing, the counterpoint itself is often enough decorous, stiff, and unprepossessing. Consider the fugue that closes the "cantata" on Grillparzer's *Mirjams Siegesgesang* (D 942), composed in March 1828 (ex. 4.4).

What must strike us first are the ponderous accents of the subject. If the answer satisfies Marpurg's ground rules, its exposed F♯s point up an awkwardness in the subject itself. Later on, the F♯s, caught in a false stretto, induce a doubling of the leading tone that in turn implicates parallel oc-

31. Robert Winter, "Paper Studies and the Future of Schubert Research," in *Schubert Studies: Problems of Style and Chronology*, ed. Eva Badura-Skoda and Peter Branscombe (Cambridge: Cambridge University Press, 1982), 242.

32. Kurt von Fischer, "Bemerkungen zu Schuberts As-dur-Messe," in *Franz Schubert: Jahre der Krise, 1818–1823*, ed. Werner Aderhold, Walther Dürr, and Walburga Litschauer (Kassel: Bärenreiter, 1985), 121–28, esp. 123. The two versions are published in Franz Schubert, *Neue Ausgabe sämtliche Werke* I/3, parts a and b, ed. Doris Finke-Hecklinger (Kassel: Bärenreiter, 1980).

33. Fischer, "Bemerkungen," 123.

34. Winter, "Paper Studies," 242. Of particular interest is the draft for the Fantasy, published in facsimile together with the *Reinschrift* as Franz Schubert, *Fantasie in f-Moll D 940 für Klavier zu vier Händen. Faksimile-Ausgabe*, ed. Hans-Joachim Hinrichsen (Tutzing: Hans Schneider, 1991). It includes two folios (fols. 11 and 12), separated from the draft at the Morgan Library and now in private hands, that record of the fugal section "mehrer übereinandergeschriebene Schichten der Komposition, ohne daß eine der früheren ausgestrichen worden wäre" (several layers of the composition written on top of one another without the earlier layers having been crossed out), writes Hinrichsen (27). In the brief history of Schubert's late encounters with fugal procedure, these pages deserve a closer look.

EX. 4.4. Schubert, *Mirjams Siegesgesang*, D 942, from the final strophe.

taves in the outer voices. Elsewhere, the texture thins without good formal reason—and it is precisely these passages *a due* that are the most vulnerable. Here again, as with the masses, the fugue seems tacked on, not really part of the piece in any integral sense.

Integrity of this sort is not at issue in the Fugue in E Minor for Organ or Piano Four Hands, D 952. The "Baden am 3 Juny 1828" penciled at the top of the autograph seems to confirm Franz Lachner's testimony that the fugue was composed in one night, in preparation for a friendly competition to try the organ at Baden the next day.[35] But the date is not in Schubert's hand, and its veracity has been questioned on several grounds. Robert Winter

---

35. *Schubert: Memoirs by His Friends*, 195–96; original in *Schubert: Die Erinnerungen seiner Freunde*, 2nd ed. (Leipzig: Breitkopf & Härtel, 1966), 224–25.

observes that the paper is of a kind that Schubert used between September 1826 and May 1827.[36] Maurice J. E. Brown, studying the autograph, argued that its format in score (unlike the lateral arrangement of all the four-hand publications) and its rough, draft-like appearance invoke a clean copy that has not survived, and suggested further that the two manuscripts could not have been prepared in a single evening.[37] Brown also drew attention to a sheet of fugal studies, now at the Sächsische Landesbibliothek in Dresden, which contains the subject of this E-minor fugue among them. Brown could not have known a sheet of similar studies that Christa Landon was busy discovering even as Brown wrote, and which contains corrections and original entries by Simon Sechter, with whom it is known that Schubert had begun to study in the few weeks remaining to him before his death in November 1828.[38]

Whatever the circumstances of its composition, the Fugue in E Minor, a late work in any case, is testimony that the genre conjured no new eloquence in Schubert. The rigors of fugal texture do not excite him. The subject, a retread of the subject of Bach's Fugue in F♯ Minor, *WTC* I, purged of its idiosyncratic grit, is only a symptom of the problem. Schubert does not hear in fugue subjects. In a similar way, the two "Cum sancto spiritu" fugues seem rather to spring from some notion of historical restoration than from the aesthetic arguments of the works to which they belong.

What prompted Schubert to visit Sechter in November 1828? Here we might wish to imagine that in 1828, at age thirty-one, Schubert had come to where Beethoven stood in 1801, an age at which Beethoven was resolving to put all his earlier music behind him, to address a new style. I do not mean to suggest that the Heine and Rellstab cycles in *Schwanengesang* would mark the end of an early phase had Schubert lived another twenty-five years. But it is plausible that Beethoven's death might have been felt both as a release from the grip of a daunting father figure, and as a call to carry forth the tra-

36. Robert Winter, "Schubert's Undated Works: A New Chronology," *Musical Times* 119 (1978): 449–500.

37. Maurice J. E. Brown, "Schuberts Fuge in E moll," *Oesterreichische Musikzeitschrift* 23 (1968): 65–70. The draft of the Fantasy (see above, note 34) is also in score.

38. Christa Landon, "Neue Schubert-Funde: Unbekannte Manuskripte im Archiv des Wiener Männergesangs-Vereines," *Oesterreichische Musikzeitschrift* 24 (1969): 299–323; repr. in *Christa Landon zum Gedächtnis*, ed. Internationalen Schubert-Gesellschaft Tübingen (Private printing by Bärenreiter, 1978), 19–43; trans. as "New Schubert Finds," *Music Review* 31 (1970): 215–31. The counterpoint exercises are the topic of a study by Alfred Mann, "Zu Schuberts Studien im strengen Satz," in *Schubert-Kongress Wien 1978: Bericht*, ed. Otto Brusatti (Graz: Akademische Druck- u. Verlagsanstalt, 1979), 127–39; trans. as "Schubert's Lesson with Sechter," *19th-Century Music* 6 (1982): 159–65. Mann, on the other hand, did not know the Dresden leaf that Brown described.

dition, much as Haydn's death seemed to flash similarly conflicting signals to Beethoven. The turning to Sechter—the admission that there might still be something lacking in his technique—is a decision that seems inevitably to implicate a revelation in reaction to the novelty of voicing and texture in Beethoven's late quartets.

The connection with Beethoven is made tangible in another way. Josef Hauer, in a letter to Kreissle von Hellborn, testified to Schubert's obsession with Handel's music in his last years: "How often did he say: 'My dear Hauer, do come to my place and let's study Handel together.'"[39] And Karl Holz, writing in Beethoven's conversation book in April 1826, put down these suggestive lines (Beethoven's replies were of course viva voce):

> Schubert was just with him, and they were reading one of Handel's scores. He was very pleasant, and at the same time rendered thanks for the pleasure milord's quartets gave him. He was always present. He has great powers of conception in song. Do you know the Erlkönig? He always talked very mystically.[40]

Deutsch thought that Rafael Kiesewetter might have been Schubert's partner in that Handel session—a provocative notion. The editors of the conversation book argue more persuasively for Ignaz Franz Edler von Mosel.[41] No less compelling is the question of why Holz should have thought the incident to be of interest to Beethoven, whose enthusiasm for Handel must have been well known to his inner circle. Did Schubert wish it to be conveyed that he shared this devotion? Reading the terse, telegraphic entries in the conversation books is a frustration; we cannot know if Holz had been prompted to plant the news that Schubert had been following the public performance of the recent Beethoven quartets (opp. 127, 132, and 130) by the Schuppanzigh Quartet. We cannot read Holz's expression.

Schubert's complicity in the activities of such early music *collegia* as Kiesewetter's has not been adequately investigated.[42] If we must remain

---

39. Deutsch, *Memoirs*, 177; *Erinnerungen*, 204.

40. *Ludwig van Beethovens Konversationshefte* 9, ed. Grita Herre, with assistance from Günter Brosche (Leipzig: Deutscher Verlag für Musik, 1988), 160. The English is from Otto Erich Deutsch, *Schubert: A Documentary Biography* (London, 1946), 536, whose original text is O. E. Deutsch, *Schubert: Die Dokumente seines Lebens* (*Neue Ausgabe sämtliche Werke*, VIII/5) (Kassel, 1964), 352.

41. See *Konversationsheft* 9:391, note 494.

42. Schubert's place in the Kiesewetter circle is described in Herfrid Kier, *Raphael Georg Kiesewetter* (*1773–1850*): *Wegbereiter des musikalischen Historismus* (Regensburg: Gustav Bosse, 1968), esp. 91–93.

uncertain regarding anything like an awakening in Schubert of antiquarian appetites, it may be safe to say that the exposure to Kiesewetter's archaeological digs must have altered Schubert's perception of the limits of style, and perhaps led him to reassess his technique in this new context.

It was Handel's music that seems to have provoked the immediate decision to retool. Katerina Fröhlich, who was in close contact with Schubert during his final months, and, with her sisters, an active participant in Kiesewetter's house concerts, reconstructed her final encounter with Schubert. "A wonderful thing has happened to me today," Schubert tells her. "I have been given the works of Handel.—Ye gods! Now I see what I still lack, what a lot I still have to learn."[43]

The incident will call to mind a very similar one. In December 1826, Beethoven received the forty volumes of the Arnold edition of Handel's music from Johann Andreas Stumpff in London—"a royal gift," he wrote in gratitude.[44] Gerhard von Breuning, who published the Fröhlich recollection in 1884, was in a position to register the irony of coincidence in Beethoven's "same reaction and similar remark."[45] And in his account of Beethoven's last years, von Breuning tells of having been asked to carry the quarto volumes from the piano to Beethoven's sickbed: "I have wanted them for a long time," Beethoven told von Breuning, "for Handel is the greatest, the ablest composer; I can still learn from him."[46]

Leopold von Sonnleithner, in a biographical notice of 1857, gave the Fröhlich story a different twist. "A few months before his death Schubert visited the Fröhlich family and told them he had got the scores of Handel's oratorios. He added: Now for the first time I see what I lack; but I will study

---

43. Deutsch, *Memoirs*, 255; *Erinnerungen*, 292. Evidence for Schubert's intimacy with the Fröhlichs is enhanced in the discovery by Otto Biba of a Waldmüller sketch from 1827 showing Schubert together at the piano with Josephine Fröhlich; see Otto Biba, *Franz Schubert und seine Zeit*, catalogue of an exhibition at the Gesellschaft der Musikfreunde in 1978 (Vienna: Gesellschaft der Musikfreunde in Wien, 1978), entry no. 70, the drawing shown on p. 30.

44. The volumes were delivered by Stumpff's nephew to Johann Baptist Streicher in Vienna; see *Jahrbücher für musikalische Wissenschaft*, ed. Friedrich Chrysander, I (Leipzig, 1863), 449. Beethoven's note of receipt to Streicher, in a copyist's hand with Beethoven's signature, dated 14 December 1826, is at Bonn Beethoven-Haus, Sammlung H. C. Bodmer, HCB Br 254. A translation is given in Anderson, *Letters*, 1433. The more poignant document is the letter of gratitude to Stumpff, dated 8 February 1827: Brandenburg, *Briefwechsel Gesamtausgabe* 6:347–48; Anderson, *Letters*, 1332–33.

45. Deutsch, *Memoirs*, 255–56; *Erinnerungen*, 292–93.

46. Gerhard von Breuning, *Memories of Beethoven: From the House of the Black-Robed Spaniards*, ed. Maynard Solomon, trans. Henry Mins and Maynard Solomon (Cambridge: Cambridge University Press, 1992), 96.

hard with Sechter so that I can make good the omission."[47] Deutsch took von Sonnleithner's account as probable evidence that the study of Handel's music prompted the turn to Sechter. He went further: "It is possible that Haslinger made Beethoven's copies of the Arnold edition accessible to [Schubert]."[48] John Reed smartly doubted that speculation.[49] It is well known that the Arnold edition excited the heaviest bidding at the auction of Beethoven's *Nachlaß*, that Haslinger did in fact make off with the prize, and that he put it up for sale very soon thereafter at a price more than four times what he paid for it.[50] It is not likely that Haslinger, all too aware of its value, would have let any of these volumes out of his shop.

More likely, Reed thought, Schubert had access to some of the miscellaneous volumes of Handel's music that were found in Beethoven's library at his death; and he suspected that these "may well have passed to Schindler . . . and have found their way into Schubert's possession towards the end of 1827."[51] Schindler, in fact, seems to have made off with none of Beethoven's Handel scores. Lichnowsky laid prior claim to six volumes of Handel's music (these were not itemized in the *Nachlaßverzeichnis*), one of which was acquired by Fischhof from Lichnowsky some years later, and is now at the Berlin Staatsbibliothek.[52] The other Handel volumes listed in the *Nachlaßverzeichnis* went to other bidders.[53]

47. Deutsch, *Memoirs*, 114; *Erinnerungen*, 133.

48. Deutsch, *A Documentary Biography*, 819; *Dokumente*, 545. Deutsch put it less equivocally elsewhere: "Schubert had received Handel's works, obviously in Samuel Arnold's edition, shortly before the studies he began with Sechter; but they were a loan, not a gift. . . ." (*Memoirs*, 258; *Erinnerungen*, 296)—but he did not say how he knew this.

49. John Reed, *Schubert: The Final Years* (London: Faber, 1972), 204–5.

50. In the account of the auction of Beethoven's *Nachlaß* in the *Allgemeine Musikalische Zeitung* 30 (1828), 27–30, the sale of the Arnold edition was described in some detail. A translation was published in the *Harmonicon* for April 1828, and repr. in Anton Schindler, *The Life of Beethoven, Including his Correspondence with His Friends, Numerous Characteristic Traits, and Remarks on his Musical Works*, ed. Ignace Moscheles (London: Henry Colburn, 1841), 2:373–76; and in Thayer-Forbes, 1070–72.

51. Reed, *Schubert: The Final Years*, 205.

52. Beethoven autogr. 46. Fischhof's inscription is given in Eveline Bartlitz, *Die Beethoven-Sammlung in der Musikabteilung der Deutschen Staatsbibliothek: Verzeichnis* (Berlin: Deutsche Staatsbibliothek, 1970), 217–18. The "angesprochene Werke" in the *Nachlaß* are given in Th. von Frimmel, *Beethoven-Studien II: Bausteine zu einer Lebensgeschichte des Meisters* (Munich: Georg Müller, 1906), 185–86. The catalogue is given as well in Thayer-Forbes, 1061–70.

53. On the surviving manuscript copies of the auction catalogue, see JTW, 567–81; but the transcription here excludes the printed music in Beethoven's *Nachlaß*. Aloys Fuchs, writing to Schindler in 1852 of a recent visit to the widow of Dr. Wawruch, who tended Beethoven in his final illness, told of finding a score of *Messiah* "in der *engl. Orig*: Ausgabe"

92 CHAPTER FOUR

The evidence, then, does not support the contention that Beethoven's Handel was also Schubert's. And yet the picture of Schubert studying Handel from the very volumes that quickened Beethoven in his final illness, its pages stained with the abdominal fluids sprung from Beethoven during those ghastly surgical tappings, is irresistible—of mythic potential—and Deutsch did not resist it. The facts of the matter were very different. It was Giacomo Meyerbeer's wife, finally, who purchased the set from Haslinger as a gift for her husband.[54]

The chronicle of Schubert's final years portrays a composer at once at the height of his powers, finally taking hold in the critical press—Reed speaks of the review of 29 March 1828 in the *Theaterzeitung* of *Winterreise*, part I, as "the first critical notice of Schubert's work which seems to take the measure of his genius"[55]—haunted at the same time by the specters of Beethoven and Handel, seeking the rapprochement with the past that nourished the music of Beethoven's final decade. The decision to work with Sechter must be understood not simply as an admission that the fugues of 1828 were in some measure inadequate in that company, but that fugue as a strategy for controlling the thematics of a piece seemed to him significant enough to be pursued in a formal curriculum.

Fugue in 1828 must have appeared an elusive sign, at once archaic and progressive. Perhaps Schubert had in mind a notion that Tovey expressed with considerable eloquence: "The forms of Beethoven's last works show, the more we study them, a growing approximation to that Bach-like condition in which the place of every note can be deduced from the scheme."[56] Tovey, romanticizing Bach, captures an aesthetic nurtured in the nineteenth century on a very few works, and largely those which approach a manner we have come to know as *stile antico*.[57] Aptly, Tovey's formulation

---

with a letter from Beethoven confirming that the score was a New Year's gift. That would have been in January 1827, a few weeks after the complete Arnold set arrived. The Fuchs letter is given in Martin Staehelin, "Aus der Welt der frühen Beethoven-'Forschung': Aloys Fuchs in Briefen an Anton Schindler," in *Musik, Edition, Interpretation: Gedenkschrift Günter Henle*, ed. Martin Bente (Munich: G. Henle, 1980), 432–33. Beethoven's copy of the Breitkopf & Härtel edition of *Messias* in Mozart's orchestration was purchased at the auction by Ferdinand Piringer.

54. See Chrysander, *Jahrbücher für musikalische Wissenschaft*, I, 452; and Rudolf Kallir, "A Beethoven Relic," *Music Review* 9 (1948): 173–77.

55. Reed, *Schubert: The Final Years*, 209.

56. Donald Francis Tovey, "Some Aspects of Beethoven's Art Forms," in *Music & Letters* 8 (1927): 131–55; repr. in his *Essays and Lectures on Music* (London: Oxford University Press, 1949), 297; and *The Main Stream of Music and Other Essays* (New York, 1959), 297.

57. Erich Doflein speaks of the Palestrina renaissance and the *Bachpflege* as "transplantations" (*Verpflanzungen*): "Die Ideen vom 'wahren Kirchenstyl' und von der 'Reinheit der

comes at the end of his classic study of the Quartet in C♯ Minor, the work which, perhaps more than any other, captures the depth of Beethoven's investment in the music of Bach. The appropriation of Bach is evident in much of the late music, an obsession that reaches out to the name itself, elevated to a kind of topos in those entries, canonic and otherwise, which recur in the sketch papers and conversation books from the last years.[58]

Consider a famous passage toward the end of the *Große Fuge* (ex. 4.5). On the face of it, it is perhaps the least explicitly fugal moment in the piece, and yet paradoxically, even the exotic asynchronic quality of the harmonization is *about* the subject, playing out its inclination to slip away from an initial B♭. The weighing of the pitches B♭, A, and G♯ even consolidates the sense in which the subject is only an aspect of the greater thematics of op. 130, reaching back to the opening pitches of the first movement, and again to the enigmatic gesture with which the Andante con moto reluctantly begins. Here too, as in the first movement of op. 74, the harmony has thematic meaning, for it is this particular configuration that alludes to those tonal maneuverings in the *Overtura* from which the *Große Fuge* will summon its arguments. To suggest—as the piece surely does—that the subject of the fugue has been tending toward some apotheosis, expressed in these harmonies, is to invite us to construe it not as a fugue subject in any conventional sense, but as some inchoate intervallic substance—"pure interval music," in Stravinsky's memorable phrase—an aspect of whose significance is made luminous at this moment of final, almost inaudible contemplation.[59]

Tonkunst' waren Interpretationen; sie entwickelten sich aus klingenden Interpretationen, die sich nicht an die alte Singweise, sondern an eine neue Lesart der wiederentdeckten Stimmbücher und der daraus neu geschaffenen Partituren anschlossen; die Semibrevis der Mensuralnotation wurde als ganze Note, also als langer Notenwert aufgefaßt." (The ideas of a "true church style" and of the "purity of music" were interpretations; they were developed from sounding interpretations which attached not to the old mode of singing but to a new reading of rediscovered part-books and the scores that were created from them; the semibreve of mensural notation was apprehended as whole note, a note value of greater length.) See his "Historismus in der Musik," in *Die Ausbreitung des Historismus über die Musik*, ed. Walter Wiora (Regensburg: Gustav Bosse, 1969), 13.

58. See, for example, the sketch for the BACH canon "Kühl, nicht lau" (WoO 182) in *Ludwig van Beethovens Konversationshefte* 8 (1981), 82, and subsequent discussions on 90, 112, and 123. Sketches on a BACH theme course through the late sketchbooks: Artaria 197 (1821), Grasnick 4 (1824), Autograph 11/2 (1824), Autograph 9/1 (1825). For particulars, see JTW, passim. Hans-Werner Küthen develops the evidence for such a topos in "Quaerendo invenietis. Die Exegese eines Beethoven-Briefes an Haslinger vom 5. September 1823," in *Musik, Edition, Interpretation*, esp. 296–313.

59. Igor Stravinsky and Robert Craft, *Dialogues and a Diary* (Garden City, NY: Doubleday, 1963), 24. The idea that one might care to "reinstate" the *Große Fuge* in op. 130 is challenged by Warren Kirkendale in *Fugue and Fugato in Rococo and Classical Chamber*

EX. 4.5. Beethoven, *Große Fuge*, op. 133, mm. 609–20.

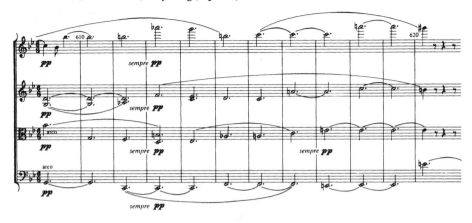

Perhaps it is grotesque to mention the two in the same sentence, but this passage in the *Große Fuge* brings to mind that modest piece of counterpoint "in freie Satz" shown in example 4.1, where the constraints of the exercise excite a part-writing and a root motion that at once obscure the plain sense of the cantus firmus and explore its harmonic implications. In the end, even Beethoven's most abstruse harmonies spring from a thematic process that is fundamentally contrapuntal.

In the final days before Schubert's death, the Quartet in C♯ Minor was performed for him in his rooms. It had yet to be heard in public. Karl Holz recorded the reaction: "Schubert was sent into such transports of delight and enthusiasm and was so overcome that those present all feared for him."[60] Again, the mythic intimations are powerful. What expressions of "delight and enthusiasm" were these that led his friends to fear for him? We cannot know. "There seems little doubt," Maynard Solomon suggests, "that Schubert would have come to terms—in his own way—with the implications of Beethoven's last style had he been given time to do so."[61] What would it have meant for Schubert to come to terms with such implications?

Music (Durham, NC: Duke University Press, 1979), 256–57, where the central argument rests on the "incontestable proof" that Albrechtsberger's *Gründliche Anweisung* served as the "point of departure" for Beethoven's fugue. This is to confuse the *Zierlichkeiten* of fugal procedure with the deeper meanings inherent in a work such as op. 130, and even to misconstrue its genre. I take the issue further in "Between Cavatina and Ouverture: Opus 130 and the Voices of Narrative," *Beethoven Forum* 1 (1992): 165–89, and return to it in chapter 8 below.

60. Deutsch, *Memoirs*, 299; *Erinnerungen*, 344.
61. Maynard Solomon, "Schubert and Beethoven," *19th-Century Music* 3 (1979): 125.

The masterpieces of Schubert's final years, those works which touch a nerve in us as does no other music, are most eloquent where the evidence of a coming to terms with Beethoven is negligible. But the C♯ Minor Quartet broadcasts implications of another kind.

The lesson with Sechter, symptom of some deeper inquiry, suggests that Schubert had begun to follow Beethoven in this fraught direction.[62] Hearing the quartet will have taught him the magnitude of the enterprise. It is not given to us to know whether a year or more in pursuit of these exalted models might finally have translated into a new manner, or would merely have deepened those aspects of Schubert's style which set him at greatest remove from Beethoven. The distinction between the exercise of counterpoint in some orthodox, even antiquarian mode, as exemplified in those retrospective fugues by Schumann and Mendelssohn, and the concept of counterpoint as a theoretical abstraction, realized in the profound new voicings of Beethoven's late quartets, would in the course of the long nineteenth century evolve well beyond these differences that fix a telling moment in the endgames of Beethoven and Schubert.

---

62. Peter Gülke has proposed that the technique in Beethoven's late work "may have appeared to Schubert as a step into territory in which he himself felt deeply incompetent." At the same time, Gülke is concerned whether the "wunderbare Gelöstheit" of a Romantic counterpoint that sprang from the need for heightened cantabile—a concept developed by him in a number of other studies—would have been compromised had Schubert attended with greater diligence to the poverty of his earlier training. "Unquestionably," Gülke concludes, "there was a deficiency here, and the turn to Sechter cannot be perceived simply as an untimely acquiescence to academicism." See his "Neue Beiträge zur Kenntnis des Sinfonikers Schubert: Die Fragmente D 615, D708A und D 936A," in *Musik-Konzepte. Sonderband Franz Schubert*, ed. Heinz-Klaus Metzger and Rainer Riehn (Munich: Edition Text + kritik, 1979), 185–220, esp. 205–6.

✳ CHAPTER 5 ✳

Con alcune licenze

On the Largo before the Fugue in Op. 106

Once more it is a challenging insight from Gustav Nottebohm's *Beethoven's Studien* of 1873, his groundbreaking exposition of the profuse and complex body of work in strict Fuxian counterpoint that Beethoven undertook with Haydn in 1793 and in both strict and less strict counterpoint and in fugue with Albrechtsberger in 1794, that will set things in motion. Assiduous students of that classic text may recall Nottebohm's harsh conclusion:

> So viel steht fest, dass Beethoven bei Albrechtsberger keine Durchbildung in der Fugenform gewonnen hat . . .

. . . and further,

> dass Beethoven einen grossen Theil der ihm von Albrechtsberger aufgegebenen Fugen nachlässig gearbeitet habe und dass durch seine Schuld der Unterricht nicht eigentlich zu Ende geführt worden sei. Es läuft darauf hinaus, dass der Eine nicht konnte, der Andere nicht wollte.[1]

And in rough translation:

---

1. Gustav Nottebohm, *Beethovens Studien* (Leipzig: J. Rieter-Biedermann, 1873), 200. Nottebohm's first exposition of these papers was in a critical response to Ignaz Seyfried's *Ludwig van Beethovens Studien im Generalbasse, Contrapuncte und in der Compositions-Lehre* (Vienna: Tobias Haslinger, 1832), a falsification of Beethoven's study papers, first reported in a series of contributions to the *Allgemeine Musikalische Zeitung* for 1863 and 1864, and then synthesized in the final essay in his *Beethoveniana* (Leipzig: C. F. Peters, 1872), 154–203. And see above, p. 80, note 17.

On the Largo before the Fugue in Op. 106   97

This much is clear: that Beethoven achieved no thorough development in the composition of fugue, that the greater part of Beethoven's work with the fugal assignments given him by Albrechtsberger was carelessly done and that it was his fault that the instruction was not really brought to conclusion. It comes down to this: that the one was not capable, the other not willing.

This stern indictment both of Beethoven's negligence in the pursuit of his fugal studies and of Albrechtsberger's limitations as an instructor must be taken very seriously, coming as it does from the sharp pen of the magisterial Nottebohm, a scholar and musician whose command of the literature and practice of eighteenth-century theory and its historical foundation had few equals, and whose control of the Beethoven *Nachlass*, and most notably his indefatigable work with a massive body of Beethoven's workshop papers, was an achievement mythic in scope and of a significance to which all subsequent studies have been indebted.

Intolerant of Albrechtsberger's recourse to an antiquated modal practice in the teaching of how fugal subjects are to be answered—his "plagal" models, for one, elicited only wry skepticism[2]—Nottebohm's summary judgment of Albrechtsberger's work with Beethoven yet seems rather too swift. The copious worksheets that record Beethoven's studies with Albrechtsberger—more than 160 closely written pages, generated in three lessons a week over a span of fifteen months, in Nottebohm's calculation[3]— these worksheets picture Beethoven and Albrechtsberger embraced in combat (or so it often seems): Beethoven, composing fairly complex fugues for two, three, and four voices on Albrechtsberger's routine text-book subjects; Albrechtsberger, scribbling corrections, catching the usual solecisms (consecutive fifths, *mi contra fa*, unprepared sevenths, and the like) and noting what he labeled "licenzen," chromatic licenses that would not have passed muster in the chaste world of Fuxian counterpoint (see, for one, ex. 4.1 in the previous chapter); Beethoven, then taking the trouble to rewrite a fugue, incorporating Albrechtsberger's corrections even as he took the occasion to tinker with his own counterpoint. As one might have expected, there are omissions and errors on both sides, and yet the overall impression is of a productive and vibrant collaboration of which we have only the written record, now painstakingly restored in Julia Ronge's authoritative edition published in 2014 for the new *Gesamtausgabe*. In a corrective to such views as Nottebohm's, Ronge writes: ". . . die Quellen bezeugen

2. *Beethovens Studien*, 194, the footnote at the bottom of the page.
3. *Beethovens Studien*, 203.

Beethovens Ernst, großen Eifer, Fleiß und Engagement bei der Bewälti-
gung der ihm gestellten Aufgaben" (the sources testify to his earnestness,
his great passion, his diligence and engagement in the accomplishment of
the assignments that were put to him).[4]

For all Nottebohm's penetrating scrutiny, one might wonder whether
his sovereign control of eighteenth-century theory, filtered through the
distant perspective of the 1860s and 1870s, isn't somewhat deaf to the
sense of inquiry evident in Beethoven's approach to fugue, driven in part
(and increasingly) by a challenge to the conventions of fugal procedure.
Beethoven, when not doing his homework for Albrechtsberger, was after
all busy developing a unique identity that was about to impose itself on
the Viennese scene, both as virtuoso pianist and as a composer at the cutting edge.

This intensive work for Albrechtsberger during these critical years
of Beethoven's first maturity was undertaken at a time when it might no
longer have seemed self-evident how the conventions of an earlier fugal
practice were to be reconciled with the new boundaries that Beethoven's
music, advancing a bold poetic and dramatic program, had begun to explore. The models of *The Well-Tempered Clavier* were at hand from his earliest instruction, recalling the report on Beethoven's progress published in
Cramer's *Magazin der Musik* for 1783: "Er spielt größtentheils das wohltemperirte Clavier von Sebastian Bach, welches ihm Herr Neefe unter die
Hände gegeben" (He plays for the most part the *Well-Tempered Clavier* of
Sebastian Bach, which Herr Neefe has put in his hands).[5] And he continually writes out passages from it, transcribing several for string quartet or
quintet, even into his final decade.[6] But the greater challenge would be to
forge large-scale works from an idea of fugue that would enable new ways
of construing theme and texture, extending tonal trajectories as alternatives to the protocols of sonata.

In the decade following the studies with Albrechtsberger, however,
fugue was limited either to internal moments of thematic development
or to such conventional, even archaic exercises as the closing chorus of
Christus am Oelberge (1803) and the "Cum sancto spiritu" fugue in the Gloria of the C-Major Mass (1807). Rather less conventional is the ambitious

---

4. [Ludwig van] Beethoven, *Kompositionsstudien bei Joseph Haydn, Johann Georg Albrechtsberger und Antonio Salieri*, ed. Julia Ronge, 3 vols. (Munich: G. Henle, 2014), 1 Tran-
skriptionen: xiii.

5. The account is to be found in the *Magazin der Musik*, ed. Carl Friedrich Cramer,
I/1 (Hamburg: 1783; repr. Hildesheim: Georg Olms, 1971), 394.

6. For a valuable checklist, see Warren Kirkendale, *Fugue and Fugato in Rococo and
Classical Chamber Music* (Durham, NC: Duke University Press, 1979), 212–14.

EX. 5.1. Beethoven, sketches for the "alla fuga" in op. 35. Wielhorsky Sketchbook, p. 32; transcription in Fishman, ed. (Moscow, 1962).

"Finale alla fuga" of the so-called "Eroica" Variations, op. 35 (1802), whose tonal answer inflecting the subdominant drew Nottebohm's red pencil.[7] Entries in the Wielhorsky Sketchbook capture Beethoven's ambivalence on this very matter, shown in transcription in example 5.1.[8] Here, in a nutshell, is the struggle to reconcile a tension between intervallic integrity and tonal imperatives. The famously subdominant answer in the fugue at the outset of the Quartet in C♯ Minor some twenty-five years later is evidence only that the dialectic of fugal theory was a lifelong inquiry for Beethoven.[9] Who, after all, would think to challenge the legitimacy of any note in that totemic work?

But in 1810, in the midst of the Allegretto ma non troppo of the String Quartet in F Minor, op. 95, comes a critical turn, fugue now moving boldly to appropriate the discourse of this deeply affecting movement, the chromatic inflections of its tortuous subject engaging both the simple diatonic scale with which the movement opens and the tune that follows from it.[10]

7. *Beethovens Studien*, 197.

8. N. L. Fishman, *Kniga eskizov Beethoven za 1802–1803 gody* [The Wielhorsky Sketchbook in facsimile and transcription, with commentary] (Moscow, 1962), facsimile, p. 32; transcription, p. 39.

9. Of the subdominant answer in op. 131, Robert Winter describes a score draft that "bears the scars of repeated attempts to bend the answer to the dominant," providing "a remarkably clairvoyant example of the conflict between Beethoven's creative muse and his deep-seated respect for tradition." See *The String Quartets of Haydn, Mozart, and Beethoven: Studies of the Autograph Manuscripts*, ed. Christoph Wolff (Cambridge, MA: Harvard University Department of Music, 1980), 272.

10. Seow-Chin Ong has argued convincingly that the date "1810" on the autograph score is to be believed (against a revisionist dating of 1814 proposed by Alan Tyson). See

At what seems a symmetrical midpoint in the movement, there comes a stunning interruption at a full close in A♭ major, a tritone distant from the D major at its inception. The fugue starts up again, its entries now compressed in stretto and inversion, a witty countersubject, *staccatissimo*, further complicating the texture and altering the tail of the subject itself. No formal closure here, but rather an amplification, the opening notes of the subject now isolated in extreme dissonance marked by characteristic *sforzandi*, dissolving finally into a reprise of the opening scale, now *sotto voce*. Here fugue breaks free of the constraints of an eighteenth-century script.

In his probing study of 1978, "'Von zwei Kulturen der Musik': Die Schlußfuge aus Beethovens Cellosonate opus 102, 2," Carl Dahlhaus reminds us of the escape clause with which Beethoven inaugurates the opening of the *Schlussfuge* in the Hammerklavier Sonata, op. 106: "con alcune licenze," Beethoven writes.[11] One imagines Beethoven reaching back to the Albrechtsberger sessions, where the term "licenz" may have come to signify in Beethoven's mind instances where the creative impulse drove the music against the unforgiving rigors of strict counterpoint, of *strenge Satz*.

But of course the *licenze* in op. 106 are of a magnitude, a significance, a frequency that affect every aspect of the work, and not least the subject itself, whose initial exposition refuses to respect the formal dimension that will define the full subject in each subsequent return. As it unfolds in the expansive ten measures up to the entry of the answer, this initial statement of the subject, through the 390 measures that commence with the Allegro risoluto, never once replicates itself.

One template that takes the measure of the subject in its truest, stripped-down form is that remarkable passage in which the subject is given in retrograde, whose beginning fixes the close of the subject.[12] A device rarely invoked, this is the solitary occasion of its use by Beethoven. (Nor is there a single instance of it in the entirety of *The Well-Tempered Clavier*.) What is revelatory here is the syntactical coherence of the theme in this permutation, even in its keen rhythmic reversals. (The retrograde is shown against the proper subject in ex. 5.2.)

What, then, can have provoked Beethoven to this initial *licenz*? In its

---

his "Aspects of the Genesis of Beethoven's String Quartet in F Minor, Op. 95," in *The String Quartets of Beethoven*, ed. William Kinderman (Urbana: University of Illinois Press, 2006), 132–67.

11. *Die Musikforschung* 31 (1978), esp. 403–4.

12. Ferruccio Busoni, in a detailed analysis of the fugue, may have been the first to offer this "proof" (as he calls it). The analysis constitutes the third appendix of volume 1 of his remarkable edition of J. S. Bach, *The Well-Tempered Clavichord* [sic] (New York: G. Schirmer, [1894]), 195–205.

EX. 5.2. Beethoven, Piano Sonata in B♭, op. 106, Allegro risoluto. Subject in retrograde, at m. 153.

quest to establish itself, this windy, pleonastic exposition of the subject hints at a searching process set in motion through the Largo that precedes it, an *introduzione*, as Beethoven refers to it in several documents (if not in the text of the published score), whose three fugue-like fragments, in G♭ major, B major, and G♯ minor, suggest a narrative in which the emergence of the true subject, coincident with the retaking of the overarching tonic of the sonata, will be understood as a final station in that process. No conventional introduction, this bold fantasy-like excursion continues to draw profuse commentary, most notably by such recent authors as Martin Zenck, Hans-Werner Küthen, and Tom Beghin.[13] "One of the most astonishing pages in the history of music," concluded Charles Rosen, after some brilliant reflections of his own in *The Classical Style*.[14] As I wrote about it in 1992 (here slightly altered):

> A process of memory is engaged here, but it extends beyond the piece itself, to genre set out historically. Three quasi-fugal passages are called up, each seeming to recall some imaginary monument from the past. The improvisatory nature of the scene only contributes to a phenomenon of the piece contemplating its own evolution. The act of authorship, the presence of the author, is strongly felt. The lines of demarcation between the work and its genesis are smudged, if only in metaphor.[15]

---

13. Martin Zenck, *Die Bach-Rezeption des späten Beethoven: Zum Verhältnis von Musikhistoriographie und Rezeptionsgeschichtsschreibung der "Klassik"* (Stuttgart: Franz Steiner, 1986), with special attention to the subchapter "Die vermittelte Stilantithese von Fantasie und Fuge in Op. 106 und Op. 110," esp. 199–213. Hans-Werner Küthen, "Quaerendo invenietis. Die Exegese eines Beethoven-Briefes an Haslinger vom 5. September 1823," in *Musik, Edition, Interpretation: Gedenkschrift Günter Henle*, ed. Martin Bente (Munich: G. Henle, 1980), 282–313. Tom Beghin: see below, note 19.

14. Charles Rosen, *The Classical Style: Haydn, Mozart, Beethoven* (New York: W. W. Norton, expanded ed., 1997), 429.

15. "Between Cavatina and Ouverture: Opus 130 and the Voices of Narrative," *Beethoven Forum* 1 (1992): 171–72.

But there is another aspect to this that must weigh heavily in our hearing of the *introduzione*, and that is its position in the larger sonata, opening out from an Adagio sostenuto (Appassionato e con molto sentimento) in F♯ minor that is by far the longest movement in the work: an extreme twenty-five minutes and seventeen seconds, as recorded by Christoph Eschenbach in 1976.[16] This monolithic, even tragic F♯ minor, a kind of anti-tonic in the sonata, is transformed in its closing bars to F♯ major (where in fact much of the recapitulation had been cast), its final chord arpeggiated from the deepest F♯, now shifted from *una corda* to *tutte le corde* but marked triple piano (*pianisissimo*), the resonance of the full string choir amplified by the open damper pedal across the final rests, even as the keys are barely touched.[17] (See ex. 5.3A.) Of interest here is the autograph of op. 101, where Beethoven writes "tutto il cembalo ma piano," at the return of the opening phrases of the sonata after an Adagio ma non troppo performed entirely "sul una corda."[18] And it is from this faintly sounded quiescence at the end of the Adagio of op. 106 that an arpeggiated octave on F-*natural* initiates the Largo. It, too, is pedaled, settling finally into the deepest F on Beethoven's keyboard.[19]

Beethoven failed to write "attacca" at the end of the Adagio. And yet, to perform the opening of the Largo without the gravitational pull of F♯ major still resonant in the mind would be to dismiss the powerful inflection that redefines this F♯ as, in effect, an appoggiatura G♭ in anticipation of the inevitable return to B♭ major. More pointedly, those octaves which open into the Largo make sense only as afterbeats, manifest as a revelatory return

16. I take this from Basilio Fernández Morante, "A Panoramic Survey of Beethoven's *Hammerklavier* Sonata, Op. 106: Composition and Performance," *Notes. Quarterly Journal of the Music Library Association*, 71, no. 2 (December 2014): 237–62, a remarkably thorough review of the history of the sonata from several perspectives, and including a table of durations for each movement drawn from fifty-one recorded performances, from 1935 through 2007.

17. A marginal note in the Artaria first edition, at the bottom of the first page of the Adagio, reads: "Una corda (U : C) bedeutet Eine Saite, Tutte [le] Corde (T : C) bedeutet Drey Saiten, poi a poi due tre Corde nach und nach 2. Und 3. Saiten." Artur Schnabel, in his edition of the sonatas ([New York: Simon and Schuster, 1935], 736), argues that the designation *tutte le corde* must apply to the opening of the Largo, but the earliest editions are very clear that it applies to the final chord of the Adagio.

18. The autograph is today at the Beethoven-Haus Bonn, and has been published in a fine facsimile edition (Munich: G. Henle, 1998) with commentary by Sieghard Brandenburg.

19. With the arrival of the six-octave Broadwood in late May or early June 1818, the deepest note for which Beethoven could write was lowered by a fourth to CC, a note that Beethoven now writes in the final movement (m. 112) of op. 106. In fact, he writes a DD in the Adagio (m. 63). The problem of keyboard range in op. 106 is among the topics in Tom Beghin, "Beethoven's *Hammerklavier* Sonata, Opus 106: Legend, Difficulty, and the Gift of a Broadwood Piano," in *Keyboard Perspectives* 7 (2014): 81–121.

EX. 5.3A. Beethoven, Piano Sonata in B♭, op. 106. Final bars of the Adagio sostenuto.

from the darkness of F♯ minor. The relationship is palpable. (The complete *introduzione*, from the end of the Adagio and into the opening statement of the subject, is shown as ex. 5.3B.)

And here it will do well to recall that remarkable letter of March 1819 to Ferdinand Ries in London:

> —sollte die *sonate* nicht recht seyn für *london*, so könn[te ich] eine andere schicken, oder sie können auch das *Largo* auslaßen u. gleich bei der *Fuge*
>
>
>
> das lezte Stück anfangen, oder das erste Stück alsdenn das *Adagio* u. zum 3-ten das *Scherzo* u. N⁰ 4 sammt *largo* u. A^{llo} *risoluto* ganz weglaßen, oder sie nehmen nur das erste Stück u. *Scherzo* als [ganze Sonate.] ich überlaße ihnen dieses, wie sie es am besten finden . . . [20]

and in the Anderson translation:

> Should the sonata not be suitable for London, I could send another one; or you could also omit the Largo and begin straight away with the Fugue [see example] which is the last movement; or you could use the first movement and then the Adagio, and then for the third movement the Scherzo—and omit entirely no. 4 with the Largo and Allegro risoluto. Or you could take just the first movement and the Scherzo and let them form the whole sonata. I leave it to you to do as you think best.[21]

20. *Briefwechsel Gesamtausgabe*, ed. Sieghard Brandenburg (Munich: G. Henle, 1996), 4:262.

21. Emily Anderson, trans. and ed., *The Letters of Beethoven* (London: Macmillan & Co; New York: St. Martin's Press, 1961), 804–5.

EX. 5.3B. Beethoven, Piano Sonata in B♭, op. 106. Largo; and opening bars of the Allegro risoluto and subject of the Fuga.

A year earlier, George Thomson wrote him from Edinburgh: "Everyone in this country finds that your works are too difficult; and there is only a very small number of first-class masters who can play them."[22] Perhaps these hard words prompted Beethoven to offer Ries various alternatives to the publication of a sonata that he must have feared would be rather

---

22. Letter of 22 June 1818. For the original text (in French), see *Briefwechsel Gesamtausgabe* 4:196. Cited and discussed in Barry Cooper, *Beethoven's Folksong Settings: Chronology, Sources, Style* (Oxford: Clarendon Press, 1994), 128.

too demanding for his British clientele. It is the very first proposal in that letter that is the most troubling: "sie können das *Largo* auslaßen u. gleich bey der Fuge das lezte Stück anfangen." By what process of argument can Beethoven have convinced himself to take back this breathtaking music? Could he have thought the Largo too radical in concept, too vulnerable to misunderstanding? And of course this would destroy any sense of continuity from the end of the Adagio to the onset of the Allegro risoluto. (As it turns out, the first British edition was issued in two parts, the second of which was titled "Introduction and Fugue."[23] In Part I, the Adagio was made to precede the Scherzo, evidently following a proposal spelled out in Beethoven's letter. So much for the sense of an "attacca" from Adagio to Largo!)

As though to confirm a relationship with the Adagio, and indeed to complicate it, G♭ major is established as the setting for the first of these fugal fragments. This is a nostalgic, wistful G♭, at once recalling, enharmonically, the final measures of the Adagio even as it alludes to some distant historical moment, its close imitation and toccata-like repetitions hinting at some imaginary keyboard canzona of the seventeenth century. Tellingly, G♭ has a role to play in the body of the *Fuga propria* itself. Here, seventy-five bars into the fugue, G♭ major is made the locus of its first full, and power-

---

23. See Alan Tyson, *The Authentic English Editions of Beethoven* (London: Faber and Faber, 1963), 102–7.

EX. 5.3C. Beethoven, Piano Sonata in B♭, op. 106. From Allegro risoluto, the new episode in G♭ major, at m. 75.

EX. 5.3D. Beethoven, Piano Sonata in B♭, op. 106. From Allegro risoluto, subject in retrograde, at m. 153.

ful, cadence, and of a lyricism, fleeting as it may be, in relief of the spiked, dissonant intensity of this driven music, intimating however briefly the second group of a sonata movement. (See ex. 5.3c.) Here is fugal texture, but of a different kind, and it takes no great leap of imagination to hear in it a reminiscence, an echo, if not quite a continuation of that fugal fragment in the *introduzione*.[24]

The next station in this *introduzione* is B major, a fragmentary two-part invention that invokes Bach but then intensifies toward a half cadence whose dominant seventh on F♯ once again calls up the closing bars of the Adagio, as though to revisit the enharmonic implication of an augmented sixth that would negotiate between Adagio and Largo. And here, too, the fragment has its echo in the *fuga propria*, this at the inception of the cancrizans in B minor, at m. 143, together with the three sixteenths that serve as an upbeat to the subject (shown in ex. 5.3D).

The third fragment bursts onto the stage, no fermata to soften the blow, and in a brisk new tempo: a rough-hewn *Klavierstück* in G♯ minor extend-

---

24. At this critical turn, the music (to my ear) wants the slightest relaxation, *quasi dolce*. Of the many recorded performances that I've studied, the one that comes closest is the performance by Ernst Lévy, recorded in 1958 for Kapp Records, and remastered on Marston Records, CD 52007–2.

ing for five full bars. The pull to a subdominant C♯ minor is so strong as to throw into question the priorities of subject and answer.

Each situated in a distant tonal area—G♭ major, B major, G♯ minor/ C♯ minor—the three fragments together perform a tonal sphere of the remote, a remoteness captured in the descent through the chain of thirds (major and minor) that finally link those octave Fs at the outset to the powerful cadencing on A, as dominant in D minor, just before the Allegro risoluto.

The impulse to situate these three fragments in a linear narrative that will prefigure the *Fuga a tre voci* is seductive. Rosen, for one, reads them to suggest what he calls "The Birth of Counterpoint, or The Creation of a Fugue."[25] Others have sought to identify sources, even specific models, in the music of earlier composers. Most provocatively, Martin Zenck hears a *Beziehung* (a word that allows some fluidity between reference and relationship) between the Largo and J. S. Bach's *Chromatische Fantasie*.[26] To my mind, such illuminating comparisons, for all that we might learn from them, threaten to over-determine what we can ever retrieve of Beethoven's internal dialogue with the iconic figures of the past. Quite beyond what we might detect of its antecedents, the entire *introduzione* seems an improvisation, a *Probestück* in search of fugue. And it is precisely this exploratory adventure that is conveyed at the outset of the *fuga a tre voci, con alcune licenze*: the feel of a subject in search of itself.

*

As it happens, several preliminary drafts for the *introduzione* have survived, illuminating a process of discovery that I am tempted to characterize as improvisatory, recognizing, as we must, a distinction between the real-time act of composing, improvisatory as it may seem, and a musical text designed to play out in mimesis the wonder of discovery in the act of improvisation, sudden and unpredictable in all its concentrated disorder: a narrative of creation. Here, both phenomena are in play, inscribed in manuscripts today housed in the William Scheide collection at Princeton University: two fascicles, purchased separately, that have no demonstrable relationship to one another. (Their contents are given in the Appendix.) The earlier of the two (Scheide 132) comprises a nested gathering of four leaves in two bifolia.

---

25. Rosen, *Beethoven's Piano Sonatas: A Short Companion* (New Haven, CT: Yale University Press, 2002), 226.

26. Martin Zenck, *Die Bach-Rezeption des späten Beethoven*, 211–13.

A later draft is to be found on a single leaf among a loose miscellany of six leaves of five different paper types that constitute Scheide 131.

On what must be the earliest entries for this music, at Scheide 132, fol. 1r, Beethoven scribbles a few terms in an effort to formulate the essence of what he is about to compose: "prelu[dium]," "Einle[i]t[ung]," and finally "introduction aus" (the meaning of "aus," preposition or adverb, if that is what Beethoven has written, remains something of a puzzle). The opening arpeggios display that improvisatory disorder, not perfectly under control. The music then comes more sharply into focus, its bass staking out the familiar descent by thirds: F, Db, Bb, pausing at Gb, where a fermata interrupts the action, signaling the advent of something new: a tentative bit of imitative counterpoint. The page is turned. At fol. 1v Beethoven begins again, now finding the broken octaves that will set the Largo in motion. Again, much is made of the arrival at Gb, and here the imitative fragment is developed into something more substantial. The descent by thirds resumes, now fixing Ab minor and another arpeggiation, rejected in favor of a more complex idea suggestive of the invention-like fragment that would finally emerge in B major, while the key of Ab minor would re-emerge as G# minor. (The two pages are shown in fig. 5.1.)

The draft continues on the recto and verso of what is currently numbered fol. 4, continuing from 4v to some space left at the bottom of fol. 3r, in a remarkable imbroglio of sketches toward the fixing of the arrival at Bb coincident with the onset of the fugue. (Some of this is disentangled in ex. 5.4. A reordering of these leaves, correcting the pagination given at the Princeton site, is explained in the Appendix.) The intensity of thought concentrated at this critical turn at the inception of the fugue leaves its mark on the page, picturing Beethoven consumed in the moment, even before the subject of the fugue in its final version had been established, much less a design for the entirety of the movement. Setting itself off from the *introduzione* proper, the music seeks to locate the metrical downbeat that will establish the "allegro risoluto," and from there, the powerful downbeat that will set the fugue in motion. In the final version, this downbeat, *fortissimo* and *sforzando*, precedes by one bar the incipit of the subject, ensuring that the leap of a tenth up to the trill will behave as an upbeat, fixing the resolution of the trill on a strong measure even as a free counterpoint of sixteenths, anticipating the subject itself, drives the music to that powerful downbeat. The sketches, then, capture the struggle to establish this ultimate stage in the unfolding of the *introduzione*. In the latest of these entries, at staves 15/16 on fol. 3r, the principal motive of the subject, sounded twice, is made to anticipate the true incipit two bars early and in the wrong

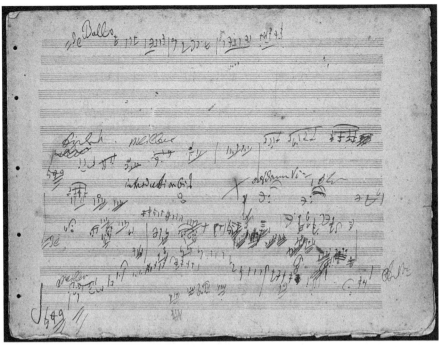

FIGURE 5.1. Beethoven, op 106, sketches for Largo. Princeton University Library, Scheide ms. 132, fols. 1r and 1v. By kind permission.

EX. 5.4. Beethoven, sketches for Largo, op. 106, in Scheide ms. 132, fol. 4v → 3r. Princeton University Library.

register, evidence again of an intent to write into the music an intuitive process of discovery in the fixing of a subject.

A later draft, on a single leaf of eight-stave paper in Scheide 131, records a next stage in the evolution of our three fragments. (Fols. 1r and 1v are shown as fig. 5.2.) But it's the broken octaves at the outset that will come as a surprise. Barely visible because Beethoven wiped them away while the ink was still wet, what they reveal is the pitch class A. Why A? Did Beethoven wish to anticipate the powerful cadencing whose octave As explode in an intense cadenza fraught with dissonance that will provide the gateway to the Allegro risoluto? Of great interest is the continuation into the grand cadenza on A, but from here, the draft trails off tentatively, the sequence of thirds in the bass seeming to find a weak dominant on C: no trace of the clinching return to the dominant on A, *fortissimo* and *prestissimo*, that will diminish to an octave on A before slipping to the true dominant before the Allegro risoluto. If the tied notes at the very end of the draft on fol. 1v would suggest a continuation on an adjacent page, none is to be found on the ten remaining pages in Scheide 131—nor anywhere else among the extant sketches for the finale, roughly seventy-eight pages dispersed among seven archival collections.[27]

Among the diffuse and scattered entries among the remaining pages of Scheide 131, one page in particular offers another glimpse of the mind in search of inspiration from other sources. This is fol. 2r (see fig. 5.3, and Appendix B below), its twenty staves ruled in a rough hand from top to bottom, as though in preparation for some massive work for orchestra, presumably with chorus. At the top margin, Beethoven writes, provocatively, "Zulezt 4-stimmig in allabreve takt" (finally, in four voices, *alla breve*), answered at the bottom of the page with "4-stimmiges Stück sul clavicembalo"—an

---

27. In addition to these large-format leaves are three pocket sketchbooks that contain work on the finale: the so-called "Boldrini" sketchbook, missing since the later nineteenth century, but described in some detail in Nottebohm, *Zweite Beethoveniana* (for details, see Douglas Johnson, Alan Tyson, and Robert Winter, *The Beethoven Sketchbooks: History, Reconstruction, Inventory*, ed. Douglas Johnson, 347–50 [hereafter JTW]); and Vienna, Gesellschaft der Musikfreunde, Beethoven A 44 and Beethoven A 45. For a checklist of the loose sketches, see Robert Winter's "Sketches for the Piano Sonata, Opus 106 (1817–1818)," in JTW, 535–38, a conspectus augmented in Norbert Gertsch, "Ludwig van Beethovens 'Hammerklavier'-Sonate op. 106: Bemerkungen zur Datierung und Bewertung der Quellen," *Bonner Beethoven-Studien* 2 (2001): 63–93, esp. 89–91. The account in Nicholas Marston, "Approaching the Sketches for Beethoven's 'Hammerklavier' Sonata," *Journal of the American Musicological Society* 44, no. 3 (Fall 1991): 404–50, concerns mainly the third movement, with interesting speculation on what Marston believes to be the earliest intimations of the transition to the fugal finale.

FIGURE 5.2. Beethoven, op. 106, sketches for Largo. Princeton University Library, Scheide ms. 131, fols. 1r and 1v. By kind permission.

On the Largo before the Fugue in Op. 106   113

FIGURE 5.3. Beethoven, copy of passages from J. S. Bach, *Well-Tempered Clavier* II, among sketches for op. 106 fugue. Princeton University Library, Scheide ms. 131, fol. 2r. By kind permission.

antiquated term, *clavicembalo*, that Beethoven continued to use now and then, mostly in sketches, as a generic term for the keyboard instrument at hand. Alas, there is no further evidence in support of a temptation to imagine Beethoven here conjuring a radical swerve as a closing component to this *fuga a tre voce*. Other entries on the page, fragmentary attempts at the subject of the fugue, do indeed draw op. 106 into the picture.

And then, at the bottom of the page, Beethoven scribbles two passages from *The Well-Tempered Clavier*, Book II. The more substantial is from the fugue in C♯ minor: measures 14 and 15. Unlike a number of citations from Bach to be found in Beethoven's papers over the years, this one is copied neither from Albrechtsberger's *Anweisung* nor from Marpurg's *Abhandlung*. Identifying its precise source is frustrating. We know only that Beethoven owned a copy of Book I of the *WTC*, in the edition published by Nägeli in Zurich in 1801 (the year that saw as well the first editions of Simrock in Bonn and Hoffmeister & Kühnel in Leipzig), a missing segment of some

114 CHAPTER FIVE

thirty pages replaced with pages from the Hoffmeister edition.[28] The volume belongs to a larger *Sammelband* from the *Oeuvres complettes* [*sic*] of Bach's keyboard works published by Hoffmeister and Kühnel, and which came to the Berlin Staatsbibliothek from the estate of Anton Schindler. And here we might remind ourselves of Neefe's testimony that Beethoven as early as 1783 is playing "größtentheils das wohltemperirte Clavier von Sebastian Bach." Can we imagine that he was ever without some text, in manuscript or print, of these paradigmatic works that served as a resource and an inspiration in Beethoven's lifelong quest to master the rhetoric of fugue, not least in its poetic aspect?

Why these few bars? What would have led Beethoven to single out, to commit to ink and paper, this measure-and-a-half of a modulation up to the return of the subject in the tonic? The fugue itself is a seductive one for the keyboard player, the difficulties of its seamless and exquisite partwriting obscuring deeper formal subtleties. It is, however, the C♯-minor fugue "a 5 voci" of Book 1, in its severe *stile antico*, that has drawn all the attention—and indeed, as Schmid reports, Beethoven annotated his copy with "all manner of numberings [allerlei Zahleneintragungen]" which, in Schmid's reading, appear to bear on fingerings from which one might draw conclusions as to Beethoven's legato playing.[29] If we cannot know with similar confidence what might have drawn Beethoven to this passage in the C♯-minor fugue from Book 2, perhaps it is enough simply to imagine Beethoven interrupting the composing of his *fuga con alcune licenze* to read through the fugue solely for the pleasure of the thing, pausing to notate these few bars whose deft voicing in its harmonic swing from E major back to C♯ minor caught his ear—and enough to happen upon Beethoven turning once again to this inexhaustible compilation, ever in dialogue with his venerated ancestor, believing, even in late maturity, that there might be something more to learn from him.[30]

There was work to be done before the Largo would be brought to its

28. The copy in Beethoven's possession was first described in some detail in Ernst Fritz Schmid, "Beethovens Bachkenntnis," *Neues Beethoven-Jahrbuch* 5 (1933): 64–83, esp. 64–66; and then in Eveline Bartlitz, *Die Beethoven-Sammlung in der Musikabteilung der Deutschen Staatsbibliothek: Verzeichnis* (Berlin: Deutsche Staatsbibliothek, 1970), 215. See also Warren Kirkendale, *Fugue and Fugato*, 213–14.

29. Schmid, "Beethovens Bachkenntnis," 65.

30. For a probing and exhaustive study of the two Bach passages on the Scheide leaf, see Hans-Werner Küthen, "*Quaerendo invenietis*," 299–302. In its pursuit of some specific relationship between a motivic device in the Bach fugue and a passage in the fugue of op. 106, the argument invests too heavily in the assumption of Beethoven in need of a model: "die Idee seiner Recherchen ist die Auffindung eines aufsteigenden Drei-Ton-Modells" (the idea of his research is in the discovery of a rising three-tone model). Perhaps the

EX. 5.5. J. S. Bach, *Well-Tempered Clavier* II, from the Fugue in C♯ Minor.

finished state. In the classic conundrum in Beethoven scholarship, we are left to postulate the missing documents where such work might have been captured on the page. The loss of an autograph score for op. 106, its existence ex post facto never established in the literature, will continue to hold such postulates prisoner to speculation.[31]

These Princeton drafts for the *introduzione* picture a mind engaged, as though seeking to retrieve an *Augenblick* in the long memory of fugal practice that would situate the Allegro risoluto at its resolute end. Each seemingly constructed from some imaginary model, these three fragments yet convey a concentration of thought born of a tension with the past. In the *fuga con alcune licenze*, the distant gaze of the Capellmeister Albrechtsberger may still be felt, not as a reprimand to his wayward pupil but as a reminiscence of a past against which Beethoven's music struggles to invent its future.

Appendix

Digital images of the manuscripts described below may be retrieved at the website of the Princeton University Library. I am grateful to the curators of

---

sleight-of-hand fluidity of Bach's voicing was sufficient to draw Beethoven's wish to capture it in writing.

31. For an account of Heinrich Schenker's attempts to locate the autograph, see Nicholas Marston, *Heinrich Schenker and Beethoven's "Hammerklavier" Sonata* (Farnham, Surrey, UK; and Burlington, VT: Ashgate, 2013), 10–16.

116 CHAPTER FIVE

the Scheide archive for permitting the reproduction of several pages from these manuscripts.

A Scheide Library, Dept. of Rare Books and Special Collections, Princeton University Library. M132. From Otto Haas via Sotheby's 1958 (Otto Albrecht: from Stargardt sale in 1958). Not in Hans Schmidt, *Skizzenverzeichnis*. 16-stave, a full sheet (4 leaves), originally two nested bifolia. The order in which the leaves were used seems to have been fols. 1, 4, 3, 2.

> Fol. 1. Early ideas for the "Einleitung" (the word "prel[ude]" is crossed out). Then, on the staff below: "introduction aus [?]". Continues on verso.
>
> Fol. 4. Verso, st. 15/16: "=de" continues from 4/5 and 6/7, showing the cadence eliding with the opening motive of the subject.
>
> Fol. 3. Recto, st. 15/16: Shows the high G♭, with fermata, then the same elision as at bottom of 4v.

B Scheide Library, M131. 6 leaves. Obtained by John Scheide in 1935 from Gottschalk. Schmidt, *Skizzenverzeichnis* 365. Formerly in possession of Johann Andreas Stumpff, then living in London, who annotated some of the leaves in English. These are separate leaves of different paper types. The order in JTW, 538, differs from the current order at the Princeton website.

> Fol. 1. 8-stave, recto and verso. Exclusively for the "Introduzione," as someone (Stumpff?) has written in pencil at the top of the recto. The draft comes close in many details to the final version, showing the counterpoints in G♭, B major, and C♯ minor. The draft runs to the bottom of the verso, evidently continuing on another leaf no longer present.
>
> Fol. 2. 20-stave, hand-ruled bar lines through the page, both sides.
>> Recto: Notation at top: "Zulezt 4-stimmig in allabreve takt." At bottom: "4-stimmiges Stück / sul clavicembalo." Entry st. 19/20, left: from *WTC* II fugue in C♯ minor, mm. 14–15; st. 18, right: from *WTC* II fugue in B♭ major, m. 5.
>> Verso: scattered entries include a sketch for the trills ascending as in final bars of the fuga.
>
> Fol. 3. 12-stave. Begins with a trial for a subject in $\frac{6}{16}$
>> Other fairly primitive entries for subject on both sides of the leaf.
>> Verso: subject and answer approaching the final version.

Fol. 4. 12-stave.

> Verso: bottom of page shows subject in its continuation, then
> in inversion, and then in retrograde.

Fol. 5. 10-stave (piano format). Recto: sketches for subject with a
counterpoint.

> Continuation in triplets. Other entry for a moderato in
> E major.
> Verso blank.

Fol. 6. 16-stave. Both sides blank.

Sonata and the Claims of Narrative

Beethoven

✳ CHAPTER 6 ✳

On a Challenging Moment in the Sonata for Pianoforte and Violoncello, Op. 102, No. 2

Preamble: Two Anecdotes

A well-known professional cellist is at our home, trying out an instrument that my wife is hoping to purchase. The expansive phrase with which the cello introduces itself in the first movement of Beethoven's Sonata for Piano and Violoncello, op. 102, no. 2, splays across its two-and-a-half octaves, prompting our cellist to recall that when she performed the work many years ago for the eminent music theorist Ernst Oster, he took aim at those two As that establish the octave breach in the middle of the phrase. Which of them, he is said to have asked, was "the more important"?[1] It would be easy enough to dismiss the question as mischievous, since each A has a stake in the internal counterpoint of this lavishly convoluted phrase, each its own claim to "importance." Oster, I suspect, was after bigger game, and in any case, the question inspires us to work through those differences in the play of theoretical abstraction against the immediacy of performance. (The opening of the sonata is shown in ex. 6.1.)

Some weeks later, moments after a performance of the sonata with another cellist at a chamber music workshop, a sharp-eared friend accosted me: "You played a wrong note!" The stern inflection in his voice hinted that this wasn't merely a question of the inevitable dropped note in the heat of performance. A larger issue was at stake. Ironically, it was another A, in yet another register, that was in question, this at the recapitulation in the

---

1. I am indebted to cellist Susan Salm, of the Raphael Trio, for sharing her memory of this session with Oster, which, Salm recalls, took place at his New York apartment in roughly 1975/1976.

EX. 6.1. Beethoven, Sonata in D Major for Piano and Violoncello, op. 102, no. 2, first movement, mm. 1–7.

first movement (shown in ex. 6.2). To my eternal mortification, I now saw that from a first slapdash reading of the passage I had misread those ledger lines, answering the grace note F♯ at m. 92 with an F♯ an octave higher. This fugitive high F♯ always troubled me, in the main because it would exacerbate the pile-up of F♯s, tripled (indeed, with the grace note, quadrupled) above the deep F♯ in the bass. But I failed to make the correction, and the loss of that A, a betrayal of what may be thought of as the crux of the work, sticks in the mind with a tenacity that resists the fleeting evanescence of performance.

Quite beyond the trivial embarrassment of the moment, these isolated incidents took on a life of their own. For it brought home all the more emphatically the sense in which these two moments in the sonata are inextricably bound up in one another, and that an answer to Oster's question would be lodged somewhere in the unfolding of the work, in that territory that Oster himself staked out in a probing essay titled "Reg-

EX. 6.2. Beethoven, Sonata in D Major for Piano and Violoncello, op. 102, no. 2, first movement, mm. 88–95.

ister and the Large-Scale Connection."[2] There will be more to say about this shortly.

1

The sonata, along with its companion in C major, figured prominently in the midst of Beethoven's 1815.[3] Its autograph score, now at the Staatsbibliothek zu Berlin, is inscribed "Sonate anfangs August 1815," though it

2. *Journal of Music Theory* 5, no. 1 (1961): 54–71—though op. 102 does not figure in the study. Reprinted in *Readings in Schenker Analysis and Other Approaches*, ed. Maury Yeston (New Haven, CT: Yale University Press, 1977), 54–71.

3. Among the substantial writings provoked by these two sonatas, an essay by Lewis Lockwood makes a compelling argument that work on the 1814 revision of Beethoven's only opera can be heard to play into the "lyrical intensity" (305) of in particular the C-Major Sonata, finding the new voice that will nourish the music of Beethoven's

124 CHAPTER SIX

has been proposed that while this date may fix the composition of the first two movements, it does not accord well with the surviving sketches for the third movement.[4]

Those sketches are to be found in two sources. The more substantial of them is the so-called Scheide Sketchbook, whose richly varied contents include intensive work on the Piano Sonata in A, op. 101, the song cycle *An die ferne Geliebte*, op. 98, an unfinished Piano Concerto in D Major, and an unfinished Piano Trio in F Minor.[5] The other is a large "pocket" sketchbook (Cracow, Biblioteka Jagiellónska [formerly at the Berlin Staatsbibliothek], Mendelssohn 1), evidently in use concurrently with Scheide.[6] Nearly one-half of its sixty-some pages is given over to sketches for the fugal finale of the D-Major Cello Sonata, and this reinforces the distribution in Scheide, where again the sketching is almost exclusively for the final movement. And in this connection, one other document is of considerable significance: a draft in four-stave score for much of this same movement.[7]

But it is the opening page of sketches for the sonata in the Scheide Sketchbook (p. 37) that claims our attention here, in part for what it seems

---

final decade. See his "Beethoven's Emergence from Crisis: The Cello Sonatas of Op. 102 (1815)," *Journal of Musicology* 16 (1998): 301–22.

4. See, for one, Douglas Johnson, Alan Tyson, and Robert Winter, *The Beethoven Sketchbooks: History, Reconstruction, Inventory*, ed. Douglas Johnson (Berkeley: University of California Press, 1985) [hereafter JTW], 244. In an undated letter to Joseph Xaver Brauchle, tutor to the children of the Countess Marie Erdödy, Beethoven writes: "ich werde die beyden violon*schel* Sonaten mitbringen," which can have referred only to op. 102. The Countess, a fine pianist to whom the Artaria edition of the sonatas was dedicated, left Vienna with her family on 30 September for Croatia, which gives us a date by which the sonatas must have been completed. The cellist in the ensemble would have been Joseph Linke. See Ludwig van Beethoven, *Briefwechsel Gesamtausgabe*, ed. Sieghard Brandenburg (Munich: G. Henle, 1996), 3:167–68.

5. Now housed at the Scheide Library, Department of Rare Books and Special Collections, Princeton University Library, under the signature M130 (WHS 30.14), the sketchbook is accessible in digital facsimile at the library website. For a description of the sketchbook, its dating, and its contents, see JTW, 241–46.

6. See JTW, 340–43. The earliest transcriptions of extracts from the book are to be found in Gustav Nottebohm, "Ein Skizzenheft aus dem Jahre 1815," in *Zweite Beethoveniana: Nachgelassene Aufsätze*, ed. E. Mandyczewski (Leipzig: C. F. Peters, 1887), 314–20.

7. Bonn, Beethoven-Haus, HCB Mh 92 [SBH 648]: a gathering of eight leaves (sixteen pages), of which ten pages are for the most part ruled into score, the last six pages entirely blank. Related to this fascicle is a bifolium today at the Koninklijke Bibliotheek in The Hague, SV 327 in Hans Schmidt's "Verzeichnis der Skizzen Beethovens," Beethoven-Jahrbuch 6 (1969): 103, of the same paper type as the Bonn manuscript. The score draft on IV shows signs of continuity with the first page of the Bonn draft. For a facsimile and transcription, see Jos van der Zanden, "A Beethoven Sketchleaf in The Hague," *Bonner Beethoven-Studien* 3 (2003): 153–67.

to capture in snapshot of an extended moment during which ideas for the first and third movements are brought into focus. At the top of the page is a bold entry for the initial bars of the first movement, in strikingly close approximation of the finished version: the opening salvo in the piano, with its flurries of sixteenths and those great intervallic leaps; the stunning entrance of the cello, torn from its deepest D, arpeggiating across all four strings and blossoming, finally, into the contrapuntal lyricism spurred by those octave As that provoked Oster's question.[8] Its appearance on the page gives the impression of an initial putting to paper of an idea for the first movement, the furnishing of a key signature normally signaling the onset of a fresh project. Indeed, the layout of this first page of sketches (shown as fig. 6.1) argues that we are witness here to a recording of what may be the earliest entries for the sonata, something of a scratch pad that preserves the untidy crossing of ideas for the outer movements. Had there been earlier sketches for the first movement, we'd expect to find evidence at this stage of more advanced probes into the interior of the work, traces of draft-like continuities beyond this statement of the opening theme.[9] To further complicate how we might think to situate the entry, it remains the single surviving sketch for the first movement, with the exception of a fleeting scribble in Mendelssohn 1 for the few bars of a second theme corresponding to mm. 31–33 in the piano.[10] No further sketches for the first movement have come to light.

Apart from a single clutch of variants for the D-major theme in the Adagio, the remaining sketches in Scheide, across some ten pages, address aspects of the fugal finale: in the main, trials of various permutations of the primary subject in stretto and in combination with the cantus-like secondary subject, with little evidence of anything resembling a continuity draft. But perhaps the most puzzling entry of all is the very first one, written just

8. The entry was transcribed by Nottebohm, *Zweite Beethoveniana*, 325.

9. It has been proposed (JTW, 244) that earlier sketches for the first two movements might have been written on some of the seventeen leaves that were removed from the sketchbook before Nottebohm examined it. The leaves were removed between the current folio 31/32 and 33/34. The first entries for op. 102, no. 2, are on p. 37. Of the three leaves believed to have been removed from the book between those pages, none contains entries for op. 102.

10. The page is shown in facsimile in Martina Sichardt, *Entwurf einer narratologischen Beethoven-Analytik* (Bonn: Verlag Beethoven-Haus Bonn, 2012), 58, 60. Sichardt (58) writes that here "erkennt man eine fragmentarische Fassung des Seitensatz-Themas des 1. Satz ... dazu die Worte 'zum ersten mal und weiter [?]' so" (one recognizes a fragmentary version of the second theme in the first movement ... and in addition, the words "at the first time and the same later"). I read the inscription rather as "2te mal u. i[m] Clavier so" (thus the second time and in the piano).

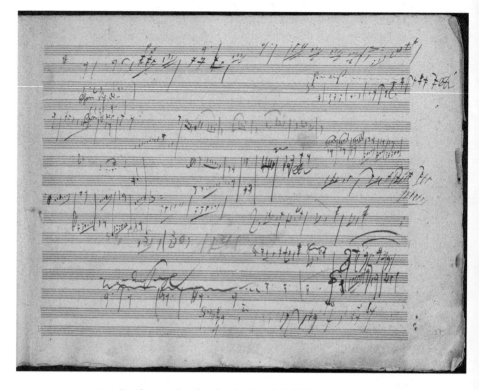

FIGURE 6.1. Beethoven, sketches for the Sonata in D Major, op. 102, no. 2. Princeton University Library, Scheide ms. 130 (the "Scheide" Sketchbook), p. 37. By kind permission.

beneath that telling entry for the first movement (see the illustration above, and ex. 6.3). Beethoven's inscription, difficult to decipher with certainty, seems to say "hier erst," a clue, perhaps, to the function and placement of this curiously distended display of the scale with which the fugal subject will open.[11] It is tempting to understand it as another of those preambles in which Beethoven invites us to meditate on the inchoate substance of the music that is about to unfold: in this case, a fragment of theme before it formulates itself as the subject of a fugue. We are reminded once again of those two iconic examples: the "Ouverture," as Beethoven named it in the autograph of the finale of the String Quartet in B♭, op. 130, that introduces (apparently in reverse order) paraphrases of the subject in the four permutations that will constitute what would come to be known as the *große*

---

11. I have profited from an exchange about this entry with Federica Rovelli, who is preparing an edition of the Scheide Sketchbook for the Beethoven-Haus series.

EX. 6.3. Beethoven, from the Scheide Sketchbook, p. 37.

Fuge;[12] and that extraordinary page of quasi-fugal incipits, so many alternatives to the proper one, in the finale of the Piano Sonata in B♭, op. 106, that was the topic of our previous chapter.

If that were the intention of this puzzling entry, its place on the page is suggestive in yet another respect, for it allows that this transformative slowing of the subject occupied Beethoven's imagination even before the labors of fugal composition are undertaken. And here it is worth recalling that in the final version the onset of the Allegro fugato is preceded by two isolated attempts at its opening phrase—one each for the cello and the piano. Instructive in what it does not specify, Beethoven's autograph score establishes that these four bars were an afterthought, squeezed into space left empty at the end of the slow movement, tellingly without tempo indication. The "At[t]acca" scribbled after the double bar was clearly intended to direct the reader to a quick turn of the page following the fermata on the dominant with which the Adagio closes.[13] (The autograph page is shown as fig. 6.2.) And in the *Stichvorlage*, a score prepared by the copyist Wenzel Rampl from the autograph in preparation for the printer, these four bars were again entered late in the process, and in the hand of a different copyist. Here, too, a tempo indication is missing; beneath the cello entry is written simply "*leggiermente*"[14]—evidently penciled in by Beethoven (and only in

---

12. I am much taken with an idea, proposed by Lewis Lockwood in a private exchange, that the order of things in the *Ouverture* is the proper one, the fugue then taking up its four topics in reverse order, moving from the brutal dissonances and rhythmic complications of the long opening panel toward the clarity of the subject in its purest form, ultimately in a harmonization that conjures a poetic essence of the subject. For more on this, see my "Between Cavatina and Ouverture: Opus 130 and the Voices of Narrative," *Beethoven Forum* 1 (1992): 165–89.

13. The autograph score is at the Staatsbibliothek zu Berlin–Preußischer Kulturbesitz, Mus. ms. autogr. Beethoven Art. 192; it is accessible digitally at the website of the library.

14. Of interest is an entry for the word in Heinrich Christoph Koch, *Musikalisches Lexikon* (Frankfurt am Main: August Hermann, 1802; repr. Hildesheim: Georg Olms, 1985), 894: "leicht, ohne studierten und schwerfälligen Vortrag"—to be performed lightly, without studied or ponderous execution. The point is only to suggest that the word had some currency in the contemporary vocabulary of music performance.

FIGURE 6.2. Beethoven, Sonata in D Major, op. 102, no. 2, autograph score, p. 16. Staatsbibliothek zu Berlin, Mus. ms. autogr. Beethoven Artaria 192. By kind permission.

the cello part) and then inked over, perhaps by the copyist—an instruction that hints at a process of tentative discovery, a listening for the subject before the rigors of the Allegro fugato.[15]

Something else leaps out in the formulation of this puzzling entry in Scheide: its isolation of the pitch dyad A–B that will articulate a central motive within the fugue subject, and then the further isolation of those pitches three octaves higher. Their prominence in this intervallic configuration only exaggerates an internal relationship to the draft for the opening

15. The copy is in the Sammlung H. C. Bodmer at the Beethoven-Archiv. Two additional authentic copies exist. On these matters, see Jens Dufner's fine account in *Auf den Spuren Beethovens: Hans Conrad Bodmer und seine Sammlung*, ed. Nicole Kämpken and Michael Ladenburger (Bonn: Verlag Beethoven-Haus Bonn, 2006), 188–92. For a different understanding of these measures, see Rudolf Bockholdt, "Der letzte Satz von Beethovens letzter Violoncellosonate, op. 102 Nr. 2," in *Beethovens Werke für Klavier und Violoncello*, ed. Sieghard Brandenburg, Ingeborg Maas, and Wolfgang Osthoff (Bonn: Verlag Beethoven-Haus Bonn, 2004), 265–82, esp. 265–69.

of the first movement, pointing up the centrality of those pitches in the thematic design of the two movements.

In the sketchbooks, the appeal of a page such as this, in its capturing of what seems a moment in the coming to life of the sonata, carries with it a temptation to transpose from the sketches into the finished work an intentionality of design, a coherence of infrastructure, that may over-clarify the obscurities of an intuitive process through which such music is conceived. A coming to terms with this conundrum, in regard to this very work, was pursued in the course of a challenging study by Martina Sichardt, who probes the Allegro fugato in search of the "poetic element" that Beethoven himself was alleged to have acknowledged in these words:

> To create a fugue is [in itself] no art. I've made dozens in my study years. But Fantasy will also assert its claim, and nowadays something else, a truly poetic element must enter into the old established form.[16]

How, in Beethoven's imagination, might this "poetic element" have been understood? Perhaps he meant nothing more, nor less, than his own life-long project to assimilate fugal texture, fugal device, fugal rhetoric into the larger discourse, whether poetic or dramatic, or even epic, of many of his most significant works. No longer primarily an academic exercise of the kind that Beethoven assiduously prepared during his studies with Albrechtsberger in 1794–1795, fugue would now serve as an intensification of thematic idea.[17] For Sichardt, this "poetic element" is expressed in the plural, and identified with some specificity, the most prominent manifestation of which is a motivic figure for which Sichardt, after Warren Kirkendale, invokes the term "*Pathotyp*," a figure often meant to convey "the affect of deep sorrow [dem Affekt der tiefen Trauer], for which it becomes a symbol, and to which its name attests."[18] In its purest form, this *Pathotyp* isolates the descending diminished seventh, framed by scale degrees ♭6 and 7; but the figure, as Sichardt construes it in the sonata, is a transformation in which this defining interval is made over into something quite different, the flatted sixth degree made major. For Sichardt, the motive is embed-

---

16. "Eine Fuge zu machen ist keine Kunst, ich habe deren zu Dutzenden in meiner Studienzeit gemacht. Aber die Phantasie will auch ihr Recht behaupten, und heut' zu Tage muß in die alt hergebrachte Form ein anderes, ein wirklich poetisches Element kommen." This is how Karl Holz, in a letter to Wilhelm von Lenz many years after the fact, recalled Beethoven's words. See Lenz, *Beethoven. Eine Kunst-Studie* (Hamburg: Hoffmann & Campe, 1860), 219. The passage is cited in Sichardt, *Entwurf*, 30.

17. The topic is explored from other perspectives in chapters 4 and 5 above.

18. Sichardt, *Entwurf*, 30.

ded in the subject of the fugue (see ex. 6.4a), and then isolated in a new counterpoint (suggesting, for a moment, a second subject, in the manner of a double fugue) at m. 143, the inception of the second part of the finale (ex. 6.4b). If there were good reason to expect a proper "tonal" answer to this new subject, as *comes* to *dux*, we are disabused: the answering phrase here plays the role of the obedient respondent in a classical sonata.

Of this secondary subject itself, much has been made (by Sichardt and others) of its putative kinship with the subject of "And with His Stripes," from *Messiah*, Handel's F minor transmuted to B major (shown as ex. 6.4c). That Beethoven knew the oratorio is confirmed in a number of extracts copied in various sketch sources that date back to 1806–1807.[19] His handwritten copy of the voice parts of the Handel chorus in its entirety can be dated in the vicinity of 1821.[20] A responsible criticism would, however, seek to establish some plausible relationship between sonata finale and Messiah chorus in which the "poetic element" of the latter would demonstrably inform the narrative of the fugue. In its absence, we are left with mere semblance, an intervallic abstraction.

As its title portends—in rough translation: "Draft of a Narratological Beethoven Analysis"—Sichardt's study will propose that such *topoi* as this *Pathotyp* constitute the elements of a narrative-like unfolding, and further, that (in her words)

> the transformation of this thematic cell [Kern] in the course of the sonata, more than evidence merely of an inner unity [Geschlossenheit], rather narrates a "story" [Geschichte] of this thematic cell—a "story" that can be abbreviated on the frame of a sequence in three steps: Movement 1: happiness, untroubled reality; Movement 2: sadness and an imagined happiness; Movement 3: an overpowering at once insolent and humorous [trotzig-humoristische Bewältigung] (not, however, a victorious conquest). This three-stage sequence can be designated as a narrative scaffold of the sonata.[21]

19. For a conspectus of Beethoven's extracts from *Messiah*, see Warren Kirkendale, *Fugue and Fugato in Rococo and Classical Chamber Music* (Durham, NC: Duke University Press, 1979), 216. On the dating of the earliest entries, see JTW 525.

20. The manuscript, previously in the collection of Arturo Toscanini, was auctioned by Sotheby's on 6 December 1991, with a facsimile of the first page of the manuscript in the auction catalogue, p. 56, and is currently in the Karpeles Manuscript Library, a consortium of museums and libraries across the United States with apparently no central depository of its collection. The dating of the manuscript is based solely on the watermark of its paper, which is drawn from the dating of its paper in JTW.

21. Sichardt, *Entwurf*, 43.

EX. 6.4A. Beethoven, Sonata in D Major for Piano and Violoncello, op. 102, no 2, third movement, mm. 5–10.
EX. 6.4B. Beethoven, Sonata in D Major for Piano and Violoncello, op. 102, no 2, third movement, mm. 143–50.
EX. 6.4C. Handel, *Messiah*, from the chorus "And with His Stripes."

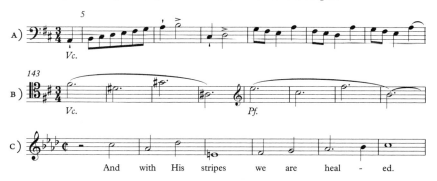

For all the original insight in the course of Sichardt's richly detailed study, there is yet something troubling in this reduction of narrative to the transformation of a thematic cell. To interpret the substance of the sonata in these terms—to hear, for one, the first movement as an expression of "happiness," of "untroubled reality," oblivious of a manic intensity, interrupted by moments of concentrated lyricism, that drives this music—is to impose on the sonata rather a caricature of narrative, dismissive of the complex unfolding of idea, of character and voice, and indeed of that expressive narrative thread conveyed in a purely musical diction that, whatever its allusion to cognitive experience, resists translation into the prose of literary discourse.[22]

A further distinction is pertinent here. The narrating voice tells its story in its own time, distinct and distant from the time of the story itself—the distinction between *Erzählzeit* (the narrator's present time) and *erzählte Zeit* (the multiple pasts captured in the story), in the lingo of the narratologist.[23] Music is clearly incapable of that kind of distinction. Either it

---

22. Carl Dahlhaus understands the "process" of the fugue very differently, underscoring an aggregate "thematic substance" constituted in the subject and its various permutations, and arguing persuasively that this new theme at m. 143 acts as a formal marker that stands in for the "erhobenen Augenblick" (the heightened moment) that articulates the point of reprise in Beethoven's sonata movements. See his "'Von zwei Kulturen der Musik': Die Schlußfuge aus Beethovens Cellosonate opus 102, 2," *Die Musikforschung* 31 (1978): 397–405, esp. 403–4.

23. The classic exposition of the difference is Gérard Genette, *Narrative Discourse: An Essay in Method*, trans. Jane E. Lewin (Ithaca, NY: Cornell University Press, 1980), 33–35 and elsewhere.

132   CHAPTER SIX

engages in a mimetic parody of the storyteller, or it acts out, in a first-order mimesis, a sequence of purely musical events that does not in itself possess the cognitive matter necessary for genuine narrative even if the traces of some narrative-like discourse might be signaled in the coded semiotic vocabulary of musical gesture.[24] The play between the narrating agent and the story that it tells, a commonplace in literary discourse, is a subtlety unavailable even to the most sophisticated elocutionary voice of music.

2

And that returns us to the second of those two anecdotes with which I began: to the misplayed note at m. 92 as "a betrayal of what might be thought of as the crux of the work." What, precisely, is at stake? The problem is illuminated in an entry dated 30 November 1929 in the diary of Heinrich Schenker, who records his impressions of a performance of this very sonata by Pablo Casals. Of the first movement, he writes: "an arbitrary double-bar set by the printer in the development allows C[asals] to commit an offense against the sense [of the work]: he begins the reprise with g^2, and then a second time after 4 bars with $f\sharp^2$! C[asals] never lets the pianist come forth, and thus the work seems deprived of all its illuminating power."[25]

In fairness to Casals and his pianist, one might wonder how the impact of this feigned recapitulation in the subdominant (m. 84) might have been finessed toward the playing of the trump card at the true moment of recapitulation at m. 89. Beethoven's notation doesn't give its hand away until the C$\sharp$ at m. 88 with which the cello initiates its swerve toward the true tonic. And this brings us to the telling F$\sharp$ at m. 92, sounded from the deepest note in the bass to the grace note four octaves above that will find

24. The question is explored in, for one, Carolyn Abbate, *Unsung Voices* (Princeton, NJ: Princeton University Press, 1991), 54–55. And it is central to the arguments around the positioning of the songs in Schubert's Hölty settings (see above, chapter 1). For further on these matters, see my "Between Cavatina and Ouverture: Opus 130 and the Voices of Narrative," 165–89, esp. 179–84.

25. "Ein von den Stechern willkürlich gesetzter Doppelstrich in der Durchführung läßt C[asals] einen Verstoß gegen den Sinn begehen; er fängt die Reprise mit g^2 an, nach 4 Takten mit fis² zum zweitenmal! Den Klavierspieler läßt C[asals] nirgend hervortreten, deshalb erscheint dem Werk alle Leuchtkraft entzogen." Helmut Federhofer, *Heinrich Schenker: Nach Tagebüchern und Briefen in der Oswald Jonas Memorial Collection* (Hildesheim: Georg Olms, 1985), 227. See also the entry in Schenker Documents Online. The double bar to which Schenker alludes is a notational convention in later editions, but is to be found in neither the two earliest "authentic" editions, by Simrock (1817) and Artaria (1819, with the dedication to the Countess Marie Erdödy), nor the autograph score and the copyist's *Stichvorlage*.

FIGURE 6.3. Beethoven, Sonata in D Major, op. 102, no. 2, autograph score, p. 6. Staatsbibliothek zu Berlin, Mus. ms. autogr. Beethoven Artaria 192. By kind permission.

its target yet another tenth higher. The leap up to the high A is clearly meant to invoke—indeed, to stand in for—the grand arpeggiation with which the cello announces itself at m. 4. How, precisely, the pianist might think to perform this leap, how to set the F♯ and the A in some meaningful acoustical relationship, is a challenge that might be read even in the calligraphy of Beethoven's autograph, the generous gap between the two notes captured graphically, Beethoven's pen seeming to choreograph the leap in the act of writing. This is to be seen in the final measure of system 2 in figure 6.3.

To stigmatize this F♯ as a "grace" note (as it is commonly called), vesting it as an auxiliary to a principal note, is to trivialize its pivotal and pointedly graceless function at m. 92: a powerful downbeat whose momentum seems to drag the bass with it. Indeed, the coupling of this F♯, in all its registers, with A is surely meant to be heard as an extreme compression of that lavish arpeggio with which the cello makes its entrance at mm. 4–5. In fact,

EX. 6.5. Beethoven, Sonata in D Major for Piano and Violoncello, op. 102, no. 2, first movement, showing the opening cello arpeggiation and the octave at m. 5, and the transformation of these motives at mm. 92–93.

everything about m. 92 will be heard as transformative. Those octave As which so provoked Oster now span three octaves, further broken between piano and cello, as though in answer to his inscrutable question. No less transformative is the harmonic underpinning of these measures, the D♯ appoggiatura on the downbeat of m. 6 now given full bass support above this deep F♯. The diminished seventh at m. 92 is an elaboration of that appoggiatura, C♮ displacing a root B. And so the sense of F♯ now sustained in the bass comes clear (ex. 6.5).

And it is precisely here that Beethoven's challenging music provokes us to probe the condition of narrative as an explanatory tool. At this moment of reprise, that expansive phrase with which the cello announces itself is now filtered through memory: not in nostalgic reminiscence of a lost moment of lyrical beauty, but rather in a brutal restructuring, a rehearing of its elements. The grand arpeggio with which the cello discovers its high A is now redundant, and so the piano seizes the moment in a precipitous leap to its highest A. In the taxonomies of sonata, the moment would be explained away in terms of the spatial symmetries of sonata form. Unfolding in time, in tension with a structural design that occupies its space, the sequential moments of music seem cognate with the events of literary narrative, whether as story told or drama enacted. Yet while the temptation to impute narrative meaning to the catastrophic reversals at m. 92 is powerful, the claim to have identified that meaning in cognitive terms is an exercise in futility. This is not to say that the signposts of narrative might not have figured in the conceiving of the work, but rather to suggest that what they seem to say is never demonstrable, never given to verification, even that they interfere inevitably with a meaning resident in the music, truer to the work and inseparable from it. And yet the urge to explain the expressive force of the music in cognitive terms is irrepressible. How to reconcile this narrative impulse both in the literary sense and in the pure discourse of music is the unforgiving challenge of the critical enterprise.

Epilogue: Another Little Buck Out of Its Stable

The curious phrase above refers to the title of a brief study by Albi Rosenthal that illuminates a marginal note that Beethoven scribbled at three points on a copy of the Simrock print of the sonata before us.[26] The first of them, against the cello part in the first movement, reads "cis ein Böcklein aus S[imrocks] Stall" (C♯: a little buck out of Simrock's stable).[27] This refers to the final note in m. 7, which, in all later editions and in the copyist's score that served as a text for the printer, is given as D. (The exception is the Artaria edition, authorized by Beethoven in 1819.) But Beethoven's autograph, from which this copyist's score was surely made, is ambiguous. The notehead seems originally to have found C♯, which is then absorbed into a larger notehead that covers the D line. What is, however, indisputable is Beethoven's correction in the Rosenthal copy of the Simrock edition.[28] In its leading of the lower-voice A–B toward a meeting with the upper voice, this C♯ is a critical player. Its significance is only heightened in the transformation of the passage at mm. 93–95, where C♯ is made the downbeat toward which the phrase now cadences.

That *other* little buck out of its stable, neither a copyist's error nor an engraver's, is the momentous A that managed to escape the reach of these

26. See Albi Rosenthal: "'A Little Buck Out of Its Stable': Some Corrections by Beethoven in a Copy of the First Edition of Opus 102," in *Pianist, Scholar, Connoisseur: Essays in Honor of Jacob Lateiner*, ed. Bruce Brubaker and Jane Gottlieb (Stuyvesant, NY: Pendragon Press, 2000), 147–50; for the more elaborate version, see Rosenthal, "'Ein Böcklein aus dem Stall': Beethovens Anmerkungen in einem Exemplar der Erstausgabe von op. 102," in *Beethovens Werke für Klavier und Violoncello. Bericht über die Internationale Fachkonferenz Bonn, 18–20. Juni 1998*, ed. Sieghard Brandenburg, Ingeborg Maaß, and Wolfgang Osthoff (Bonn: Beethoven-Haus, 2004), 229–38.

27. For the corrected reading of the note, see Beethoven, *Sonaten für Klavier und Violoncello/Sonatas for Pianoforte and Violoncello*, ed. Jonathan Del Mar (Kassel: Bärenreiter, 2004), Critical Commentary, 55.

28. The matter is exhaustively treated in Del Mar, *Sonaten für Klavier und Violoncello*, 62.

wayward fingers, setting loose this excursion into the theoretical consequences of the act. If the misplaying of that critical A at m. 92 as an F♯ is
a deed that can never be undone (at least in the mind of this humbled author), there is yet some consolation in the irony that a wrong note, and the
inquiry into its wrongness, will have set off in bolder relief the merits of the
right one.

Schubert

✳ CHAPTER 7 ✳

Against the Grain

The Sonata in G (D 894) and a Hermeneutics of Late Style

Extreme in the unremitting lyricism of its ruminative first movement, Schubert's Sonata in G Major, op. 78 (D 894), composed in October 1826, unaccountably provoked the critic of the Leipzig *Allgemeine musikalische Zeitung* to warn the young composer against following too closely on the path set out in Beethoven's later music.[1] In 1827, an acute ear would have heard Schubert's music on its own terms, resistant to the overpowering resonance of Beethoven's last works. In 1928, Adorno returned to this very condition: to situate Schubert in the year after Beethoven's death, asking us to imagine a world framed in the silence after Beethoven. Adorno taught us to rethink Schubert, to problematize the idea of the lyrical, to visualize his vast tonal landscapes over against the "puzzling out of dissociated elements" endemic to Beethoven.[2]

Heine's Weltriß, *Adorno's* Hohlräumen

In the midst of his probing interrogation of the great String Quintet in C Major (D 956)—an essay called "Zum Bilde des späten Schuberts"

---

1. [Leipziger] *Allgemeine musikalische Zeitung* for 26 December 1827. For the entire review, see Otto Erich Deutsch, *Franz Schubert: Die Dokumente seines Lebens*, rev. ed. (Kassel: Bärenreiter, 1964; rev. Wiesbaden: Breitkopf & Härtel, 1996), 467–69; *The Schubert Reader: A Life of Franz Schubert in Letters and Documents*, trans. Eric Blom (New York: W. W. Norton, 1947), 693–97. Deutsch suggests the author to have been G. W. Fink.

2. Theodor W. Adorno, "Schubert," in *Moments musicaux* (Frankfurt am Main: Suhrkamp, 1964), 18–36. A translation by Jonathan Dunsby and Beate Perrey served as the incentive for six essays in an issue of *19th-Century Music* 29, no. 1 (2005). The Adorno essay is on pp. 7–14.

EX. 7.1. Schubert, String Quintet in C, D 956 (op. post. 163), first movement, beginning of development, mm. 155–72.

(Toward an image of the late Schubert)—Peter Gülke takes in hand the "shocking interruption" that sets in motion the *Durchführung* at m. 167 in the first movement.[3] (See ex. 7.1.)

For Gülke, the moment has something to do with what seems a violent repudiation of this "lyrische Singen" that so permeates the exposition, coincident with the finding of F♯ minor, as the "am weitesten entfernten Punkt" (the point of furthest remove) from C major. And this inspires Gülke to an insight that cuts to the bone of what might be called the Schubert problem.

As a terrifying look at a reality inimical to singing, this interruption ... exposes the obligatory force of the music to reflect, always freshly, upon the presuppositions and risks of its own sounding. In a broader sense, the music consummates Heine's "*Weltriß*," often reclaimed by Schubert,

3. Peter Gülke, "Zum Bilde des späten Schubert," in *Musik-Konzepte. Sonderband Franz Schubert*, ed. Heinz-Klaus Metzger and Rainer Riehn (Munich: Edition Text + kritik, 1979), 111. "Dergestalt in einer schockierenden Verstörung angekündigt, setzt die Durchführung im engeren Sinne mit dem Takt 167 ein." Unless otherwise noted, all translations are my own.

Schubert: Sonata in G and a Hermeneutics of Late Style 139

and not simply by chance. In the stricter, compositional sense this accords with that which the lyrical singing, in sonata movements above all, would tear violently from his innermost being.[4]

This "Heinesche Weltriß" that Gülke hears reclaimed in Schubert is worth a moment's reflection. The term is embedded in a remarkable passage from Heine's "Die Bäder von Lucca" (1829): "For since the heart of the poet is the focal point of the world, it must be wretchedly torn these days. But it is the great cleft of the world that tears through my heart."[5] Less, perhaps, about rupture and upheaval within the political Europe of the 1820s than of a German society that Heine, torn between his sense of himself as insider/outsider, observed with the poet's trenchant irony, this *Weltriß* penetrates to the heart of the poet. In Heine's metonymy, the heart of the poet *is* the throbbing center of the world. *Weltriß* and *Herzriß* are reciprocal—essential, and not symbolic.

If Schubert's music, seemingly oblivious of world politics, fails to traffic in such ironies, there is yet something compelling in Gülke's appropriation of Heine's dark conceit to explain those antinomies that find their expression in a music often enough driven to poetic extremes. *Poetic*: in talk about music, the word has a shadowy, fraught birthright. I use it here as an entry into my topic, for I want to explore, however tentatively, the vexed question how, in Schubert's music, the poetic is to be understood, both in song and in sonata: in song, in its performative aspect, as a rehearing of the poem to which it is coupled; in sonata, as a hearing of the poem that is not there. Anyone who has engaged seriously with the Schubert lied repertory will understand my hesitation in proposing how music and poem might speak to one another. In one of his unpublished notebooks, Adorno confronts the problem with bold insight:

---

4. Gülke, "Zum Bilde," 111: "Als erschrockener Blick auf eine dem Singen feindliche Realität [exponiert] diese Verstörung . . . erstmals den dieser Musik auferlegten Zwang, die Voraussetzungen und Risiken des eigenen Erklingens immer neu zu reflektieren. Im weiteren Sinne ist es der nicht zufällig oft für Schubert reklamierte Heinesche 'Weltriß', den die Musik nachvollzieht; im engeren kompositorischen Sinne entspricht dem, daß das lyrische Singen zumal in Sonatensätzen kaum anders als gewaltsam seinem Fürsichsein entrissen werden kann."

5. "Denn da das Herz des Dichters der Mittelpunkt der Welt ist, so mußte es wohl in jetziger Zeit jämmerlich zerrissen werden. . . . Durch das meinige ging aber der große Weltriß." Heinrich Heine, "Die Bäder von Lucca," chapter 4, in *Reisebilder*, "Dritter Teil. Italien 1828," in (for one) Heinrich Heine, *Werke*, ed. Stuart Atkins (Munich: C. H. Beck, 1973), 1:535. On this passage, see also Katrin Becker, *"Die Welt entzwei gerissen": Heinrich Heines Publizistik der 1830er Jahre und der deutsch-französische Kulturtransfer* (Inaugural Dissertation, Albert-Ludwigs-Universität, 2008), 6.

Music comes to the aid of the poem in its fallibility. It doesn't duplicate its content but rather dwells in its hollow spaces. Music delivers the poem from its residual meaning. It interprets the poem, performs it, just as good music is itself performed. It actualizes the poem.[6]

If we are inclined to hear in the music merely a replication of the poem, Adorno disabuses us, unsettling the complacency with which the relationship between music and poem is commonly explained. Adorno's *Hohlräumen* will remind us of A. B. Marx's *dichterischen Pausen*, the unspoken *Idee* in the poem to which music will have to address itself (see above, chapter 3).

Fantasie oder Sonate

It is toward a hearing of this formidable Sonata in G Major that these provocations in Gülke and Adorno are now turned, in a venture to understand something of the deeper meanings inscribed beneath the placid surface of a work whose introspective probing may have inspired its publisher, Tobias Haslinger, to entitle it "Fantasie oder Sonate."[7] Its opening bars are shown in example 7.2.

Schubert's "molto moderato" invites an expansiveness beyond the gait of an andante. The extreme tempo concentrates the mind.[8] We are drawn

---

6. "Musik springt dem Gedicht in seiner Fehlbarkeit bei. Sie verdoppelt nicht seinen Gehalt sondern wohnt in seinen Hohlräumen.—Sie erlöst das Gedicht vom Rest seines Sinnes.—Sie interpretiert es, trägt es vor, so wie gute Musik selber vorgetragen wird.—Sie realisiert es." The passage, apparently from a notebook written in 1959, is given in Beate Perrey, "Exposed: Adorno and Schubert in 1928," in *19th-Century Music* 29, no. 1 (2005): 18. I have altered the translation in several places.

7. This, on the first page of the music. Haslinger's title page reads "Fantasie, / Andante, Menuetto und Allegretto / für das Piano-Forte allein." On the title page of the autograph, Schubert wrote simply "IV. Sonate fürs Pianoforte allein." The autograph is published in facsimile as *Franz Schubert. Piano sonata in G major, op. 78 (D. 894). Facsimile of the autograph manuscript in the British Library Add. MS 36738*, with an introduction by Howard Ferguson and a note on the paper of the manuscript by Alan Tyson. British Library Music Facsimiles II (London: British Library, 1980). For Robert Schumann, writing in the *Neue Zeitschrift für Musik* 29 (December 1835), of the three sonatas published during Schubert's lifetime, this "Phantasiesonate" he declared to be "seine vollendetste in Form und Geist. Hier ist alles organisch, atmet alles dasselbe Leben" (his most perfect in form and spirit; here everything is organic and breathes the same life).

8. These thoughts were inspired in part by a famously provocative interpretation by Sviatoslav Richter, recorded in two performances that I know of: a "live" performance at the Aldeburgh Festival of 1977 (and available both on DVD and via YouTube); and a recording of 1979, available on Decca, "Richter the Master," vol. 5. On the recording, the first movement takes nearly twenty-seven minutes.

EX. 7.2. Schubert, Piano Sonata in G, D 894 (op. 78), first movement, mm. 1–17.

into a narrative whose unfolding seems ever on the verge of rupture. In its chaste utterance, we listen for the unspoken poem within whose *Hohlräumen* this music seems to find its voice. The opening phrase of the sonata, in a simplicity commonly identified with the lyrical, and by extension with the songlike (Gülke's "lyrische Singen"), is yet challenging in just this aspect. Listening for a mimetics of song in such a phrase, in pursuit of some imaginary text whose diction, whose articulation and scansion, might be read in the music, these first bars are difficult to parse, their drawn-out tones suggesting a meta-lyricism in search of some poetic meaning not reducible merely to words.

If we are attuned to narrative breaches, to tears in the fabric of the story, the music does not disappoint. Perhaps the most unsettling of these follows upon the opening paragraph. At first encounter, the new phrase at m. 10 seems merely an elaboration of the doubled third, the B♮ of the triad with which the sonata begins: doubled thirds always harbor the threat of their own tonicity. There is, however, something otherworldly about this phrase: the deep octave F♯ that accrues a touch of its own tonicity; the quickened pace of the diction; the triple *piano—pianississimo*—in which this music is cast, as though in further retreat from the quiet of the opening music into a whispered, ghostly silence. And precisely here Schubert writes "Ped" with no signal for its release—the only such marking in the entire sonata. What can he have meant by it? The damper pedal will surely have been working from the outset, but perhaps Schubert wants the passage drenched in an undamped blur. When he wants "una corda," he will write "mit Verschiebung," a marking not found in Schubert before 1821, but employed in the two sonatas that precede op. 78: in the trio of the scherzo of the A-Minor Sonata, D 845 (op. 42), and in the slow movement of the D-Major, D 850 (op. 53), both from 1825.

Of our passage at m. 10, it has been proposed that it is the "moderator" pedal, which applies a layer of felt between the hammers and the strings, that is wanted.[9] When, however, Schubert specifies this muted effect, he writes "sordini"—as he does against the little turn figure, marked triple *piano*, in the Andante of the Sonata in A Minor, D 784 (op. post 143), of

---

9. And this is precisely how the passage is played in a remarkable interpretation by Stefan Litwin, recorded in 2002 on Telos Music Records. Litwin performs on a modern concert grand, but one that, as he reports in his program notes, is fitted out with the moderator device, which "inserts between the hammer and the strings a felt that is mounted on a wooden strip extending the entire length of the keyboard." For more on Schubert's presumed use of the moderator pedal, and an otherwise balanced analysis of Schubert's various markings for the use of the pedals, see David Rowland, *A History of Pianoforte Pedalling* (Cambridge: Cambridge University Press, 1993), 138–39.

1823. The opening bars of *Der Tod und das Mädchen* (D 531), in a copy in Stadler's hand, presumably from 1817, are inscribed "pp (sempre con Pedale e Sordino)," suggestively ambiguous in what it will allow. If, in op. 78, we cannot know precisely which pedal is to be brought into play, perhaps it is sufficient to read Schubert's marking as an impulse to do *something*: as a signifier in search of meaning beyond the ephemera of timbre.

When the bass slips to its deep octave F♯ at m. 10, the narrative seems to engage another gear, the prosody another mode, its mordant inflection of G major conjuring an aura of poetic introspection. Inevitably, a passage such as this puts us in mind of song—but beyond the mechanics of prosody to the less clinical topic of poetic meaning.

Schwestergruß

If there is a song that springs to mind for its resonance with this passage in an almost literal and tactile sense, it is the setting of Franz Bruchmann's *Schwestergruß*, D 762, an alternately somber and ecstatic threnody on the death of the poet's sister Sybille, who died in 1820 at age twenty-one. Dated November 1822 on its autograph—within weeks of the composition of the Symphony in B Minor (D 759, "Unfinished") and the Fantasy in C Major (D 760, "Wanderer")—the song was very likely intended for a "Schubertiada" (as it was called) planned for 10 November by the two surviving Bruchmann sisters, "in order to dispel as far as possible the sorrowful recollection of the departed Sybille," as we learn from a letter of 22 October from Moritz von Schwind to Franz von Schober.[10] Schubert's music grounds the poet's hallucinatory effusions in a lament of controlled grief in somber F♯ minor, its deliberate $^{12}_{8}$ meter measuring out its pedal tones and its tolling bells. (The opening is shown as ex. 7.3; the full poem is given here.)

SCHWESTERGRUSS	SISTER'S GREETING
Im Mondenschein	In the moonlight
Wall' ich auf und ab,	I wander up and down
Seh' Totenbein'	seeing bones of the dead
Und stilles Grab.	and a silent grave.
Im Geisterhauch	In the spirit's breath
Vorüber bebt's,	it trembles
Wie Flamm' und Rauch	and like flame and smoke,
Vorüber schwebt's;	drifts past;

---

10. Deutsch, *Die Dokumente*, 167; Blom, *Schubert Reader*, 239.

Aus Nebeltrug	From the deluding mists
Steigt eine Gestalt,	a shape rises up
Ohn' Sünd' und Lug	and floats past
Vorüber wallt,	without sin or deceit,
Das Aug' so blau,	the eyes as blue,
Der Blick so gross	the gaze as great
Wie in Himmelsau,	as in the fields of heaven,
Wie in Gottes Schoss;	as in the lap of God;
Ein weiss Gewand	A white garment
Bedeckt das Bild,	clothes the apparition,
In zarter Hand	in its tender hand
Eine Lilie quillt.	a lily springs up.
Im Geisterhauch	In a ghostly whisper
Sie zu mir spricht:	she speaks to me:
"Ich wand're schon	"Already I wander
Im reinen Licht,	in the pure light,
"Seh Mond und Sonn'	"see moon and sun
Zu meinem Fuss	at my foot,
Und leb' in Wonn',	and live in bliss,
in Engelkuss;	kissed by angels.
"Und all' die Lust,	"And all the joy that
Die ich empfind',	I feel, your breast
Nicht deine Brust	cannot know,
Kennt, Menschenkind!	child of man,
"Wenn du nicht lässt	"unless you were to relinquish
Den Erdengott,	the false earthly god
Bevor dich fasst	before grim death
Der grause Tod."	seizes you."
So tönt die Luft,	Thus the air resounds,
So saust der Wind,	the wind soughs,
Zu den Sternen ruft	the child of heaven
Das Himmelskind.	calls to the stars.
Und eh' sie flieht,	And before she flees,
Die weiss' Gestalt,	her white figure
In frischer Blüt'	is enfolded
Sie sich entfalt':	in fresh blossoms:

In reiner Flamm'	She floats up
Schwebt sie empor,	in pure flame,
Ohne Schmerz und Harm,	without pain or grief,
Zu der Engel Chor.	to the choir of angels.
Die Nacht verhüllt	The night veils
Den heil'gen Ort,	the holy place,
Von Gott erfüllt	filled with God
Sing ich das Wort.	I sing the Word.

Muted grief, this is. An opening *pianissimo*, sustained for thirty-eight bars, recedes to a triple *piano* for the fourteen bars of an interior strophe in which this spectral vision speaks to the poet in *Geisterhauch*—in ghostly tones. The opening music returns, the tune now intoned deep in the bass. (See ex. 7.4.) The music flares in a final epiphany, the poetic apparition now enfolded "in fresh blossoms," rising up to the heavens in a purifying flame. Bruchmann's mawkish imagery is redeemed in the intensity of Schubert's music, the voice edging up chromatically over the single crescendo in the song to its peak F♯ at m. 62, further underscored by a hairpin—and by a singular harmony equivalent in pitch, if not in function, to the aggregate later (and ever after) identified with Wagner's *Tristan*. *Wort-Ton* analysis can be a devious game with Schubert. At this telling moment, the music delivers its extreme harmony coincident with "sich," not the word that one might have chosen for overwrought emphasis. Here, in Adorno's phrase, music does indeed "deliver the poem from its residual meaning." Schubert's music internalizes the moment, repressing the pictorial image of the levitating sibylline spirit in favor of the poet's ecstasy at having been witness to this vision. A further ecstasy of cadencing, still *pianissimo*, gives way to an epilogue of arching intervals deep in the piano, echoed in the voice, an incessant pedal tone on F♯ receding one final time into a triple *piano*.

The Poem in the Sonata

Back to the sonata, to that passage shrouded in *its* pedal tone on F♯. To suggest, however cautiously, that its meaning might somehow be linked to the setting of Bruchmann's poem in any literal sense would likely incite the agnostic's skepticism, and deservedly so. I've placed the two on the same stage merely to frame how one might begin to talk about these things: how music grounded in a shared lexicon of tropes and figures, even across the drafty partitions that define genre, seeks the expression of some deep well of sentient experience.

EX. 7.3. Schubert, *Schwestergruß* (Bruchmann), D 762, mm. 1–17.

EX. 7.4. Schubert, *Schwestergruß*, D 762, mm. 55–63, 73–79.

How, then, do we come to terms with the passage in the sonata? The plaintive music of these six bars never returns. In its isolation, it sounds a solitary moment that yet lingers in the mind, attuned to its pedal-tone F♯ even as we wait for some reply to it. Rather, in its first movement the sonata seems bent on exploiting a polarity between the sharp side and the flat side. In the lengthy, and leisurely, exposition there is not a single tone from the flat side. This idyllic scene is shattered at the first double bar, the opening phrase now reheard *fortissimo*, and in G *minor*. (See ex. 7.5.) The *Durchführung* forfeits the lyrical calm of the narrative for violent juxtapositions of the principal themes transformed, and nowhere more radically than in the mutation of the introverted music of the opening bars into a phrase of massive breadth, first in B♭ minor (at m. 73) and then, eighteen bars later,

following upon a more emphatic preparation, in C minor, here deployed more expansively across the keyboard. *Fortississimo*—triple *forte*—each is marked, within which a hairpin suggests a further crescendo up to the dissonant ninth at its peak (see ex. 7.6).

Like the music on F♯ at m. 10 that has no issue in the first movement of the sonata, this magisterial phrase, too, is without sequel. The isolation of these two extreme moments, the one withdrawn in recessive *pianississimo*, the other exploding in triumphant, even violent *fortississimo*, only points up the polarity compassed in the sharp-side reach to B major and the flat-side pull to B♭ minor and C minor. The theorist will construct an explanatory model to accommodate these tonal extremes, even as the hermeneut seeks to understand them as metaphors for a poetic dissonance played out in a rupture of the narrative fabric in the sonata—Heine's "Weltriß" projected into the throbbing lyrical heart of the sonata, to appropriate Gülke's conceit.

Is it, however, the metaphorical that is at play here? Does the music *stand for* something poetic, or is it to be understood as the thing itself, as the expression of a sensibility, an emotion, an action of mind or body that might, in some literary genre, be given specificity even as the language of the

EX. 7.5. Schubert, Piano Sonata in G, D 894 (op. 78), D 894, first movement, mm. 65–76.

EX. 7.6. Schubert, Piano Sonata in G, D 894 (op. 78), D 894, first movement, mm. 87–96.

literary must inevitably fail to capture the quality of expression inherent in the music? I put these as questions and that is what they must remain, and yet in asking them, it seems to me that we are led to approach with greater caution the poetics within Schubert's music in an effort to come closer to an understanding of how a passage such as that at m. 10 might gloss the music of *Schwestergruß*—might, that is, illuminate those "Hohlräumen" of which Adorno speaks—as though Schubert's singing were less *of* the language of Bruchmann's mawkish poem (its prosody, its bathos) than an expression of some deeper musical and indeed poetic image. Inspired perhaps by his own feeling of loss—the loss of a young friend, in sympathy with the poet's loss—Schubert composes, one might imagine, in anticipation of this occasion on 10 November, where his own inner mourning would be exposed. Loosening the grip of Bruchmann's poem frees Schubert's song from the prison house of the poet's language, opening the music into deeper wells of experience. Experience, however, is frustratingly intangible, a stimulus, perhaps, that might explain why composers compose: to reify experience, to cast in tone as fiction the ineffable experience of living. Inner existence is given language, embodied in a music where fiction and autobiography bedevil one another.

The Sonata in G is a long work. That isolated passage at m. 10, its deep F♯ still unanswered, continues to reverberate beyond the boundaries of the first movement: certainly, in the explosive interruption in B minor that sets off the middle section of the Andante, and its lyrical epilogue that discovers B major; but perhaps nowhere so tellingly as in the Trio of the Menuetto— rather, a grim *anti*-menuetto in B minor that sets in stark relief this "aller-liebstem Trio" (as the critic for the *Allgemeine musikalische Zeitung* calls it), a touching *Ländler* in B major. (The Trio is shown in ex. 7.7.) Marked triple piano, and with pedal tones on F♯, the Trio seems a time-lapsed echo of the earlier passage, even in its rehearing of the shift from B minor to B major.[11]

For Schubert, the trio is often a special place, a retreat into that other world, an internal *Fürsichsein* purged of the antinomies with which Schubert's music must otherwise contend. In a sense, the true dance is here, in this *Ländler*, with its tender hints of the intimacies of Schubert's social circle. The finding of that place, the finding of B *major*, is scripted in the two languid phrases written into the Trio but sounding as though afterbeats, trailing behind the Menuetto. The hesitant ambivalence of those

11. Litwin's interpretation (see above, note 9) enhances the relationship, for both passages—first movement, mm. 10–16; and the Trio—are performed with the moderator pedal. For all the novelty of the effect—"as if one were hearing music from a music box," as Litwin describes it—the music of the Trio is to my ear trivialized, made mechanical, expressionless ("ohne Empfindung," it might have been inscribed).

EX. 7.7. Schubert, Piano Sonata in G, D 894 (op. 78), D 894, third movement, Trio.

phrases is recalled in the second part of the Trio, but recalled in no conventional mode. The reprise is prepared on the dominant of G♯ minor. Here we would expect a conventional correction to the true dominant, on F♯, the reprise sounding in B major. Instead, the reprise is begun in G♯ *major*—in the tonal spectrum of the sonata, the extreme point, seven fifths removed from G major. The return to the tonic is subtle. Those fugitive phrases between Menuetto and Trio, now recast as G♯ major and G♯ minor, are worked into the narrative, setting off the final phrase where B major sounds as an afterthought, an obligatory correction, more denouement than resolution.

There is something *other* about the Trio, a condition only exaggerated when, as in the Litwin recording, it is heard through the scrim of the moderator cloth. And yet, for all the novelty of the effect, it seems critical to apprehend the Trio as integral to the larger sweep of the sonata: together with the passage at m. 10 in the first movement, as music in search of some inner place.[12] The music of *Schwestergruß*, written four years earlier for a special occasion and a special person, opens into a similar place, inspired by Bruchmann's poem but moving beyond its delusional images to an expression of something more profound, both in the abstraction of its syntactically complex narrative and in the visceral reality of its tonal language.

Mein Traum; Mein Gebet

To place this song and this sonata together in the hermeneutical theater, so to say, is to provoke larger questions about any plausible reciprocity between works that differ so vastly from one another in genre, in purpose, in the circumstances under which they were composed. In an effort to understand how these works might be understood to speak to one another, I take shelter in a few well-rehearsed lines from Harold Bloom's *Anxiety of Influence*, whose central thesis is that every poem—every great poem—is in effect a rewriting, a revision of some precursor poem: not consciously so, nor inspired by an intention that can be documented. "The meaning of a poem," Bloom writes, "can only be a poem, but *another poem—a poem not itself*."[13] This in turn brings to mind something that the literary critic and

---

12. I'm reminded here of what Lawrence Kramer identifies in Beethoven's "tempest" sonatas (op. 10, no. 1; op. 13; op. 31, no. 2; op. 57) as places of "(sym)pathetic reserve," passages in which the music projects an interior subjectivity distinct from (in these cases) an otherwise "tempestuous" environment. See his "Primitive Encounters: Beethoven's 'Tempest' Sonata, Musical Meaning, and Enlightenment Anthropology," *Beethoven Forum* 6 (1998): 31–65, esp. 50–56.

13. Harold Bloom, *The Anxiety of Influence: A Theory of Poetry*, 2nd ed. (New York: Oxford University Press, 1997), 70.

philosopher Walter Benjamin wrote in 1923, in a letter to a colleague: "The research of contemporary art history always amounts merely to a history of the subject matter or a history of form, for which the works of art provide only examples and, as it were, models. There is no question of there being a history of the work of art as such." And yet (Benjamin continues), "there remains an intense relationship among works of art. The specific historicity of works of art is the kind that can be revealed not in 'art history' but only in interpretation."[14] For both Benjamin and Bloom, it is how works of art speak to one another, often across vast temporal and cultural spaces, that constitutes the argument of criticism.

In the instance before us, the more incestuous relationship among works by the same composer, such anxieties are only complicated by another, with which all authors must contend: an internal struggle in which the powerful impulse to sing the same song—the creative project as one great continuity—is challenged by the no less powerful instinct to "clear imaginative space for [oneself]," here turning Bloom's famous words to the condition of the composer rewriting his own past.[15] In this scenario, we take the works before us, song and sonata, each as a sounding, a depth charge into the life, staking out the four intensely lived years between November 1822 and October 1826. The haunting prose narrative "Mein Traum" (My Dream) of July 1822 is now read as a confessional of the "family romance" and for the disturbing signs of what Walther Dürr has identified as "Jahre der Krise"—the years of crisis.[16] The autobiographical signs in Schubert's poem *Mein Gebet* (My Prayer), dated May 1823, are no less troubling. Here are its final quatrains:

Sieh, vernichtet liegt im Staube,	See, undone in dust now lying,
Unerhörtem Gram zum Raube,	Victim to unheard-of grief,
Meines Lebens Martergang	The martyrdom of my life
Nahend ew'gem Untergang.	Approaching eternal downfall.

14. From a letter of 9 December 1923 to Florens Christian Rang. See *The Correspondence of Walter Benjamin, 1910–1940*, ed. and annotated by Gershom Scholem and Theodor W. Adorno, trans. Manfred R. Jacobson and Evelyn M. Jacobson (Chicago: University of Chicago Press, 1994), 224.

15. Bloom, *Anxiety of Influence*, 5.

16. See Maynard Solomon, "Franz Schubert's 'My Dream,'" in *American Imago* 38, no. 2 (1981): 137–54. This "Traumerzählung" figures prominently in Walther Dürr, "Franz Schuberts Wanderjahre," an introduction to the collection titled *Franz Schubert: Jahre der Krise 1818–1823*, ed. Werner Aderhold, Walther Dürr, and Walburga Litschauer (Kassel: Bärenreiter, 1985), 11–21.

Tödt' es und mich selber tödte,	Kill it and kill myself,
Stürz' nun Alles in die Lethe	Plunge now all in the Lethe
Und ein reines kräft'ges Sein	And let, O Lord, a pure
Lass', o Großer, dann gedeih'n.[17]	Powerful Being flourish.

Pleading for divine intervention, the poet wishes his anguished life drowned in the river of oblivion, of *Vergessenheit*. The prayer is for a transformative reincarnation, for "ein reines kräft'ges Sein"—a purer, stronger self. Only months earlier, in December 1822, Schubert set Goethe's *Am Flusse*: "Verfliesset, vielgeliebte Lieder," the poet sings, "zum Meere der Vergessenheit": flow off, beloved songs, into the sea of oblivion. (The opening bars are shown in ex. 7.8.) The setting is in D major, but for a wistful moment the harmony swells toward F♯ minor, toward a *Vergessenheit* that does not come—and reminiscent of that other unanswered $^6_4$ on C♯, another F♯ minor unsounded, in the second setting of *Meeres Stille*, at the word "Todes."

By the autumn of 1826, all the external signs were of a life engaged in vigorous productivity, the ghastly, fatal symptoms of venereal disease apparently in recession. External signs, however, often mask the truer self. If one might imagine Schubert willing himself through the catharsis portrayed in *Mein Gebet*, the resolve to a process of forgetting is more difficult to conjure. Memory persists. This, I think, is what we hear in later Schubert: the ambivalent engagement with *Vergessenheit*, the purging of memory, played out beneath the struggle toward a "reines kräft'ges Sein."

Epilogue

With the death of Schubert a mere two years after the composition of op. 78 comes the inevitable mythologizing of the life and, as corollary, the construction of a late style. The vulnerability of such a construct would be self-evident were it not that much of this late music conveys something of what Edward Said would detect as a voice "against the grain": "the experience of late style that involves a nonharmonious, nonserene tension, and above all, a sort of deliberately unproductive productiveness going *against*. . ."[18] It was Adorno's "Spätstil Beethovens" that established a rhetorical ground-

17. For the full text, see Deutsch, *Dokumente*, 192–93. The translation is my own, but drawing upon Blom, *Schubert Reader*, 279.

18. Edward W. Said, *On Late Style: Music and Literature Against the Grain* (New York: Pantheon Books, 2006), 7.

EX. 7.8. Schubert, *Am Flusse*, D 766, mm. 1–11.

ing for talk about late style, and preeminently in the paradox of an isolated music in which (to paraphrase Adorno) the objectivity of its fissured landscape is illuminated in a subjectivity that yet fails to heal.[19] For Adorno, the idea of landscape deeply informed by the lyrical is central to an apprehending of Schubert's music: "It is the shared participation of the subjective and the objective newly directed toward the lyrical that constitute

---

19. "Objektiv ist die brüchige Landschaft, subjektiv das Licht, darin einzig sie erglüht. Er bewirkt nicht deren harmonische Synthese." Theodor W. Adorno, *Beethoven: Philosophie der Musik*, ed. Rolf Tiedemann (Frankfurt am Main: Suhrkamp, 1993), 184. For one translation, see Adorno, *Beethoven: The Philosophy of Music*, ed. Tiedemann, trans. Edmund Jephcott (Stanford, CA: Stanford University Press, 1998), 126.

Schubert's landscape."[20] This abstruse tension between the subjective and the objective, between the expanse of landscape and the centered voice of the lyrical, finds its extreme expression in the "molto moderato e cantabile" of op. 78. And yet, to suggest that this music might be parsed into oppositions such as these, that one might discriminate object from subject, the objective from the subjective, is to presuppose a specificity contrary to the condition of art.

Finally, there is the conundrum of late style. The densely saturated chronology of Schubert's work invites a narrative toward lateness that would in part explain why we hear these last works as poignant reflections of a life lived, in all its concentrated brevity. And here we are returned to that reviewer for the *Allgemeine musikalische Zeitung* in December 1827, unable to hear this "young" Schubert unencumbered by late Beethoven. A century later, in the disquieting opening lines of his Schubert essay—"He who crosses the threshold between the years of Beethoven's death and Schubert's will shiver, like someone emerging into the painfully diaphanous light from a rumbling, newly formed crater frozen in motion," it begins—Adorno captures in apocalyptic moonscape a moment sealed in historical memory, its protagonists locked in iconic embrace. The image is difficult to repress, even as we now have a better sense of the extent to which the music of Schubert's final years moves into its own world, cutting across the grain of Beethoven's last works, conjuring a subjectivity that we are no less at pains to demystify. In this inscrutable narrative we are challenged to interrogate the condition of a late style without lateness.

---

20. "Damit wird der Anteil des Subjektiven und Objektiven am Lyrischen, das Schuberts Landschaft ausmacht, neu bestimmt." "Schubert," in Theodor W. Adorno, *Moments musicaux. Neu gedruckte Aufsätze 1928–1962* (Frankfurt am Main: Suhrkamp, 1964), 20. For a very different translation, see Theodor W. Adorno, "Schubert (1928)," trans. Jonathan Dunsby and Beate Perrey, in *19th-Century Music* 29, no. 1 (2005): 7.

Last Things, New Horizons

✴ CHAPTER 8 ✴

Final Beethoven

". . . we are challenged to interrogate the condition of a late style without lateness." Inspired by Adorno's reflections on Schubert's last works, these words that close the previous chapter might provoke us as well to revisit Beethoven's last works as expressions of what would come to be construed as his late style. But then, the very notion of late style, as distinct from (though bound up in) a chronological lateness, seems to have been conceived in the nineteenth century as a means of coming to terms with the challenging music of Beethoven's final decade.[1] With the completion of the *Leonore/Fidelio* project in 1814 as a convenient watershed, the works of 1815 (Beethoven at age forty-five)—preeminently the Piano Sonata in A, op. 101, and the two Sonatas for Piano and Cello, op. 102—are commonly taken to inaugurate this final stage in Beethoven's project. The reaction to the often intimidating originality, the deviant traces, the quiddities of this music brings to mind Charles Burney's astute insight into the music of Carl Philipp Emanuel Bach, who "used to be censured for his extraneous modulations, crudities, and difficulties; but, like the hard words of Dr. [Samuel] Johnson, to which the public by degrees became reconciled, every German

---

1. The signal inquiry into the phenomenon of a late stye, and of Beethoven's place in it, is Theodor W. Adorno's "Spätstil Beethovens," conveniently available and set in a rich context of fragments and notes, in Adorno, *Beethoven: Philosophie der Musik*. Fragmente und Text, ed. Rolf Tiedemann (Frankfurt a.M: Suhrkamp, 2nd ed., 1994), 180–84; and in English as "Beethoven's Late Style," in *Beethoven: The Philosophy of Music*, ed. Tiedemann, trans. Edmund Jephcott (Stanford, CA: Stanford University Press, 1998), 123–26. Adorno's writings on late Beethoven served as an inspiration for the chapter "Timeliness and Lateness," in Edward W. Said, *On Late Style: Music and Literature Against the Grain* (New York: Pantheon Books, 2006), 3–24.

composer takes the same liberties now as Bach, and every English writer uses Johnson's language with impunity."[2]

But if we are inclined to read the symptoms of lateness in Beethoven's music from 1815, we might remind ourselves that Haydn at age forty-five had not yet composed the string quartets of op. 33 (1781), written, as he himself advertised them, "auf eine gantz neue besondere art," and which indeed established a critical basis for a defining of the Classical style:[3] a new beginning. "Art demands of us that we shall not stand still," Beethoven is said to have remarked to Karl Holz, upon completion of the first three of the last quartets: "You will notice a new kind of part-writing, and thank God there is less lack of invention [*Fantasie*] than ever before."[4] From this one might theorize the attribution of late style as a critical misprision of works conceived as so many ventures into new territory, the condition of lateness no impediment against the challenge to conceive ideas of bold originality.

The five string quartets composed in the years 1824–1826 constitute their own stylistic world, a unique idiolect whose *Entstehungsgeschichte*— the complex history of their composition—is documented in well over a thousand pages of sketches, more than six hundred pages of which have been aligned with the Quartet in C♯ Minor alone.[5] Of the drafts in quartet score, a category exhaustively cataloged and described by Robert Winter, some 450 leaves (or 900 pages) have survived for these late quartets.[6]

---

2. Charles Burney, *A General History of Music*, with Critical and Historical Notes by Frank Mercer, 2 vols. (New York: Dover Publications, 1957), 2:955. In quite another context, I called on the Burney passage in *Unfinished Music* (Oxford: Oxford University Press, rev. 2012), 36.

3. The phrase is contained in a letter to the Prince Kraft Ernst zu Öttingen-Wallerstein, and, in slightly different wording, in a letter to Johann Caspar Lavater, both letters dated 3 December 1781, offering handwritten copies of the quartets. See Joseph Haydn, *Gesammelte Briefe und Aufzeichnungen*, ed. Dénes Bartha (Kassel: Bärenreiter, 1965), 106–7. It was Charles Rosen, *The Classical Style: Haydn, Mozart, Beethoven* (New York: W. W. Norton, expanded ed., 1997), who (116) spoke of the opening page of the Quartet in B Minor as "a revolution in style."

4. ". . . die Kunst will es von uns, daß wir nicht stehen bleiben. Sie werden eine neue Art der Stimmführung bemerken und an Fantasie fehlt's, Gottlob, weniger als je zuvor!" Given in Wilhelm von Lenz, *Beethoven: Eine Kunst-Studie*, 4 (Hamburg: Hoffmann & Co., 1860), 217; I take the quotation from Klaus Kropfinger, *Beethoven* (Kassell: Bärenreiter, 2001), 194. This well-traveled passage is given as well in Joseph Kerman, *The Beethoven Quartets* (New York: Alfred A. Knopf, 1967), 349; and Robert Winter, "Plans for the Structure of the String Quartet in C Sharp Minor, Op. 131," in *Beethoven Studies* 2, ed. Alan Tyson (London: Oxford University Press, 1977), 106–37: 107.

5. See Robert Winter, "Plans for the Structure," 136.

6. "Sketches in Score for the Late Quartets," in JTW, 463–502.

But within this stylistic world, the music composed in the final months of Beethoven's creative life, from roughly August through November 1826, seems a retreat from the more radical adventures that constitute the core of this empyreal repertory.

Two complexes of music, in particular, invite further interrogation. The first comprises sketches and drafts for late work on the finale of the String Quartet in C♯ Minor, op. 131, with plans for a "postscript" in D♭ major that would eventually constitute the basis for the *Lento assai* of the String Quartet in F Major, op. 135, with its own family of drafts. And then there is the String Quartet in B♭ Major, op. 130, whose original finale, now known as the "grosse Fuge," would be replaced by a second finale and then published separately both as quartet (op. 133) and in a boldly idiomatic arrangement by Beethoven himself for piano four hands (op. 134).[7] If the facts are well known, the back stories tracing the evolution of these two projects will reveal a tangled weave of underlying motives, and much else.

1

If it was once commonplace to think of the corpus of Beethoven's sketches as in some sense finite and sufficiently legible to encourage its publication in an edition of facsimiles and transcriptions—to envision a *Gesamtausgabe der Skizzen Beethovens*[8]—the vast corpus of sketches for the String Quartet in C♯ Minor is here to bedevil such utopian visions. There is, first of all, the important desk sketchbook known as "Kullak"—it was the pianist and composer Franz Kullak who in 1880 gifted the book to the Royal Library in Berlin—the last such book to have been used by Beethoven, with entries that can be dated between October or November 1825 and November 1826, and containing substantial sketches for the three quartets at the core of our inquiry.[9] Then there are the so-called pocket sketchbooks,

7. For an illuminating study of the arrangement, see Robert Winter, "Recomposing the *Grosse Fuge*: Beethoven and Opus 134," in *Variations on the Canon: Essays on Music from Bach to Boulez in Honor of Charles Rosen on His Eightieth Birthday*, ed. Robert Curry, David Gable, and Robert L. Marshall (Rochester, NY: University of Rochester Press, 2008), 130–60.

8. As it was advertised by Joseph Schmidt-Görg, then newly appointed as Director of the Archive of the Beethoven-Haus in Bonn, in *Beethoven-Jahrbuch* 1, Jg. 1953/54 (Bonn, 1954), 249—though the early volumes were limited to transcriptions, with only a few pages in facsimile.

9. Berlin: Staatsbibliothek zu Berlin, Preussischer Kulturbesitz, Mus. ms. autogr. Beethoven 24. I take these dates from Robert Winter's account in JTW, 313. For a detailed inventory of the book, see Hans-Günter Klein, *Ludwig van Beethoven. Autographe und Abschriften. Katalog*, Staatsbibliothek Preussischer Kulturbesitz, Kataloge der Musik-

assembled from loose sheets of manuscript paper, and folded so as to yield a gathering of sixteen pages and often constructed of several such gatherings. Written mostly in pencil and presumably without the stability of a writing table, its fleet telegraphic entries will challenge the competence of even the most adept readers of Beethoven's hand. For op. 131, six such gatherings have survived. And finally, there are the voluminous drafts in score—"over 200 leaves," in Robert Winter's count—whose significance during the years 1824–1826, when Beethoven "was occupied almost exclusively with the late quartets, must therefore reflect an important development in Beethoven's compositional process."[10] The prospect of an edition that would put all this in order and accessible to the casual reader seems remote if not implausible. Still, digital access, particularly of the important holdings of the Berlin Staatsbibliothek, has enabled a control of these unruly documents unimaginable even ten or fifteen years ago.

Our first stop will be at a remarkable page among the score drafts for the finale of op. 131.[11] It was Robert Winter who first called attention to this page, and its stunning revelation of an alternative close for the quartet: "Beethoven planned to conclude the quartet with a D-flat postscript—and this postscript used the theme later adopted as the basis of the 'Lento assai' variations in Op. 135."[12] (The page is shown in fig. 8.1.) In his detailed inventory of the Beethoven manuscripts then in the West Berlin Staatsbibliothek, Hans-Günter Klein even chose to identify this "postscript" as a sketch for the third movement of op. 135, a bibliographic expedient, perhaps, that leaps ahead prematurely to another stage in its evolution.[13]

For it is clear from this page, and from other entries preliminary to this point in the composition of the work, that this D♭ music was conceived to play an essential role in the denouement of op. 131. What is equally striking—baffling, even—is the absence of any sign how, in this late draft, the music (and its performers) would negotiate between those massive chords in C♯ major—three quadruple stops above the deep C♯ in the cello, marked *fortissimo* and *crescendo*—that were meant to close off the movement, and this new music in D♭ major, *adagio* and *pianissimo* (as we learn from earlier sketches) and in $\frac{6}{8}$ meter: this, in a quartet in which the liaison between movements is in each case so refined as to embody an essence

---

abteilung, ed. Rudolf Elvers, Erste Reihe: Handschriften, vol. 2 (Berlin: Merseburger, 1975), 74–89.

10. JTW, 482—this, at the outset of an extraordinarily detailed inventory (482–97) of the score sketches for op. 131, distributed across some twenty signature bundles.

11. Berlin: Staatsbibliothek zu Berlin, StPK, Artaria 216, p. 99.

12. Winter, "Plans for the Structure," 125, and the music example at 124.

13. Klein, *Katalog*, 225.

FIGURE 8.1. Beethoven, score draft for String Quartet in C♯ Minor, op. 131, finale. Staatsbibliothek zu Berlin, Mus. ms. autogr. Beethoven Artaria 216, p. 99. By kind permission.

of the quartet, each formulating the illusion of actual transformation from one state to another. In the final bars of the opening fugue, to take but one example, the close in C♯ major reduces itself to the vanishing point on an octave C♯, *pianissimo*, from which the octave D♮ emerges seamlessly as the incipit of the *Allegro molto vivace*: a defining moment (see ex. 8.1).

That Beethoven expended considerable concentration over these moments of transformation, those few notes within the interstices between movements that bring them to life, is amply confirmed in the many pages devoted to them in the sketches. The sheer novelty of the device was broached by Karl Holz in conversation with Beethoven in the last few days of August 1826, only two weeks after the quartet had been delivered to a representative of the publisher Schott on or about 12 August. Holz was second violinist of the quartet led by Ignaz Schuppanzigh, and it was Schuppanzigh who, a month earlier, had asked Beethoven when they might be able to try

EX. 8.1. Beethoven, String Quartet in C♯ Minor, op. 131, from the close of the first movement to the opening of the second.

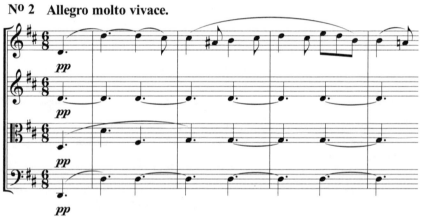

out the new quartet, offering that his players would willingly copy out their own parts.[14] Clearly, they had already read through the quartet when Holz inquired: "Must it be played through without interruption?" and then, in reply to what we must assume to have been Beethoven's impatient affirmation: "But then we shan't be able to repeat anything," referring, of course, to the repetition of individual movements often requested at performances, public or private.[15] Holz was concerned too about the need to tune their

14. "Wann werden wir denn das neue *Quartett* probieren? Wir werden unsere Stimmen selbst schreiben." *Ludwig van Beethovens Konversationshefte*, ed. Dagmar Beck (Leipzig: Deutscher Verlag für Musik, 1993), 10:47.

15. *Konversationshefte* 10:163–64.

Final Beethoven   167

instruments in the course of a performance. "Wann sollen wir stimmen?" (When are we to tune?), he asks, and in reply to Beethoven's answer, joked "We'd better order very reliable strings!"[16] Holz then offered: "Die Unterhaltung von einem Stücke zu dem andern ist nie so geistreich, daß sie ein verhältnismäßiges Intermezzo bilden könnte," a somewhat ambiguous and even ironic formulation that meant to suggest that the conversation heard between the movements of a work is never so witty that it could be taken to serve as an appropriate intermezzo. Beethoven seems to have read this as a critique of the music at these interstices, for Holz was led to clarify: "Ich meine die Unterhaltung des Zuhörers zwischen den Stücken" (I mean the conversation of the members of the audience between the movements).

The understated significance of this little exchange with Holz resides as much in what we might read between and beneath its half-written lines. For some ten years, Beethoven's music, beginning with those works of 1815, and notably in the cycle *An die ferne Geliebte*, had been tending toward a continuity that would sacrifice the self-contained perfection of the individual movement in the service of the larger work. But it is only here, in op. 131, that Beethoven creates an instrumental work whose seven disparate movements, from the lapidary tones of its opening fugue, *molto espressivo*, through to what seems a transformation of the fugue subject into a rough-hewn finale (and the afterbeats of this "postscript" in D♭ major, finally deleted before the writing of the final autograph), plot out a trajectory with narrative implications, the modulation of affect from the one movement to the next captured at a singular moment of inflection.

In pursuit of the topic, there is one scrap of evidence that has always seemed to me especially telling. In a conversation book from late June 1826, on a page otherwise given to quotidian household notes—and an inked

16. "Vor dem *Presto*," Holz wrote, perhaps in reply to a query from Beethoven. In a note to this passage in the conversation book, the editor cites Holz's recollection of 1857: "Der Absicht des Autors gemäß sollen sämmtliche Stücke dieses Quartetts *ohne* Unterbrechung ihres Zusammenhanges vorgetragen werden" [In accord with the view of the author, the entirety of this quartet is to be performed without interruption of its continuity], and affirmed that Beethoven would allow, "trotz aller Vorstellungen wegen des Nachstimmens der Instrumente, und der Ermüdung der Zuhörer, nur eine kurze Pause *nach* dem Presto E Dur (nicht etwa *vor* demselben)" [in spite of all proposals regarding the tuning of the instruments, and the tiring of the audience, only a brief pause *after* the Presto in E major (and not *before* it)]. This, however, cannot have been the case, since to act on that advice would be to ignore the *attacca* at the end of the Presto and the octave G♯s that make the connection to the following Adagio. "Vor dem *Presto*," as Holz wrote in 1826 (perhaps echoing Beethoven), does indeed make more sense, if a pause is absolutely necessary. *Konversationshefte* 10:372. The Holz quotation is taken from Lenz, *Beethoven. Eine Kunst-Studie* 5:216 and 226.

EX. 8.2A. Beethoven, String Quartet in C♯ Minor, op. 131, final bars of the sixth movement and opening of the seventh.

entry (presumably in Schindler's hand) noting the death of Carl Maria von Weber "im 40ten Jahre"—here, in the midst of these distractions, is Beethoven scribbling out those few final notes, the briefest cadenza-like pause before the emphatic downbeat on C♯ that will set the finale in motion (see ex. 8.2).[17] Away from his workshop, Beethoven is yet focused on that mo-

17. Weber died on 5 June, and it was reported in the *Wiener Allgemeine Theaterzeitung* for 20 June. *Ludwig van Beethovens Konversationshefte* 9, ed. Grita Herre, assisted by Günter Brosche (Leipzig: Deutscher Verlag fur Musik, 1988), 315.

EX. 8.2B. Beethoven, String Quartet in C♯ Minor, op. 131. Entry, ca. 20 June 1826, in *Konversationshefte* 9, p. 315.

ment at the very end of the sixth movement, this deeply moving lament in G♯ minor, *Adagio quasi un poco andante*, each repetition of its constrained principal phrase repositioned and revoiced, up to the last eighth in its penultimate bar. The texture explodes on a seventh chord from a deep F♯ (a subdominant in C♯ minor), the cello reaching into its low register for the first time, while the violin sounds an unprepared A♮ in its high register, and then reaches up to the even higher F♯ on the final beat of m. 28. A "new kind of part-writing" indeed! And here is where that faintly scribbled entry in the conversation book finds itself. In performance, this final beat poses a challenge: played *a tempo*, it could be taken to establish the actual tempo of the *Allegro* (adagio ♪ = allegro ♩). A rubato that seems written into the notes, no violinist can resist taking time here. It, too, is a defining moment.

This then brings us back to the "postscript" in D♭ major: to an imagined transition that would move from the close of this powerful movement in C♯ minor to the D♭ music, a draft of some thirty-five measures in score that was to follow. There is first of all the choice of key: D♭ major. Did Beethoven have in mind a postlude of the kind that Schumann would compose at the end of *Dichterliebe*, whose final song, *Die alten, bösen Lieder*, is set in C♯ minor?[18] The extended postlude (*Andante espressivo*), given to the piano alone, has a subtle poetic mission, returning the cycle to some internal moment of conciliation, its D♭ grounding a tonal journey set in motion by the dominant seventh on C♯ that sounds out famously unresolved at the end of the song with which the cycle begins. Beethoven's postscript might be thought to have functioned similarly: at this relatively late stage in the composition of the quartet, we are witness to a concept of the whole that would radically alter the impact of those terrifying quadruple-stopped chords,

---

18. This and other similarities between the two works inspired Nicholas Marston to his compelling "Schumann's Monument to Beethoven," in *19th-Century Music* 14, no. 3 (Spring 1991): 247–64, a study in turn cognizant of Winter's discussion of the D♭ "postscript" in the quartet.

in its published text, as a design of teleological finality, even against the equivocations on its final page around the minor subdominant that seem to undermine that sense of finality.

There is something about the reciprocity of C♯ minor and D♭ major, the mutability between them, that seems to have intrigued Beethoven even in his Bonn days. As early as 1789, in the two modulatory "Preludes through all the major keys" (op. 39), the transition from the one to the other, a traversal up through the sharp keys and a descent through the flat side, is captured in the enharmonic mutation of C♯ (with a shift to the minor mode and a striking new texture) to D♭ major. In the second prelude, the transition between them is marked by a poignant new voicing, again making manifest the shift from the accrued dissonance implied within the sharp-side keys to the sense of return within the flat side.[19] This extreme moment in the composing out of a tonal hierarchy, inspiring passages of impressive expression in these preludes, will resonate in later works—memorably, in the magical "attacca subito," from the *Adagio sostenuto* in C♯ minor to the *Allegretto* in D♭ major of the Sonata "quasi una Fantasia," op. 27, no. 2, of 1801. And here, some twenty-five years further on, during a late stage in the composition of op. 131, this final turn to D♭ major would throw into question the hegemony of C♯ minor in a work whose bold divagations led Joseph Kerman to write of that "perfect mutual trajectory" across its seven movements.[20]

Unlike the postscript with which *Dichterliebe* closes, this new music in D♭ has no evident referent. It does not call up some earlier music, as did those cyclic works of 1815. In the innocence of a virgin performance and in feigned ignorance of the circumstances of its creation, we might even be tempted to hear it as an eighth movement, the threefold repetition of its eight-bar theme suggesting a design of some expanse—were it not for the powerful sense of closure in the music that precedes it. To put it cautiously, D♭ major would be heard enharmonically as an extension of the overarching tonic of the quartet, even as it inflects both pitch and mode, the simple stepwise diatonicism of its theme mollifying the sharp edges, the brutal energy of the true finale. Prospero's words in the epilogue to *The Tempest* come to mind: "what strength I have's mine own, / Which is most faint"—Prospero not, I hasten to add, as a stand-in for a Beethoven in the final months of his creative life, but as a figure whose parting words give voice to what would have been conveyed in the enervated music of this postscript. This is a mat-

19. For a more detailed discussion of op. 39 and its significance, see my *Cherubino's Leap: In Search of the Enlightenment Moment* (Chicago: University of Chicago Press, 2016), 16–20.

20. Kerman, *The Beethoven Quartets*, 349.

Final Beethoven 171

ter of narrative, of theater, of fiction, and not of autobiography. The narrative, however, was altered once more, restoring the finale as we know it.

2

Removed from the Quartet in C♯ Minor, this D♭ music is given new life, reconceived as the basis for the *Lento assai*,[21] the third movement of the String Quartet in F Major, op. 135, its key now sounding as ♭VI in the tonal spectrum of the quartet. If the theme is essentially intact, with a simple two-bar cadential extension that lengthens it from eight to ten bars, its repetitions are now elevated to the status of true variations, each exploring complexities of voicing without abandoning the sentiment of the theme— with one exception. The second variation, in an edgy, ominous C♯ minor, stripped down to its harmonic bones, is about something else. For those who know something of the evolution of this music, the C♯ minor of op. 131 must hover in the background, a prominent subtext brought into play with this muted variation, *più lento* and *pianissimo*, setting itself apart from its D♭ environment and consequently suggesting a relationship between the two keys that will recall in an ironic reversal the posthumous apparition, so to say, of D♭ major from those final chords of the Quartet in C♯ Minor.

The placement of the *minore* at the precise mathematical center of the movement only underscores its significance. Especially impressive, in response to the simple sequence around the circle of fifths at mm. 7–10 of the theme, harmonies are now recast in bold diminished sevenths that climax with a *rinforzato* in the middle of m. 29, the outer voices having expanded from the deep A in the cello to a high D♯ in the first violin, a diminished seventh as dominant ninth, its root, G♯, delayed and displaced over the final bars of the variation (see ex. 8.3).

What is uncommonly striking about this final cadence is the nature of that displacement, the full dominant in root position pushed to the extreme edge, to the final sixteenth of the group, *pianissimo*, in the first half of m. 32, and then answered by the silence of an eighth rest in the second half of the bar. This merely delays the resolution by an eighth, but when

---

21. The tempo designation at the opening of the movement is given as "Assai lento, cantante e tranquillo" in Beethoven's autograph and in the parts that he copied and which were sent to the publisher Maurice Schlesinger in Paris. Schlesinger altered this wording to read: "Lento assai e cantante tranquillo." On this point, see Beethoven, *Werke: Gesamtausgabe* VI/5, Streichquartette III, ed. Rainer Cadenbach (Munich: Henle, 2004); and Barry Cooper, "The Autograph Score of the Slow Movement of Beethoven's Last Quartet, Opus 135," in *The New Beethoven: Evolution, Analysis, Interpretation*, ed. Jeremy Yudkin (Rochester, NY: University of Rochester Press, 2020), 332–54, esp. 344.

EX. 8.3A. Beethoven, String Quartet in F Major, op. 135, third movement, opening theme, mm. 1–14.

EX. 8.3B. Beethoven, String Quartet in F Major, op. 135, third movement: variation in C♯ minor, from m. 26, and return to D♭ major at m. 32.

resolution comes, it comes with a difference: a triad in first inversion on the weakest eighth of the measure and notated in D♭ major. The cello waits another eighth to flesh out the harmony with an octave D♭. Tellingly, the autograph score shows a notational idiosyncrasy familiar from other works: the A♭ in the first violin at m. 32 has the value of a quarter note, but is written as two eighths tied, and then tied again to the A♭ on the first beat of m. 33, at the *Tempo Imo* of the new variation (see ex. 8.4).[22] Away at his brother's residence in the village of Gneixendorf near Krems (about fifty miles from Vienna) and without a copyist at hand, Beethoven was forced to write out the individual parts of the quartet that would serve as *Stichvorlage* for the publisher Maurice Schlesinger in Paris.[23] Here, and in all subsequent editions, the two eighths are replaced with a quarter note. Still, there is meaning to be teased out of the original notation. The first eighth together with the imperfect tonic beneath it sounds the tentative resolution of that fleeting, barely sounded dominant. The second eighth looks ahead, an anticipation of the new variation. The distinction is admittedly a subtle one, perhaps intended to guide the performer toward an articulation, if only in the mind, at this momentary juncture where C♯ minor cedes to D♭ major.[24] In the end, no doubt in the haste of copying out the parts, this fine notational detail was lost: something of value that we might wish to reclaim.

There is more to this story. Those drafts in quartet score for the third movement of op. 135, by the sheer accident of their survival and in spite of their fragmentary state, have much to tell us about a gestation thick with revision of the substance and detail of texture and voicing. The drafts are to be found in two manuscript compilations in the Berlin Staatsbibliothek, and here I follow their description in Robert Winter's inventory.[25] The first is Artaria 216:

---

22. The autograph score of the slow movement, now at the Musée Royal de Mariemont, Morlanwelz, Belgium, is given in full transcription in Cooper, "The Autograph Score," 347–51.

23. This state of affairs is corroborated in Beethoven's letter of 30 October to Maurice Schlesinger, which survives only in the two versions of Schlesinger's recollection of its text. See *Briefwechsel Gesamtausgabe* 6:304; Anderson, *Letters*, 1318, 1319. The autograph parts are today at the Bonn Beethoven-Haus (HCB Bmh 6/46) and may be consulted in its digital archive.

24. Barry Cooper reads the notational change differently, suggesting that "no special effect was intended, so [Beethoven] substituted a quarter note in the separate [violin] part." See Cooper, "The Autograph Score," 344.

25. JTW, 498–502.

EX. 8.4. Beethoven, String Quartet in F Major, op. 135, third movement, m. 32, as in the autograph score.

	pages		
A	155/156 157/158	bars 1–32	These appear to be the earliest drafts for the movement.
B	119/120 121/122	bars 1–22	Another early state, but clearly subsequent to the draft in bifolia A
C	95/96 97/98	bars 1–27	A later draft
	115/116 117/118	bars 28–48	[continued from p. 98]
D	89/90	bars 50–54	

The other is Artaria 210:

A	227/228 225/226	bars 25–32	C♯ minor, in $\frac{9}{8}$ [the two leaves of the bifolium are reversed in the MS]

176 CHAPTER EIGHT

FIGURE 8.2. Beethoven, score draft for String Quartet in F, op. 135, third movement. Staatsbibliothek zu Berlin, Artaria 216, p. 155. By kind permission.

Not the least remarkable aspect of what appears to be the earliest of these drafts, at Artaria 216, p. 155, has to do with its opening measures (shown in the illustration, fig. 8.2). In the published version, the new tonic is established across two bars, its unusual voicing unfolded in a calibrated exposition of the notes of the triad delaying till the end the foundational root as doubled octave in the cello. One could picture Beethoven finding it on his imaginary keyboard in a matter of seconds. And so it is astonishing to discover, in the earliest of these score drafts, and in the two later ones at pp. 119 and 95 in Artaria 216, evidence of a process of trial and error, written in both pencil and ink, so densely convoluted as to suggest a composer at wit's end over these bars that have so little to do with the thematic core of the piece. It is humbling indeed to witness a mind so locked into a discovery of that solitary F from which the *Lento assai* will materialize.

While this initial F in the viola would function as a liaison from the final triad (in F major) of the second movement, another train of thought suggests itself. It is clear from the sketches and score drafts that work on the finale of op. 131 and early sketches for op. 135 seem to overlap.[26] Can we then permit ourselves to imagine the impact of the postscript in D♭, a *Nachklang* to those final massive chords of op. 131, continuing to resonate in Beethoven's inner ear even after the hard decision had been made to re-purpose this music for the *Lento assai* of op. 135? Another of those conjunctions that navigate from one tonal sphere to the next, these two bars function seamlessly as an extension both of the E♯ at the end of op. 131—a transition that remained unwritten in the drafts—and no less seamlessly from the tonic F of the Vivace in op. 135. This is of course an analytic fantasy. Beethoven cannot have *intended* so blatant a textual contradiction. And yet the residue of a process, convoluted and subliminal as it may be, leaves its trace.

No less remarkable are the score drafts for the variation in C♯ minor. The draft in Artaria 210 is of particular interest. At the top, Beethoven scribbles $\frac{9}{8}$, and then, in pencil, sketches out the first-violin line alone. The music is bare: only minimal motion in the thematic voice, and long silences within each measure. But then Beethoven takes pen in hand and writes over this preliminary draft, transforming its austere lines into a music of considerable shape in a sequence of phrases synchronized to its bass. Inner voices are entered here and there (see fig. 8.3).

This, however, was not the earliest evidence of the turn to C♯ minor. Returning to that earlier draft in Artaria 216, we find an incipient entry for this variation, reduced to little more than a rhythm. At the bottom of the page, beneath the scored-up variation, Beethoven scribbles a cue to a rewriting of the passage in $\frac{9}{8}$. The effort to establish a clear rhythmic flow in $\frac{9}{8}$ leaves its traces on pages 121/122 in Artaria 216, where the intervallic transformation of the theme begins to make itself felt. The variation drifts off without conviction. The next step is the version in Artaria 210, shown above in figure 8.3. But then comes a later draft, this on p. 98 in Artaria 216, and continuing on p. 115 (the two pages once contiguous). The visual impression of these bars is astonishing. The essence of the music, as it will go in the final version, is captured in the first violin, now returned to the $\frac{6}{8}$ meter of the theme and adhering to its harmonic rhythm. But the manuscript is clotted with counterpoints and rhythmic complications that will, in the end, be stripped away. To attempt to extrapolate some orderly process from the unfolding of the entries on this page, were that even possible, would only divert attention away from the stunning impression of a first

---

26. This is perhaps most clearly the case in the pocket sketchbook Berlin Staatsbibliothek, Artaria 205, bundle 3. For the contents, see JTW, 450–52.

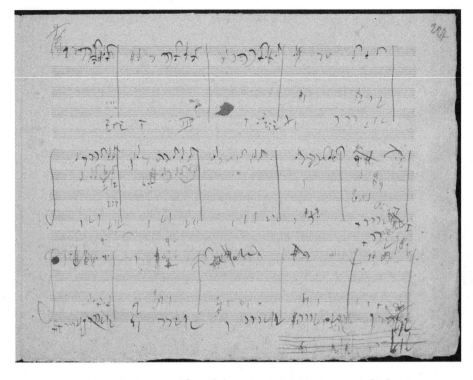

FIGURE 8.3. Beethoven, score draft for String Quartet in F, op. 135, third movement. Staatsbibliothek zu Berlin, Artaria 210, p. 227. By kind permission.

encounter with the creative moment: Beethoven, struggling mightily to identify the character, the place, the effect—the *affect*—of this moment, at once declamatory and muted, in C♯ minor. The final bar in the draft (shown in fig. 8.4) is revelatory, capturing a moment of hesitation at the return to D♭ major. The dominant itself, at the cadence, is here respelled in D♭. The final chord, a full quarter note, was first written as a dominant on A♭, then altered to a root-position triad on D♭—and no sign here of a division of that A♭ into those two tied eighths in the first violin found in the autograph score. The meaning of two words scribbled below the first violin is difficult to ascertain with any certainty: "beßer" [better] is clear enough; could the second word spell "pause" [rest]?[27] That would make good sense. But perhaps we should be content to read in these words further evidence of a composer in search of the poetic moment.

To have worked one's way through the vast expanse of Beethoven's

27. I am indebted to Dr. Jens Dufner, of the Beethoven-Archiv in Bonn, for graciously sharing his own thoughts on the reading of Beethoven's nearly illegible script here.

FIGURE 8.4. Beethoven, score draft for String Quartet in F, op. 135, third movement. Staatsbibliothek zu Berlin, Artaria 216, p. 115. By kind permission.

workshop papers, from that earliest portfolio of music gathered during his first creative decade through to these sketches and drafts for the final quartets, is to formulate quickly enough the picture of a composer in the throes of an unforgiving self-criticism—less a criticism of self than a rigorous interrogation of a process set in motion with the inception of a musical idea. We might have thought that by the late autumn of 1826, in the writing out of this *Lento assai* in op. 135, the challenges would have been met more easily. Surely, the finished version of the movement would encourage such a view. And that is why these drafts are so revealing. The music may sound "late," if that is the unintentional signifier of such studied simplicity, but the worksheets, capturing the long reach of the draft against the myriad detail of local revision, stand witness to the exercise of the robust mind thoroughly absorbed, as it always had been, in the adventure of the compositional challenge.

Inevitably, the sustained focus on the opening bars of the *Lento assai* and the calibrated placement, after considerable deliberation, of that first Db deep in the bass, will of course put us in mind of the quirky opening bars of the quartet: the incipit that sets it all in motion, etching the outlines of a minor subdominant (Bb minor) and *sixte ajoutée* with the fewest notes, the initial *gruppetto* in the viola answered by that deep, unprepared Db in the cello. And then comes the expansion of this fragile gesture at the moment of its reprise (mm. 100–102), the first violin now anticipating the *gruppetto* as an upbeat, four octaves above the viola, while the cello, refusing to surrender its Db, hammers out twenty-one iterations, *forte*, before resolving (see ex. 8.5). I don't wish to claim for this single tone—this deep Db—more than its position in a subtle play of syntax, an inflection point upon which the quartet turns. Such moments as these, flashes of uncommon wit, of the vigorous mind at play, fully engaged in the machinations of this final comedy, must give us pause in our inquiry into the idiosyncratic symptoms of late style, of lateness and its mythologies.

3

In a yet more fabled reversal, in late November of the same year, Beethoven delivered to the publisher Artaria a new finale for the Quartet in Bb Major, op. 130, replacing the original finale, a "grand fugue" of 741 measures whose daunting challenges both to its performers and to its listeners led the composer to acquiesce to the advice of close friends and to its publisher. It is a debate that Beethoven must have carried within himself for many months, beginning very likely with the first public performance of the work by the Schuppanzigh Quartet on 21 March 1826, its fugal finale having provoked puzzled reaction in several quarters. "The reasonable ones say that the last movement must be heard often to be understood, the others wish it to be removed in that it is too difficult to be understood," reported brother Johann, in the aftermath of the concert.[28] Even in the run-up to the first performance, Karl Holz (the second violinist, and a steady companion to Beethoven in these years) confessed that "with the beginning of the fugue up to the section in Gb major we are not yet 'in Ordnung.'"[29] But perhaps it was the now famous lines in the review of the concert in the *Allgemeine*

---

28. *Ludwig van Beethovens Konversationshefte* (Leipzig, VEB Deutscher Verlag für Musik, 1988), 9:137. A few days later, he reports that "the art dealer Leidesdorfer [= Maximilian Joseph Leidesdorf, partner in the publishing house Sauer & Leidesdorf] said to me that he heard the quartet [op. 130] with delight and well understood everything up to the last movement which he greatly wishes to hear again in order to understand it as well." *Konversationshefte* 9:156. My translation.

29. *Konversationshefte* 9:103.

EX. 8.5. Beethoven, String Quartet in F Major, op. 135, first movement, mm. 1–7 and mm. 99–103.

musikalische Zeitung that proved decisive: "But the reviewer dares not interpret the sense of the fugal finale: for him it was incomprehensible, like Chinese." Less often cited are his concluding thoughts: "perhaps the time will come when that which seemed at first glance opaque and confused will be apprehended as clear and in agreeable forms."[30]

The new finale is its inverse in every respect. Where the fugue bristles with dissonance in the chromatic angularities of its subject and the intensity of its rhythmic displacements, its massive and anomalous formal complexity a compressed image of the conventional four movements of a large-scale work, the new finale is all gaiety and brilliance and diatonic clarity, alternating between rondo-like repetitions of its genial theme and the scope and breadth of sonata. For all its lightness of esprit, this is a finale of real substance and of a temporal weight—in performance, roughly ten minutes in duration—to ground the dizzying flight of the five movements that precede it.

This again puts before us the critic's dilemma: to live with what may seem contradictory views of how the five disparate movements of this quartet will find a true resolution in two finales that differ so radically from one another. And yet, in spite of such differences, these contrary finales each act on the immediacy of their location, their opening notes meant to play upon the closing phrase of the cavatina, whose cadence comes to rest, *pianissimo*, on a G, the third degree, tripled, of a tonic triad on E♭. The impact of the initial octave G, struck *forte*, announces the advent of the fugue as it dispels, if it does not eradicate with some violence, the aura of the cavatina.[31] The new finale takes a very different tack, sustaining the *pianissimo* and easing gently out of the *molto espressivo* with its own octave G. In the original finale, an initial "overtura" (*ouverture*, as Beethoven writes in the autograph score) offers a brief taste, though in contrary order, of the four sections that will constitute the fugue, and in a tonal spectrum that moves from that octave G around the circle of fifths to the tonic B♭, at which point the fugue proper commences.[32] The new finale moves deftly through the same circle, building it into its opening phrases within the first ten bars.

In a terse summation of a lengthy disquisition in support of the view

30. For the original, see *Ludwig van Beethoven: Die Werke im Spiegel seiner Zeit*, ed. Stefan Kunze (Laaber: Laaber, 1987), 559–60. A fine English translation, which differs slightly from my own, is now available in *The Critical Reception of Beethoven's Compositions by His German Contemporaries, Op. 126 to WoO 140*, ed. and trans. Robin Wallace (available online at the Center for Beethoven Research, Boston University, 2018), 40–41.

31. This, in effect, is the central topic in my "Beethoven Cavatina and Ouverture: Opus 130 and the Voices of Narrative," *Beethoven Forum* 1 (1992): 165–89, esp. 178–81.

32. For more on this, see above, chapter 6, note 12.

that on the evidence of its evolution in the sketches the massive fugal finale was at the matrix of the quartet in its entirety, its *Kompositionsidee* (its fundamental "idea"), Klaus Kropfinger concludes that "only the original version concords with Beethoven's idea," and further, that "the finale subsequently composed takes up traces [of this idea] that make sense, but a sense that remains at the periphery, and which does not—as does the fugal finale—penetrate to the *Summe* of the whole."[33] Whatever one makes of his view that the sketches serve as evidence toward an analysis of the quartet, there can be no arguing with Kropfinger's view that the quartet as a whole is radically altered when this second finale replaces the original one, that something foundational in the concept of the work has been lost. That, in itself, is a condition worth pondering: a quartet whose sense of itself has undergone a transfiguration.

What can we learn of Beethoven's state of mind as he composed this surrogate finale? Turning away from the sublime extremities of the work as it was originally conceived, not least in a final coming to terms with those fugal demons that seem to have pursued him for the length of his career, Beethoven now seeks a music that touches another sensibility, no less profound, if rather more accessible. It, too, toys with fugue (see mm. 170–207), but more for the lightness and clarity of its texture and its fluid rhythm than for any deeper inquiry into the artifice that might be extrapolated from the extreme intervals of a challenging subject. There's a sensual delight in the fluency of the writing that sweeps us up in its exhilaration, a palpable pleasure in the act of composing. The shifts of mood have a quixotic feel to them. At the close of the exposition at m. 96, the music stutters a bit, and then slips almost accidentally into a lyrical Ab major, the viola taking the lead, the music continuing in this mode for some fifty bars before a return to those opening octaves. At m. 208, the fugue-like music closes in, *fortissimo*, on a dominant ninth in G minor, sixteen bars in octaves receding finally to a *pianissimo* return of those sprightly octaves, announcing the imminent recapitulation. But the octaves are a fifth away, and only through a deft sleight of hand does the music find its way to the true return. When the recapitulation has run its course, the music mimics that stuttered close after

---

33. "Geht man aber von Beethovens 'Kompositionsidee' aus, seiner kompositorische Konzeption, so wie sie sich aus den Skizzen deutlich genug ergibt, dann muß man sagen: nur die Originalversion entspricht Beethovens Idee. Das nachkomponierte Finale greift Züge auf, die Sinn ergeben: doch es ist ein Sinn, der an der Peripherie bleibt, der nicht—wie das Fugenfinale—wirklich die 'Summe' des Ganzen zieht." Klaus Kropfinger, "Das gespaltene Werk—Beethovens Streichquartett op. 130/133," in *Beiträge zu Beethovens Kammermusik. Symposion Bonn 1984*, ed. Sieghard Brandenburg and Helmut Loos (Munich: G. Henle, 1987), 296–335, esp. 328. The translation is my own.

the exposition; a reprise of the lyrical music follows, now revoiced, and in E♭ major, before slipping casually into the tonic. The coda that begins at m. 414, running on for eighty measures, is all wit and prestidigitation: first, an explosive sequence in contrary motion, *forte, piu forte, fortissimo*; then, a return to the opening tune, now *pianissimo*, that quickly dissolves into a more robust exchange, a *scena* whose players seem mock-ups of the *improvvisatori* in a *commedia dell'arte* of an earlier century.

Hearing the finale this way, as an evocation of theater, of characters who take the stage, allows us to apprehend this remarkable music as a *fin lieto*. The quartet as a whole may be about other things, touching deeper wells of thought and emotion, but it is no comedy, even if the touching *Alla danza tedesca*, in the stammered confusion of its final phrases, and the tearful cavatina might feel quite at home in a *comédie larmoyante*. At the same time, that massive fugal finale *as finale*, despite its formal exile to a life of its own, will not go quietly. I return to the idea at the root of Kropfinger's notion of the "gespaltene Werk" (the cleft, or fissured, work), of the fugue as the source of the idea of the quartet. As I put it at the conclusion of an earlier essay: "Severed from op. 130, the sublime idiosyncrasies of the fugue are debased, made eccentric. It is a finale in concept. The permutations of its thematic material echo, and its tonal proportions ground, the music of earlier movements."[34] Can Beethoven have put out of mind the prominence of the fugue, both in the unfolding of the quartet as a whole and in the extended process of its creation, any more than he could truly have sanctioned a "gespaltene" version of the Piano Sonata op. 106 in any of the alternatives offered to Ferdinand Ries in London in 1819?[35] But of course things went much further with op. 130. And it is with this in mind that I want to pry a bit into Beethoven's creative subconscious. In that private, inaccessible inner world, we might conjure the *personaggi in maschera* of this dexterous, vibrant new finale at play against the fearful symmetries of the fugue, figuring a world closer in tune with some *Fantasiestück* of E. T. A. Hoffmann, in its extreme contradictions of the human condition, than with the balanced sensibilities of Enlightenment drama. I don't, of course, propose this as a literal rendering of what might have taken place in a mind as profoundly complex as Beethoven's, but rather as an attempt to grasp how these two extraordinary finales, and the quartet that they finalize, might have coexisted in the mind—his and then ours—if only subliminally.[36]

34. "Between Cavatina and Ouverture," 189.

35. On the equivocations surrounding op. 106, see above, chapter 6.

36. For an intriguing study of relationships between the two finales, see Megan Ross, "The Power of Allusion: Beethoven's *Grosse Fuge* and Opus 130 VI," in *Philomusica Online*, vol. 18, no. 1 (2019).

Final Beethoven 185

In the new finale of op. 130, we hear the exuberance of a composer in the moment, taking pleasure in the act of making music and reluctant to bring it to a close. As it turns out, this would be the last work that Beethoven lived to complete. The finale was delivered on 22 November to Matthias Artaria (via Tobias Haslinger) from Gneixendorf, where Beethoven had been domiciled since the end of September. Beethoven returned to Vienna on or about the 27th, and about a week later fell ill. On the 7th of December, at the onset of this final illness and confined to his bed, he crafted a lengthy and touching letter to Franz Wegeler, a dear friend from his Bonn days. Toward the end, he writes:

> Es heißt übrigens bey mir immer: *Nulla dies sine linea* , u. lase ich die Muse schlafen, so geschieht es nur, damit sie desto kräftiger erwache. Ich hoffe noch einige große Werke zur Welt zu bringen, u. dann wie ein altes Kind irgendwo unter guten Menschen meine irdische Laufbahn zu beschließen.[37]

> My motto has always been: *Nulla dies sine linea* [no day without its line]; and if I let my Muse go to sleep, it is only that she may be all the more active when she awakes. I still hope to create a few great works and then like an old child to finish my earthly course somewhere among kind people.[38]

These are not the words of a man who, even in those grim circumstances, thought that he'd composed his last work. To read in Beethoven's final music the signs of a fading creative libido is to misread the quality of mind at play in those remarkable works.

In the nearly two hundred years that we've been given to ponder the significance of these works of Beethoven's final months, the aura of finality has taken on mythic overtones, a construct of historical narrative, of romance. The grim circumstances of their composition in the summer and autumn of 1826 are well known: in August, the grotesque suicide attempt of Beethoven's nephew and its troubling aftermath; in September and beyond, a concluding chapter of the staggeringly complex Family Romance at the brother's home at Gneixendorf; and then the horrid final illness. Astonishingly, this music that Beethoven found himself composing seems oblivious of all that. In its gruff good humor, its miraculous technical virtuosity, its uncanny touching of the deepest wells of human sensibility, this

37. *Briefwechsel Gesamtausgabe* 6: 319–21.
38. Anderson, *Letters*, 1322.

186 CHAPTER EIGHT

is the work of a composer, mind fully engaged, taking pleasure in the act of composing, perhaps even manic joy in the accomplishment of having created music so damned near perfect.

Epilogue

That quality of mind is, however, less evident in what is thought to be his final project. Among the accumulated residue of sketches and drafts to be sifted through at Beethoven's death, one fragment drew considerable interest at the auction of Beethoven's estate (the *Nachlaß*) in November 1827. This was item 173, described as "Bruchstück eines neuen Violinquintetts vom November 1826, letzte Arbeit des Compositeurs" (fragment of a new violin quintet from November 1826, the last work of the composer). It was purchased by Carl Anton Spina for his associate Anton Diabelli, paying what was then an exorbitant price of 30 florins 30 kreutzer, for music dealers at the auction were interested primarily in unpublished works, even fragmentary ones, that could be completed and sold to the public as novelties.[39]

It wasn't until 1838 that Diabelli brought forth the work in a transcription for piano alone, in versions for both two hands and four hands, and entitled "Ludwig van Beethoven's letzter musikalischer Gedanke, aus dem Original-Manuscript im November 1826," with this note at the bottom of its first page: "Skizze des Quintetts, welches die Verlagshandlung A. Diabelli u. Comp. bei Beethoven bestellt und aus dessen Nachlasse käuflich mit Eigenthumsrecht an sich gebracht hat" (a sketch of the quintet which the firm A. Diabelli & Co. commissioned of Beethoven and which it then acquired through purchase from the estate with the rights of ownership). Alas, Diabelli's source has not survived, and we cannot therefore ascertain whether his transcription is true to Beethoven's manuscript, or whether it gives finish to a fragment that would have displayed the sketch-like characteristics of most other score drafts from this period.[40] An account of the

---

39. For a detailed study of the auction catalogue in its many extant copies, see JTW, 567–72, though the transcription that follows does not include the category under discussion here. A record of the purchase can be found in Georg Kinsky, "Zur Versteigerung von Beethovens musikalischem Nachlaß," *Neues Beethoven-Jahrbuch* 6 (1935), 85.

40. "Probably no more than a score sketch," wrote Robert Winter of the manuscript purchased at the auction. See JTW, 458. We may glean something of Diabelli's intentions in another instance of a manuscript purchased by Spina at the auction of the *Nachlass*. This was item 185, a "Leichte Caprice für das Pianoforte, unbekannt," for which Spina paid the very high price of 20 florins 30 kreutzer. Diabelli published the work as Rondo à Capriccio in 1828. When the autograph (now at the Morgan Library in New York) was discovered in a private collection in 1945, and described in an illuminating essay by Erich Hertzmann ("The Newly Discovered Autograph of Beethoven's 'Rondo a capriccio,'

auction in the *Allgemeine musikalische Zeitung* describes the document as "a quintet begun in November 1826, of which alas barely twenty or thirty bars 'im Entwurfe' had been put to paper." Gustav Nottebohm, citing this account, was led to point out the apparent contradiction here to the description of the item as a "Bruchstück" in the auction catalog, a fragment suggesting something "ausgeführt" (rather thoroughly worked out) up to a certain point.[41] An "Entwurf," to the contrary, suggests a preliminary state closer to what we would call a sketch, giving the appearance of a concept in embryo. The distinction is not trivial, even if the two states often appear to converge on the page.

The scant surviving sketches for this quintet, whose identity nevertheless rests on circumstance, must be culled from several disparate sources. A prime suspect ought to have been the last of the major desk sketchbooks: the "Kullak" sketchbook invoked at the top of this chapter, whose final pages are given to the replacement finale for op. 130. But in fact it displays not a single indisputable entry for the quintet. For these we must turn to what is quite clearly the latest of the pocket sketchbooks, the second bundle of Berlin, Staatsbibliothek, mus. ms. autogr. Beethoven 10 (Heft 2). Of its twelve leaves, only the first six contain writing, and these are preliminary entries for three movements. Anton Schindler, ever prepared to insinuate himself as a witness to Beethoven's daily life, wrote after that last entry: "Dies hier auf dieser Seite sind die letzten Noten, die Beethoven ungefähr zehn bis zwölf Tage vor seinem Tode in meinem Beiseyn geschrieben" (here on this page are the last notes that Beethoven wrote, in my presence, ten or twelve days before his death).[42] But if, as seems likely, a separate leaf ruled in score for the finale of the quintet will have drawn its continuity from those sketches, Schindler's claim must be questioned.[43]

Much to our point is the more urgent question whether what has survived of these "letzten Noten" is sufficient to enable a critical assessment

---

op. 129," in *Musical Quarterly* 32 [1946]: 171–95), we learned that Diabelli's edition was a finished text of a work that Beethoven had left in an unfinished state. The differences are detailed by Otto von Irmer in the Henle edition of 1968.

41. See Gustav Nottebohm, "Beethoven's letzte Composition," in *Beethoveniana* (Leipzig: C. F. Peter, 1872), 79–81.

42. Schindler's note is transcribed in Klein, *Katalog*, 49. Robert Winter (*JTW*, 458–59) suspects that these last sketches were made during the last days of November 1826, weeks before Beethoven was confined continuously to bed in early December.

43. Bonn: Beethoven-Haus, NE 101, shown in facsimile and partial transcription in Martin Staehelin, "Another Approach to Beethoven's Last String Quartet Oeuvre: the Unfinished String Quintet of 1826/27," in *The String Quartets of Haydn, Mozart, and Beethoven: Studies of the Autograph Manuscripts*, ed. Christoph Wolff (Cambridge, MA: Harvard University Department of Music, 1980), 302–23.

of the work. The firmest basis for any such exercise hangs on an appraisal of the fragment published by Diabelli, a stately, even ceremonial intrada, *Andante maestoso*, to a first movement for which a handful of sketches offer a tentative sense how that movement might have progressed. In a freewheeling discussion that followed the presentation of Martin Staehelin's provocative study of this material at a Harvard symposium in 1979 (see above, note 43), there was little consensus. Staehelin (316) concluded that the work was inspired to some degree by the Mozart string quintets, grouping the fragmentary quintet together with op. 135 and the new finale to op. 130: "All three works visibly indicate that the composer's last quartet and quintet style, thereby also his 'Altersstil', was marked by a consciousness of tradition and the past." Robert Winter (325) noted "a real disparity between even the little bit that we hear [of the quintet fragment] and anything that goes on in Op. 135." And Christoph Wolff had "difficulties in identifying the stylistic orientation of this quintet with anything retrospective, say eighteenth-century or specifically Mozartean features." But then Lewis Lockwood (326) sagely warned of the dangers of treating these sketches and score drafts "as if we are interpreting it as a finished composition," pointing to the "somewhat regressive early phrase to which Beethoven often seems to seek refuge in getting started."

The conversation has a quaint ring to it. We no longer worry to their death the stylistic proclivities of such music, in search of some compelling argument that would clinch a thesis for or against influence. And, more to Lockwood's caveat, these remnants of the quintet, shards of an early stage in its composition, give only hints of how the work might have gone. With the rich rewards and that frisson of discovery that we may take in the study of sketches and fragments comes a twinge of conscience: this trafficking among workshop papers meant only for the eyes of the composer is to trespass in his private world. We mustn't abuse the privilege—mustn't pretend to understand how Beethoven might have brought these initial ideas to a state that would satisfy his infallible critical judgment, or to underestimate his keen wit in knowing when to abandon unpromising ones. Had he recovered from that final illness, "neue Kraft fühlend," this chapter would have read very differently.

The appeal of a "letzter musikalischer Gedanke" was the salesman's pitch. Diabelli was to use it again a year later (1839), slightly reworded and affixed to the publication of Schubert's three final sonatas for piano. And this brings us to our final chapter.

✳ CHAPTER 9 ✳

Posthumous Schubert

Last works are prized in the marketplace. Tinged in necromancy, the exhumation of Schubert's music begins at the very moment of his death. Tobias Haslinger, seizing upon *Schwanen-Gesang* as the title for a volume of Rellstab and Heine songs (with a setting of Seidl's *Taubenpost* tossed in for good measure), hastened to advertise its publication as "Letztes Werk."[1] Haslinger intended as well to publish the three last sonatas, but through some shadowy transaction, the autographs were sold to Anton Diabelli by Ferdinand Schubert in 1829.[2] And, while the plate number suggests that the sonatas might have appeared as early as 1831, publication was delayed until 1839.[3] Diabelli's title page insinuates itself into the plot of a reception history: "Franz Schubert's allerletzte Composition. Drei grosse Sonaten für das Pianoforte. Herrn Robert Schumann in Leipzig gewidmet von den Verlegern."

1. Haslinger's draft for the title page is described in Georg Kinsky, *Manuskripte, Briefe, Dokumente von Scarlatti bis Stravinsky: Katalog der Musikautographen-Sammlung Louis Koch* (Stuttgart: Hoffmansche Buchdruckerei Felix Krais, 1953), 189–90. And the title was inscribed in Haslinger's hand on the outside of the bill of sale, dated 17 December 1828, from Ferdinand Schubert. This is given in Otto E. Deutsch, *Schubert: A Documentary Biography*, trans. Eric Blom (London: J. M. Dent & Sons, 1946; New York: W. W. Norton, 1947), 842–43; and Deutsch, *Die Erinnerungen seiner Freunde* (Leipzig: Breitkopf & Härtel, 1966), 444–45.

2. Haslinger announced the purchase of "fourteen as yet wholly unknown songs . . . and three new pianoforte Sonatas (composed in September 1828)" in the *Wiener Zeitung* for 20 December 1828. See Deutsch, *A Documentary Biography*, 844; and *Schubert: Die Dokumente seines Lebens*, Neue Ausgabe sämtliche Werke, VIII/5 (Kassel: Bärenreiter, 1964), 567.

3. See Deutsch, *Franz Schubert: Thematisches Verzeichnis seiner Werke in chronologischer Folge* (Kassel: Bärenreiter, 1978), 618.

190 CHAPTER NINE

1

When Schumann journeyed to Vienna in the winter of 1838–1839, the seeking out of Schubert's unpublished works, while it may not have been the first order of business, was clearly high on his agenda. Inspired by a visit to Ferdinand Schubert, who had been designated by the family to administer the musical estate, Schumann wrote back to Leipzig, seeking to stimulate Breitkopf & Härtel's interest in the "several operas, four large masses, four or five symphonies" there awaiting discovery.[4]

Curiously, Schumann's reflections on these final sonatas, published together with an appreciation of the Grand Duo, op. 140, under the broader title "Aus Franz Schubert's Nachlaß," appeared in the *Neue Zeitschrift*, 5 June 1838, some months before the trip to Vienna, and a full year before Diabelli actually announced the publication of the sonatas. Diabelli evidently wanted the reputation of these sonatas to precede them, an annunciation before the advent. The dedication to Schumann had its pecuniary aspect, one might suspect.

Reluctant to be taken in by the puff of Diabelli's "allerletzte Composition" and the consequential mythologizing of last works, Schumann prevaricates. "Perhaps these sonatas would be judged differently by those to whom the date of composition remained unknown," he hazarded.

> Whether they were written on the deathbed or not, I cannot say. From the music itself one might dare to conclude that they were; and yet it is also possible . . . that through the melancholy word "Allerletzte" the imagination is impregnated with thoughts of impending death.[5]

In what sense do these sonatas suggest that they were composed "auf dem Krankenlager"? Schumann's equivocation on this point stems from a genuine perplexity as to their style. The gist of his thought is in a passage often enough maligned:

> These Sonatas seem to me strikingly different from his others: in a much greater simplicity of invention, through a spontaneous renunciation of glittering novelty where he is otherwise so demanding of himself, and through a spinning out of certain common musical ideas where other-

---

4. Schumann's letter to Breitkopf & Härtel is given in Deutsch, *Schubert: Memoirs by His Friends* (London: Macmillan, 1958), 391–92; and *Erinnerungen*, 451–52.

5. Robert Schumann, *Gesammelte Schriften über Musik und Musiker*, ed. Martin Kreisig (Leipzig: Breitkopf & Härtel, 1914; repr. Westmead, Hampshire: Gregg Publishing, 1969), I, 330–31 (translation mine).

wise he would combine new threads from one period to the next. Always musically rich with song, it ripples along from page to page as though it might never end, never obstructed for the sake of the effect, here and there interrupted by isolated impulses of greater vigor which, however, are quickly assuaged.[6]

Simplicity of invention ("Einfalt der Erfindung") and renunciation of novelty are ambivalent symptoms, characteristic of a late style and yet retrospective. It is the retrospective aspect that is played up in an influential study by Edward T. Cone, whose uncanny demonstration that the finale of the Sonata in A Major was modeled upon the finale of Beethoven's Sonata in G Major, op. 31, no 1, is as unsettling as it is persuasive.[7] Independently, Charles Rosen comes to a very similar conclusion about the relationship between these two movements.[8]

But Rosen and Cone do not view the enterprise in quite the same way. Schubert, in Cone's hearing, was very likely

> impelled by the same kind of insecurity that, during the last year of his life, drove him to apply to Sechter for counterpoint lessons. He felt that he had failed to master certain technical problems and needed help in solving them. . . . It is to his finales, and especially to his rondo finales, that his reputation for rambling redundancy is due.[9]

And finally:

> The contrast between the proportions of Beethoven's 275 measures and Schubert's 382 (398 with the repeats) suggests that the younger composer's more relaxed sense of form could never produce an exact imitation of the older man's concentrated structures.[10]

6. Schumann, *Gesammelte Schriften*, I, 331. For an extreme response, see Alfred Brendel, "Schubert's Last Sonatas," *New York Review of Books*, 2 February 1989, 32; reprinted in Brendel, *Music Sounded Out: Essays, Lectures, Interviews, Afterthoughts* (New York: Farrar, Straus & Giroux, 1990), 78. "It is to be hoped that Schumann, in later years, came to know the pieces better, and to regret his statements. Not even from Schumann will I accept that Schubert's sonatas 'ripple along.'" Did Schumann mean this in the pejorative sense that Brendel conveys?

7. Edward T. Cone, "Schubert's Beethoven," *Musical Quarterly* 56 (1970): 779–93, esp. 782–87; reprinted in *The Creative World of Beethoven*, ed. Paul Henry Lang (New York: W. W. Norton, 1971), 277–91.

8. Charles Rosen, *The Classical Style: Haydn, Mozart, Beethoven* (New York: W. W. Norton, expanded ed., 1997), 456–58.

9. Cone, "Schubert's Beethoven," 787; *Creative World of Beethoven*, 285.

10. Cone, "Schubert's Beethoven," 788; *Creative World of Beethoven*, 286.

For Rosen, the modeling is a rather more salubrious process, the off-spring healthier:

> What is most remarkable in this close imitation is its lack of constraint. Schubert moves with great ease within the form which Beethoven created. He has, however, considerably loosened what held it together, and stretched its ligaments unmercifully. . . . Some of the excitement naturally goes out of these forms when they are so extended, but this is even a condition of the unforced melodic flow of Schubert's music. It must be added that with the finale of this A major Sonata Schubert produced a work that is unquestionably greater than its model.[11]

The heavenly length of these finales—for Cone and Rosen no less than for Schumann—is a topic for dialectical inquiry. Beethoven's "concentrated structures" are planted in them. One might be persuaded that the modeling engages less in the cool exercise of imitation than in some precarious rite of exorcism. Still, to endure until m. 717 of the finale of the C-Minor Sonata is to demonstrate tenacity, no less so for the critic than for the pianist who pulls up lame at the finish. Was it any less the case for the intrepid composer who had to set down all those pages of music in readable script?

If this last question interests us, the script is there in abundance, for we are blessed not only with the complete autographs of the three last sonatas—*Reinschriften* (clean copies) that served as the engraver's copy for Diabelli's print—but with preliminary drafts for all three sonatas.[12] The substance of these drafts, if not their actual appearance, has been known for more than a century; generous extracts were published in the editor's supplement to the old Breitkopf *Gesamtausgabe*.[13] Hans Költzsch, in a 1927 monograph, wrote about them at some length, but only on the basis of these extracts.[14] Denied any access to the manuscripts in the Wienbibliothek im

---

11. Rosen, *The Classical Style*, 458.

12. The drafts are described in Ernst Hilmar, *Verzeichnis der Schubert Handschriften in der Musiksammlung der Wiener Stadt- und Landesbibliothek* (Kassel: Bärenreiter, 1978), 98–100. The *Reinschriften*, again in private hands, were formerly in the possession of Louis Koch and described in *Manuskripte, Briefe, Dokumente*, 177–79. For a thoughtful and thorough study, see Anne M. Hyland and Walburga Litschauer, "Records of Inspiration: Schubert's Drafts for the Last Three Piano Sonatas Reappraised," in *Rethinking Schubert*, ed. Lorraine Byrne Bodley and Julian Horton (Oxford: Oxford University Press, 2016), 173–206.

13. *Franz Schubert's Werke. Kritisch durchgesehene Gesammtausgabe*. Revisionsbericht, Series 10, Sonaten für Pianoforte (Leipzig: Breitkopf & Härtel, 1897; repr. New York: Dover Publications, 1969), 8–43.

14. Hans Költzsch, *Franz Schubert in seinen Klaviersonaten* (Leipzig: Breitkopf & Härtel, 1927; repr. Hildesheim: Olms, 1976), 137–43.

Rathaus (as the former Stadbibliothek in Vienna is now named), he was unable to ascertain even the full extent of the material that had survived. In 1960, working from photographs, Paul Mies published a characteristically methodical autopsy, something of a sequel to his well-known *Beethovens Skizzen* (1925). Categorical and quantitative, its impressive thoroughness masks a certain insensitivity to the greater, less answerable questions that such documents are likely to pose.[15]

Happily, the Schubert enthusiast today is blessed with easy access to these documents. Among the lavish rewards of the burgeoning world of digital reproduction is the impressive site *Schubert-Online*, offering lucid images of the complete Schubert holdings of the City Library of Vienna (the Wiener Stadt- und Landesbibliothek, now renamed Wienbibliothek im Rathaus), containing by far the richest collection of Schubert autographs, the Austrian National Library, the Staatsbibliothek zu Berlin, and the Norwegian National Library. Some years earlier, these drafts for the last sonatas were issued in a handsome, multicolored facsimile edition together with extensive commentary prepared by Ernst Hilmar, who was then curator of the collection.[16] The digital copy at *Schubert-Online*, even in the extraordinary clarity of its images and its capacity to magnify details, does not entirely supersede these facsimiles, whose loose leaves and unbound bifolia are grouped, unsewn, into separate fascicles, one for each sonata. No doubt troublesome for librarians, this verisimilitude has important consequences for those who will want to shuffle the loose sheets around, much as Schubert seems to have done during the composition of these sonatas.

Two instances, both from the first movement of the Sonata in B♭ and intimately linked to one another, are especially illuminating. The first of them comes toward the end of the movement, beginning at what corresponds to m. 333 in the final version (see ex. 9.1). The entry is instructive in several ways. For one, it is to be found squeezed into two blank staves at the bottom of the verso of a sheet given entirely to the draft of the exposition of the Sonata in A Major. For another, it specifies in its opening bar music that had not been heard in the analogous passage at the end of the exposition (see ex. 9.2). There is a tendency to speak of a process of expansion in such instances. Mies is very much of that mind, but the passage in question inspires in him a deeper thought as well:

15. Paul Mies, "Die Entwürfe Franz Schuberts zu den letzten drei Klaviersonaten von 1828," in *Beiträge zur Musikwissenschaft* 2 (1960): 52–68.

16. Franz Schubert, *Drei große Sonaten für das Pianoforte, D 958, D 959, und D 960 (Frühe Fassungen)*. Facsimile from the Autographs in the Wiener Stadt- und Landesbibliothek. (Publications of the International Franz Schubert Institut, vol. 1), with accompanying text and commentary by Ernst Hilmar (Tutzing: Hans Schneider, 1987).

EX. 9.1. Schubert, Sonata in B♭ Major, D 960, first movement. Draft for the coda at its opening bars.

EX. 9.2. Schubert, Sonata in B♭ Major, D 960, first movement. Draft for end of exposition.

One has the feeling now and again that Schubert had already foreseen such extensions and interpolations (*Dehnungen und Einfügungen*) during the sketching, but failed to notate them, even indeed to suggest them, in order to be able to follow the flight of thought (*Flug der Gedanken*) in the writing down. The unity (*Einheitlichkeit*) of the material was assured at the very first moment of composition. At the writing down of the final clean copy nothing of essence is changed, for that would have endangered the unity.[17]

17. Mies, "Die Entwürfe Franz Schuberts," 57.

The thought has a certain appeal. But the notion that these measures, first conceived in the drafting of the coda and only later (presumably in the writing out of final copy) inscribed at the end of the exposition, might be explained away as an extension—whether to designate an act of composition or a formal member of the phrase is never made clear—is in the end unsatisfactory. No less troubling is the notion that these new measures were part of an original conception that Schubert simply neglected to write down for fear of disturbing a train of thought. There is a contradiction here. The new music cannot be construed at once as innate to the original idea (if repressed in the first writing) and at the same time as an extension of—and therefore external to—that very idea.

As it goes in its published form, this passage at the end of the exposition has a touch of mystery about it. Enigmatic to an extreme, its profound questioning pierces to some essence of the work. The halting rhythms, the slightly unhinged harmonies, and the languid bit of narrative beginning at m. 113 are paradoxically all of a piece, together with the hesitant, profoundly inarticulate first ending. For those not yet weaned of performances that neglect to repeat the exposition, it is a crucial piece of the narrative that remains unheard.[18] It is hard to imagine how any of it might have gone differently in Schubert's mind. And it is difficult to imagine, with Mies, that in the writing of the draft, Schubert might knowingly have omitted any of it as a time-saving expedient.

If perhaps I inflate the case for this passage, it is only to cast in relief the earlier version of it. How do we explain the differences between the two? Certainly not in quantitative terms: a repetition here, a registral shift there, an extension of the phrase elsewhere. Even if there is some plain truth to such an explanation, the main issue remains unfathomed. Perhaps the difference lies somewhere between the notion of a passage that is syntactically

---

18. Brendel ("Schubert's Last Sonatas," 35) disagrees. "Those transitional bars in the first movement" he deplores as "an intrusion from the feverish regions of the other two sonatas, carried over from an earlier phase of conception that seems to me no less ill-advised than the execution of the repeat that these bars instigate." (Brendel rewrites this in *Music Sounded Out*, 83, but the idea is the same.) The point comes in the wake of a disquisition against repeats in Schubert's first movements. There is this bold insight (33; *Music Sounded Out*, 86): "In his larger forms, Schubert is the wanderer. He likes to move at the edge of the precipice. . . . To wander is the Romantic condition." To repeat the exposition, we are meant to infer, is to contradict this condition of "controlled wandering." Here is room to suggest only that the conflict between formal convention and the idiosyncrasies of style (the "edge of the precipice") is a necessary and vital one that we disavow at great risk to the authenticity of the work.

correct, even impressive in its thematic relevance, and one that approaches the imponderable—between the quotidian and the sublime.

Consider again the entry for the coda. Tucked away at the bottom of a sheet containing the draft for the Sonata in A Major, it gives every appearance of an afterthought, scribbled on whatever blank space was at hand. Inadvertently, it confirms what is otherwise rather clearly documented in these drafts: that Schubert routinely broke off work once the exposition—in this case, for the A-Major Sonata—had been put in place. And it implies something that must be inferred from poor, indeed negative evidence: that Schubert failed to draft recapitulations, or at any rate, to specify them in writing (a habit, by the way, that Beethoven shares with him often enough). Further, it will be clear to anyone who has the facsimile in view that Schubert thought to begin the entry with m. 334; what corresponds to m. 333 is squeezed into a bit of margin too small for what Schubert had to write. The script is witness to an altogether rare phenomenon in the workings of Schubert's mind. For it will strike every reader that the cusp of the phrase—its initial bar: m. 332, then m. 113—is still missing. When it is found, this elusive pair of notes sets off reverberations that transform entirely a passage meant to consume within itself and in some sense to resolve the two enigmatic endings with which the exposition closes.

But the story divulged in these drafts prompts us to ponder whether the idea for a second ending, or even the idea of transit from the fermata at the repetition sign to the fresh beginning in C♯ minor, had been thought through at this stage. From an apparent break in thought at the end of the exposition, dangerous as it may be to leap to such conclusions from the look of the writing on the page, one might even infer that the decision to compose an Andante sostenuto in C♯ minor—and perhaps even the act of composing it—was coeval with the continuation after the exposition in the first movement, if it did not in fact precede it. That is because the development, when it was finally drafted, was continued on a loose sheet of paper in "upright" format, one side of which had already been used for the closing paragraphs of the finale. On this evidence, it seems fair to conclude that the greater part of the development, if not the whole of it, was composed only after the finale had been drafted.

Precisely *how* the decision to compose a slow movement in the remote key of C♯ minor might have been linked in Schubert's mind with a decision, similarly audacious and unorthodox, to have the opening theme sound in C♯ minor at the outset of the development in the first movement is an inevitable question, but one that cannot be answered. Because it is missing in the draft, perhaps we tend to overvalue the minimal transition which, in a single bar of breathtaking music, plunges the weak, rhythmically equivocal

EX. 9.3. Schubert, Sonata in B♭ Major, D 960, first movement, mm. 113–18b, final version.

cadence at mm. 115–16 into the desolation of C♯ minor (see ex. 9.3). It *is* an important measure, and its articulation further blurs the formal line between exposition and development: syntactically, and in its diction, it must be performed as a continuation of the cadence. In the finding of m. 113, whose eloquence is cast as an isolated dissonance made to resolve to another dissonance—an appoggiatura F moves to an anticipation of an E which, no matter how we hear its underlying harmonies, will sound as a stronger, yet more dissonant appoggiatura—the E in just that register at the third beat of m. 117b takes on a resonance that suggests that the one is in some sense a response to the other.

The hunt for traces of a last style in Schubert, encouraged by the appeal of works composed in the proximity of death, is encumbered by it as well. Let us for the moment pretend (with Schumann) that these sonatas survived without the credentials that might establish their date of composition. Can we say of m. 117b (forgetting as well that we know *its* credentials) that its essence is itself evidence of a music that could only have been conceived after, say, March 1827? To pose the question in this circumlocutory mode means only to suggest that a psychoanalytic of style might begin from such interior, even recessive moments in the work. This, too, is a question that cannot be answered. We are returned to the conundrum of late style, and to those lines at the very end of chapter 7, where the music of Schubert's final years is heard to sing "across the grain of Beethoven's last works, conjuring a subjectivity that we are no less at pains to demystify." The challenge "to interrogate the condition of a late style without lateness" seems, in these last sonatas, only to echo the questions that Schumann, not so naively, asked of them in 1838.

In a final study, we encounter a major work for the stage that remained unfinished at Schubert's death. The fragment that survives has much to tell us of the place of opera in Schubert's late thinking, and of the quality of the music that it inspired. Beethoven, only months in his grave, hovers over this music, a spectral presence touching yet another aspect of Schubert's last work.

198 CHAPTER NINE

2

Der Graf von Gleichen, a failed project once thought to have occupied Schubert right up until his last days, is a work more written about than experienced in the theater. That is because, with the trivial exception of one or two numbers published in the 1860s and the enticing incipits in the Deutsch *Thematisches Verzeichnis*, none of its music had, until very recently, ever been in circulation. And for good reason, for all that has survived is a draft, itself inaccessible to the public until the publication in 1988 of a facsimile edition that would encourage a new inquiry into the place of the opera among Schubert's final projects.[19]

The draft, unique among the autograph documents in the Schubert *Nachlaß*, is nothing less than a concept of the entire opera, lacking only two final numbers: a comic duet and a finale of pomp and ceremony, both afterbeats to the essential unfolding of the dramatic action. The several internal omissions in the draft do no damage to the coherence of that concept. Further, the draft preserves intact the state of the composition before Schubert had begun to set any of it in full score. The book, by Schubert's intimate friend Eduard von Bauernfeld, was completed in May 1826.[20] It failed to win the approval of the State Censorship Office. "Der Operntext *von der Zensur verboten*," Bauernfeld noted in his *Tagebuch* in October. "Schubert will sie trotzdem komponieren."[21] There must have been a considerable interval between this expression of Schubert's intentions to compose the op-

19. The draft is in the collection of the Wienbibliothek im Rathaus, Vienna. See Hilmar, *Verzeichnis der Schubert-Handschriften*, 28–29. The facsimile edition is Franz Schubert, *Der Graf von Gleichen, Oper in zwei Akten (D 918)*, text by Eduard von Bauernfeld, Erstveröffentlichung der Handschrift, edited with commentary by Ernst Hilmar, and a contribution by Erich W. Partsch (Tutzing: Hans Schneider, 1988). And we now have a fine edition of the work prepared by Manuela Jahrmärker in *Schubert, Neue Ausgabe sämtlicher Werke*, ser. 2, vol. 17 (Kassel: Bärenreiter, 2006).

20. "So dacht' ich an den Operntext für Schubert, machte mich über den Grafen von Gleichen her," Bauernfeld notes in his diary on 2 May 1826 (*Dokumente*, 356; *Documentary Biography*, 523). "Die meisten Nummern zum *Grafen Gleichen* hab' ich auch komponiert und gesungen," he wrote to Schubert in an undated letter that Deutsch puts at early May (*Dokumente*, 357; *Documentary Biography*, 524). A diary entry for 9 May (*Dokumente*, 361; *Documentary Biography*, 530) reads: "Die Oper in acht Tagen fertig gebracht. Darüber an Schubert berichtet, der mit der Antwort nicht zögerte. Er brennt nach dem Operntext." The handing over of the libretto to Schubert is recorded in an entry dated July 1826 (*Dokumente*, 370; *Documentary Biography*, 545): "'Wo ist der Oper?' fragte Schubert.— 'Hier!'—Ich überreichte ihm feierlich den 'Grafen von Gleichen.'" The libretto is now accessible in *Franz Schubert: Bühnenwerke. Kritische Gesamtausgabe der Texte*, ed. Christian Pollack (Tutzing: Hans Schneider, 1988), 561–615.

21. Deutsch, *Dokumente*, 381.

era and the actual taking of pen (and pencil) to paper, for the date "19. Juny 1827" is inscribed at the head of his draft.

The Censorship Office will have had no difficulty defending its decision. Bauernfeld's theme, drawn from an actual account from the fourteenth century, is of bigamy. The Count von Gleichen, a crusader held prisoner in Cairo, admires Suleika, the adolescent daughter of the Sultan. Her feelings for the Count are more passionate. About to be given in marriage to one of three Indian princes who sue for her hand, Suleika seizes the opportunity to flee with the prisoners (whose departure on a "European" ship she has engineered), even while the Count explains that he expects to find his wife and child at home, deserted all these seven years.

The symmetry of the two acts is not subtle. Bauernfeld's script for act 1 reads "Orient. Frühling. Morgen"; for act 2, "Okzident. Herbst. Abend."[22] Suleika, perhaps not quite so innocent as she is made out to be, is something of a catalyst in the play. It is she to whom all the other characters are drawn. In act 1, there are the three Indian suitors. There is the Sultan, who must lose her. There is the Count, who is in turn consumed by her. In act 2, the Countess succumbs to her purity: prepared finally for the *ménage à trois*, she accepts Suleika—symbolically renamed Angelika—as sister. In each act, complex and intriguing ensembles form and dissolve around her.

What kind of music did Schubert compose for Bauernfeld's book? If a simple answer does not leap out from the pages of the draft, that is only because Schubert's concept reflects, and is to a certain extent victimized by, the unsettled condition of Viennese opera in the 1820s. Eclectic, knotted in contradictory conventions, its extremities were defined by Rossini on the one hand and Weber, whose *Euryanthe*—a "große romantische Oper," as it was titled—Schubert heard, apparently in rehearsal, in 1823.[23] Schubert's derogatory semipublic remarks after the first performance of *Euryanthe*

22. The oppositions were noted in Bauernfeld's diary entry for 2 May: "Dramatisch-musikalischer Gegensatz: Orient und Okzident, Janitscharen und Rittertum, romantische Minne und Gattenliebe usw.—kurz, ein türkisch-christliches Brouillon." Deutsch, *Dokumente*, 356–57; *Documentary Biography*, 523–24.

23. This, according to Weber's son, Max Maria, in his *Carl Maria von Weber: ein Lebensbild* (Leipzig: Ernst Keil, 1864–66), cited in Deutsch, *Memoirs*, 377. Weber himself had much to say about the state of German opera. "To be quite honest, German Opera is not at all well. She suffers from nervous cramps and can't stand properly. . . . She is so swollen by all the claims that have been made on her behalf, that she cannot get into any clothes." This, from the satirical pastiche in chapter 6 of *Tonkünstlers Leben*, given in Carl Maria von Weber, *Writings on Music*, ed. John Warrack, trans. Martin Cooper (Cambridge: Cambridge University Press, 1981), 346. The review of E. T. A. Hoffmann's *Undine*, published in the *Allgemeine musikalische Zeitung* 19 (1817): 202–8, contains within it a manifesto for an ideal German opera. The paragraphs in question were taken up again in chapter 5 of

must have concealed a deeper sense of conflict within himself, for if there is much in *Euryanthe* that opens it to serious criticism, there is also an original, theatrical, and thoroughly German voice of the new Romanticism that Schubert would have perceived as a challenge to his own enterprise.[24] No less troubling for Schubert were the ineffable models from the great Mozart operas, already canonized in the Viennese repertory, and Beethoven's *Fidelio*.

The mythologizing of Beethoven had begun long before his death. His passing (to return to a thought ventured above in chapter 4) would have released Schubert from an obsession with a patriarchal figure who inspired veneration to an extreme.[25] For Schubert, the death signals a coming of age: Beethoven's music, studied with fresh ears (arguably in the appropriation of op. 31, no. 1), is demystified. In the months after Beethoven's death, *Fidelio* was evidently much on Schubert's mind. Anton Schindler tells the story:

> Shortly after Beethoven's death [Schubert] wished to examine the manuscript of *Fidelio*. After he had been occupied with it for a long while, and had scrutinized at the piano the many alterations in harmony, instrumentation and rhythmic construction, he remarked that under no circumstances would he accede to such drudgery, and that moreover, he finds the first idea to be just as good as the emendation.[26]

Discerning truth from fiction in Schindler's reconstructions is a frustrating exercise. The circumstantial evidence allows that Schindler may well have displayed his *Fidelio* manuscripts to Schubert in those months between the death of Beethoven on 26 March 1827 and Schindler's departure from Vienna the following September.[27] These are the months during which

---

Tonkünstlers Leben and published in 1821; see Weber, *Writings on Music*, 201–2, 312–13, and 333–40.

24. In addition to the incidents reported by Max Maria von Weber, see also the report by Spaun, given in Deutsch, *Memoirs*, 137, and *Erinnerungen*, 160; and Helmina von Chézy, the author of the libretto, *Memoirs*, 259–60, *Erinnerungen*, 297. See, too, Michael C. Tusa, "Weber's *Große Oper*: A Note on the Origins of *Euryanthe*," *19th-Century Music* 8 (1984): 119–24.

25. The evidence in support of this notion is developed in Maynard Solomon, "Schubert and Beethoven," *19th-Century Music* 3 (1979): 114–25.

26. Deutsch, *Erinnerungen*, 272 (translation mine).

27. What would Schubert have seen? Among the manuscripts acquired from Schindler by the Royal Library in Berlin in 1846, the two most substantial items are (Staatsbibliothek zu Berlin [=SBK] mus. ms. autogr. Beethoven 3) a volume of 206 leaves, mostly autograph, containing four numbers for the 1805 *Leonore*; and (SBK, autogr. 26) a "Sammelband," altogether 274 leaves, comprising copyist scores of fifteen numbers for the ver-

Schubert had taken up *Der Graf von Gleichen* in earnest, and so his interest in the *Fidelio* papers would have been much to the point. However he might have expressed himself in Schindler's presence—knowing, as we now do, of Schindler's penchant for embellishment if not sheer fabrication in such storytelling—it is very likely that the engagement with these papers left in Schubert some deeper impression, one that he may not have wished to share.

The influence of *Fidelio* is felt even when Schubert is at pains to suppress it. In an opening soliloquy (act 1, sc. 2), the imprisoned Count invokes the heavens and sings for his abandoned wife and son. The Count is no Florestan, the Countess no Leonore. And Bauernfeld's scene comes at the outset of the piece, before his characters have established any claim to genuine sympathy. Still, any such situation will call to mind Beethoven's sinister dungeon. The unnerving diminished sevenths that enshroud Florestan's "Gott, welch Dunkel hier!" are done over in a music whose plaintive dissonances resolve in a phrase of Classical equipoise (see ex. 9.4). The opening strophe of the cavatina yields finally to a *stretta di tempo* that will call to mind Florestan's "Und spür' ich nicht linde." Its opening bars (see ex. 9.5a)—one imagines three horns, and inevitably the *stretta* in Leonore's "Komm, Hoffnung"—expound a motive of later significance. In the epilogue (ex. 9.5b), the decay after the ecstasy again calls up Florestan's pathetic collapse.

The symmetry of Bauernfeld's text is not lost on Schubert. In a second soliloquy (act 2, sc. 2), the Count, approaching his castle upon his return from Cairo, again invokes the Deity. The *scena* is charged with ambivalence: anxiety and gratitude together. In the opening bars before the first lines of recitative (ex. 9.6a), the horns and clarinets echo the motive earlier associated with the *stretta* ("O sehnendes Verlangen") in the cavatina of act 1. A transformation that touches more deeply is drawn out of it at the outset of the aria (see ex. 9.6b).

When finally the Count and the Countess are reunited, Bauernfeld's lines echo the famous duet of reconciliation between Leonore and Florestan:

---

sions of 1805 and 1806, with entries and revisions in Beethoven's hand. Of Schindler's other *Fidelio* holdings, the most suggestive would have been the two autographs of Florestan's "Gott, welch Dunkel hier": 1814 (SBK, autogr. 4), available in facsimile (ed. Karl-Heinz Köhler, Leipzig: VEB Deutscher Verlag für Musik, 1976); and 1805 (SBK, autogr. 5). During the summer of 1827, while the *Nachlaß* was under litigation, it had gotten around Vienna that Schindler had appropriated manuscripts to which he had no legal right. See Clemens Brenneis, "Das Fischhof-Manuskript: Zur Frühgeschichte der Beethoven-Biographik," in *Zu Beethoven: Aufsätze und Annotationen* (Berlin: Verlag Neue Musik, 1979), 1:98. Schubert must have seen the *Fidelio* papers before 15 September, the date of Schindler's departure for Pest; he next returned to Vienna in 1829.

EX. 9.4. Schubert, *Der Graf von Gleichen*, act 1, sc. 2. Draft, fol. 5r.

EX. 9.5. Schubert, *Der Graf von Gleichen*, act 1, sc. 2.

EX. 9.6. Schubert, *Der Graf von Gleichen*, act 2, sc. 2.

Count: Laß ab, laß ab! Mir sprengt's die Brust!
Countess: Unendlich, unendlich ist diese Lust!
Leonore: O namenlose Freude!
  Mein Mann an meiner Brust!
Florestan: O namenlose Freude!
  An Leonorens Brust!

Schubert's setting does nothing to dispel the similarities (see ex. 9.7).

The exotic love between the Count and Suleika is less easily rendered, and in a difficult moment toward the end of act 1 the Count prepares to abandon her. The dialogue with himself is set off in melodramatic music of touching poignancy. The encounter between them provokes a response in Suleika worthy of Donna Anna. The parallels are not trivial and extend beyond the peremptory opening phrase ("Scheiden . . . Verräter!"; see ex. 9.8A) deep into the duet. Suleika is determined to get a confession from

EX. 9.7. Schubert, *Der Graf von Gleichen*, act 2, sc. 3. Draft, fol. 24r.

EX. 9.8A. Schubert, *Der Graf von Gleichen*, act 1, sc. 11. Draft, fol. 18r–19v.

the Count. The interrogation ("Liebst du mich?") is at once seductive and obstinate (see ex. 9.8B). It is impossible not to think for a moment that we are witness to the riveting oath-taking exchange between Ottavio and Anna, and there is much in Schubert's music to suggest that the dynamics between the unequal lovers in Mozart's duet was somehow at play here as well. Tellingly, Schubert inscribes the indignant, authoritarian posture of a Donna Anna in the ingenue Suleika—a posture that Bauernfeld's scene does not altogether encourage, contradicting the figure of naive innocence that Suleika personifies. (Is some autobiographical signature to be

EX. 9.8B. Schubert, *Der Graf von Gleichen*, act 1, sc. 11. Draft, fol. 19v.

discerned here? Even the suggestion of marriage was taken as something of a threat by Schubert, we learn from more than one account.)[28]

The Countess, on the other hand, has a touch of Almaviva about her. She, too, makes her entrance in the second act, alone and lamenting. Bauernfeld gives her a lied by Goethe to sing: *Wonne der Wehmuth* (Bliss of Sadness). Did Bauernfeld know Schubert's 1815 setting?[29] This early setting is

---

28. The several sides of the issue are aired in Maynard Solomon, "Schubert: Some Consequences of Nostalgia," in *19th-Century Music* 17, no. 1 (Summer 1993): 34–46, esp. 35.

29. The song (D 260), composed on 20 August 1815, was included in the first of the autograph "Liederheften" sent to Goethe in April 1816 (discussed in chapter 3 above). Its publication by the Viennese firm M. J. Leidesdorf was announced in the press on 16 June 1829 as op. 115, together with *Sprache der Liebe* (D 410) and the exquisite *Das Lied im Grünen* (D 917), the rough autograph of which is dated June 1827; the draft for *Der Graf von Gleichen* bears the inscription "19. Juny 1827." It is tempting to imagine Schubert, hav-

resurrected here, but the alterations to it are profound. Erich Partsch, who has a brief essay among the preliminary material of the facsimile edition of the opera draft, may be right that the transposition from the C minor of 1815 to G minor "has apparently semantic implications."[30] When he claims that G minor "encompasses the affective sphere of sorrow and pain" ("umspannt das Bedeutungsfeld 'Trauer/Schmerz'"), citing Pamina's "Ach ich fühl's," one wants to believe that Pamina, too, figures in the subtext of the scene, and yet must question whether Schubert's notion of G minor can have been dictated by any such theorizing about *Tonarten* in the abstract.

The decision to transpose seems to me altogether bound up in the recomposition of the piece. For one, the earlier setting has an uncomfortably high tessitura that does nothing to enhance the gravity of the Countess's complaint. Similarly, while the new draft lacks a tempo direction, the doubling of its note values suggests something more deliberate, lingered-over, than the puzzling "etwas geschwind" of the original. But it is in the exquisite new extension that this touchingly simple song of 1815 is utterly transformed. The expansion, more than double the length of the original (the entire poem is declaimed a second time), responds to a Neapolitan sixth, a harmony that in the original is sounded for the first and last time in the final sung phrase, a dissonance without issue. Even the little epilogue in the piano is oblivious of it. That plaintive note (A♭ in the transposition) is now given new latitude, touching off a melancholy passage to the minor subdominant, and then husbanded for the high octave in the final phrase (see ex. 9.9). The epilogue in the winds is now made to absorb that note, and in some sense to resolve it. In the process, *Wonne der Wehmuth* is transformed from a lied in the locutionary manner of 1815 to a cavatina-like confession that captures some genuine aspect of the Countess and her situation. The new music defines the Countess for us in a way that the original lied could not.

If the appropriation of *Wonne der Wehmuth* distributes rich dividends in its new turns of phrase, it cuts a rather more precarious deal with the aesthetics of opera, if only that the integrity of the genre is in some sense compromised. An astonishing instance of this ambivalence emerges late

---

ing rediscovered his *Wonne der Wehmuth* in preparation for the composition of the opera, putting it together with the newly composed *Lied im Grünen* in a package for Leidesdorf, who had published another group of Schubert's songs, in January 1829, as op. 108. On the problem of verifying Schubert's role in the publications appearing shortly after his death, see Walther Dürr's commentary in Schubert, *Neue Ausgabe sämtlicher Werke*, IV/5a, xv, although op. 115 is not considered in this connection.

30. ". . . offensichtlich semantisch bedingt ist." Franz Schubert, *Der Graf von Gleichen. Oper in zwei Akten (D 918)*, Erstveröffentlichung der Handschrift, 18.

EX. 9.9. Schubert, *Wonne der Wehmut*, D 260, closing bars, shown against the expansion for the Countess's aria, *Der Graf von Gleichen,* act 2, sc. 1. Draft, fol. 21v.

in act 2. The Count has now explained to the Countess his intention to take Suleika as a second wife. The Countess offers her consent: "Muß ich sie nicht wie eine Schwester lieben, / Die dich mir gab?" (Must I not love her as a sister whom you have given to me?) The two examine this theme in a duet that sings of "Verklärung"—of an ecstatic transfiguration: "O bin ich deiner Liebe wert?" the Count wants to know. "Daß ich dich liebe, ist mein Wert," she replies, and together they consort, "Wie herrlich ist's im Arm des Gatten, / Wie rein das Leben, klar und hell!" The music to these lines will be familiar to anyone who knows *Winterreise* (see ex. 9.10). *Die Nebensonnen* is certainly not the song that springs to mind in this exchange between the Count and the Countess. But the evidence is here that, for Schubert, Müller's poem and Bauernfeld's lines evoked literally the same music—even the same pitches.

What are we to make of this disquieting echo of the duet—in some sense, the philosophical heart of the opera—in a setting of Müller's inscrutable lied, a text no less central to the meaning of Schubert's somber cycle? There can have been no intention here to allude in the one to the other. We do not better understand Müller's arcane "Ach, *meine* Sonnen seid ihr nicht! / Schaut andren doch ins Angesicht!" (You alas are not *my* suns! Gaze into others' faces!) to know that its music had been conceived to express an ecstasy of love transfigured. The transfiguration embraces all three lovers: Suleika is powerfully present even in her absence. "Dreieinigkeit" (a trinity), now cryptically, is again the message in *Die Nebensonnen*: "Drei Sonnen sah ich am Himmel stehn" (I saw three suns stand still in the sky), and then "Ja, neulich hatt' ich auch wohl drei: / Nun sind hinab die besten zwei" (Yes, not long ago I too had three suns; now the two best have set).[31] Perhaps it was only the power of this abstraction that fused the two situations in Schubert's mind.

Coincidentally, in addition to the *Reinschrift* of the twelve songs that constitute part 2 of *Winterreise*, an earlier autograph of *Die Nebensonnen* has survived, characteristically described by Deutsch as an "erste Niederschrift."[32] Undated, its watermark not visible, the paper can yet be

---

31. Arnold Feil distinguishes two sets of three suns: the first he understands as a perceptual phenomenon—the sun refracted through tears; the second, in simile, he takes to be self-evident: "die Augen des Mädchens und die Sonne am Himmel" (the eyes of the maiden and the suns in the sky). See *Franz Schubert: Die schöne Müllerin. Die Winterreise* (Stuttgart: Philipp Reclam, 1975), 146–47; in English (Portland, OR: Amadeus Press, 1988), 126–27. John Reed, in *The Schubert Song Companion* (Manchester: Manchester University Press, 1985), 457, sees no need for hermeneutics: the three suns are one of the wanderer's hallucinations, and we know from *Täuschung* that he willingly submitted to them. But perhaps it is merely the suggestive symbolism of Müller's language that lends to deluded fantasy a quality of insight much prized in Romantic poetry. Why three suns? The question remains. For a gloss on this very question, see Kristina Muxfeldt, *Vanishing Sensibilities* (Oxford: Oxford University Press, 2012), 72–74 (note 40); and further, Lisa Feuerzeig, "Elusive Intimacy in Schubert's Final Opera, *Der Graf von Gleichen*," in *Rethinking Schubert*, 353, note 23.

32. Vienna, Gesellschaft der Musikfreunde, Schubert autogr. 235. See Deutsch, *Thematisches Verzeichnis*, 576. A facsimile is shown in *Österreichische Musikzeitschrift* 27 (1972): 76; and *Zusatz-Band zur Geschichte der K. K. Gesellschaft der Musikfreunde in Wien*, ed. Eusebius Mandyczewski, Sammlungen und Statuten (Vienna, 1912), facing p. 117.

EX. 9.10. Schubert, *Der Graf von Gleichen*, act 2, sc. 9. Draft, fol. 31r.

identified with the type whose most substantial use is as a second paper in the draft of *Der Graf von Gleichen*.[33] In upright format, sixteen staves to the page, the paper was used for the most part in "pocket" format—that is, folded in half from top to bottom. The *Reinschrift* of *Winterreise*, part 2, dated October 1827, is on another kind of paper. From all this, one might speculate that work on the "Fortsetzung" of *Winterreise* may well have followed closely upon the completion of the draft of the opera, perhaps in September 1827.[34]

33. See Robert Winter, "Paper Studies and the Future of Schubert Research," in *Schubert Studies: Problems of Style and Chronology*, ed. Eva Badura-Skoda and Peter Branscombe (Cambridge: Cambridge University Press, 1982), 244–46. (The reference to *Die Nebensonnen* as item 6 on p. 256 is clearly an error for the autograph of the March in G for Piano Four Hands, D 928.)

34. For more on the autograph of *Winterreise* and its dating, see my *Distant Cycles: Schubert and the Conceiving of Song* (Chicago: University of Chicago Press, 1994), 152–

3

All this brings us back to the mysterious circumstances under which Schubert began to compose. More than a year after the book had been presented to him, and with virtually no chance that the decision of the Censorship Office would ever be reversed, Schubert yet undertook the composition of a major work for the stage—and without genuine prospects that a performance might be mounted in any case, unless Grillparzer's offer to stage the work in Berlin was to be taken in earnest.[35] Why did he do so? And can it be ascertained that Schubert decided in the end to abandon the work?

Ernst Hilmar, whose commentary to the facsimile ranges widely over the chronology of Schubert's last years, alleges that the final numbers in the draft suggest a flagging of interest in the project. The allegation is of considerable import, for its underlying assumption is not simply that the opera was left abandoned (an accident of the actuarial tables, after all), but that Schubert had determined to abandon it (11): "Work on the opera extended presumably into the spring of 1828, but to judge from the *Handschrift*, the composer seems visibly to have lost interest in the work toward the end of this *Particell*" (my translation). And again (11): "The haste with which the last entries for the opera were written signifies rather that other important compositional plans had already announced themselves." With regard to the dating of the draft, this last constitutes a revision of a view expressed with some specificity that the opera continued to occupy Schubert right up until his death.[36] This, one suspects, was an attempt to "verify" through the handwriting in the manuscript the accounts of two witnesses who reported deathbed conversations with Schubert. Writing in 1860, Franz Lachner described a visit with Schubert one day before his death:

> When I went to see him for the last time before my departure, Schubert was fully conscious and I conversed for several hours with the most un-

---

53; and Franz Schubert, *Winterreise: The Autograph Score*, with an introduction by Susan Youens (New York: Pierpont Morgan Library and Dover Publications, 1989), viii–xvii.

35. Thus Bauernfeld recalls the circumstances in his notice of 1869: "Grillparzer declared himself willing to arrange for the performance of the opera at the Königstädtische Theatre [in Berlin], in the event of its being banned in Vienna" (quoted from Deutsch, *Memoirs*, 235; *Erinnerungen*, 269).

36. See Hilmar, *Verzeichnis der Schubert-Handschriften*, 29, where it is suggested that the draft for the duet between the Countess and Suleika was begun as late as the spring of 1828, broken off after m. 4, and completed ("Soviel man aus den Schriftzügen lesen kann"—so far as one can read from the handwriting) shortly before Schubert's death.

Posthumous Schubert   211

assuming and most modest artist, with my warmest and most sympathetic friend. He still told me about various plans he had for the future and was looking forward, more than anything else, to his recovery so that he could finish his opera, "Der Graf von Gleichen". . . . A great part of the opera was already sketched out by him.[37]

Bauernfeld spoke with Schubert on 17 November, two days before his death. On 20 November, he entered in his diary: "On Monday I still spoke with him. . . . To the last he talked to me of our opera."[38] And in a memorandum written in 1869, he recalled that about one week before Schubert's death, "he had spoken . . . with great eagerness about the opera and with what richness he wanted to orchestrate it!"[39]

Hilmar's inclination to see in the hasty writing a signal that the project had lost its appeal—that Schubert (his handwriting tells us) was anxious to move on—runs up against the accounts of these witnesses. Still, it is an argument that deserves to be examined on its merits. Where, precisely, does Schubert's hand betray signs of impatience? The evidence ought logically to be found in the final numbers in act 2. For, while it can be shown that the sequence of composition now and again deviates from the sequence of the libretto, the thrust of the manuscript is clear that work proceeded from beginning to end.

But there is another issue here. The traces of a fleet hand, even of a careless scribble that trails off inconclusively, must not be taken to signify an erosion of interest in what was being written. Often enough, these are the signs of an impatience to keep pace in the writing with the rush of ideas, this "Flug der Gedanken" (flight of ideas) that inspired Mies to his thoughts on the "Einheitlichkeit," the uniformity, of works conceived on the grand scale. In this regard, the document itself is illuminating. Altogether rare among Schubert's papers, it is a draft by definition, from first note to last. Its structure is similarly unorthodox, for the manuscript comprises two functionally distinct kinds of paper. On the one hand is (A) a run of thirty-six leaves of sixteen-stave paper, all—with the exception of a bifolium containing the "namenlose Freude"–like duet between Count and Countess—in oblong format, its entries written in ink; on the other, (B) three "pocket-sized" gatherings, altogether thirty-six leaves, whose entries are written alternately in pencil and ink.

There is a temptation to read the entries in B as in some sense less formal

37. Deutsch, *Memoirs*, 195; *Erinnerungen*, 224.
38. Deutsch, *Documents*, 824; *Dokumente*, 549–50.
39. Deutsch, *Memoirs*, 238; *Erinnerungen*, 272.

than those in A. Entries in pencil have often a sketchy, hip-pocket look to them. What, then, is the relationship between the contents of A and B? It turns out that an entry in B is never a rough preliminary take for a cleaner one in A. Further, it cannot be claimed that Schubert reserved desk and pen for the more significant and challenging numbers. One senses the contrary often enough. Some of the conventional ensembles of lesser dramatic import are drafted in A, while certain problematic confrontations whose dramatic implications Schubert may have approached with some insecurity are entered tentatively, in pencil, on the pocket leaves. The scene in which Suleika and the Count first address one another is a case in point. The Count casually offers Suleika a purple rose, unaware of the heavy symbolism in the act.[40] Any Muslim, he learns too late, will take this as a declaration of love. The duet breaks off in mid-phrase at Suleika's stunned response. A march— one of Schubert's quirky "Turkish" numbers—is heard in the distance, against which the Count completes his lines. Schubert's music for all this, sketchy as it may look on the page, conveys genuine dramatic engagement.

The music seems to gain in poise toward the end. The two ensembles at the close are exceptionally fine, even moving. In the *terzetto* which is the penultimate number in Schubert's score, the *ménage à trois* is finally consummated: the three sing together for the first time. The opening music is tentative. Suleika, *ängstlich*, is ready to leave, and Schubert's bass tones edge away from the harmony. (Beware the faulty incipit in the Deutsch *Verzeichnis*.) But the Countess reassures her, and the reconciliation is joined in a new music (ex. 9.11) at once sensual and chaste. Is this the music of a composer whose mind is elsewhere?

4

In the end, *Der Graf von Gleichen* is a fragment. A good deal more than the orchestration remains unfinished. Just how this is so can perhaps be suggested in the draft for the opening of the Sonata in A Major (ex. 9.12). What

---

40. Erich V. Partsch, overly laconic, offers: "Die Purpurrose gilt als Symbol der Liebe"—the purple rose is considered as the symbol of love (*Der Graf von Gleichen*, 19, note 3). For a rich study on the topic, see Jutta Hecker, *Das Symbol der Blauen Blume im Zusammenhang mit der Blumensymbolik der Romantik* (Jena: Frommann, 1931): "Auch die Erwähnung der mystischen Erzählung von der Liebe der Nachtigall zur Purpurrose entstammt dem Orient. Dieses Motive, das in der 'Kreisleriana' schon auftauchte als Liebe der Nachtigall zur Purpurnelke, ist . . . als häufig besungenes Motiv der Perser erwähnt"— the mention of the mystical tale of the nightingale's love for the purple rose comes from the Orient. This motif, which appears in the "Kreisleriana" as the nightingale's love for the purple carnation, is mentioned as a frequently sung motif of the Persians (59).

EX. 9.11. Schubert, *Der Graf von Gleichen*, act 2, sc. 10. Draft, fol. 34r.

EX. 9.12. Schubert, Sonata in A Major, D 959, first movement. Draft for opening phrase.

astonishes us here is not that the structure of the phrase is in place, ready for all those elegant diminutions that will shape it, but that what we might have taken to be the generating idea of the piece—its rhythm, and even the sheer tactile anticipation in making the bass tones speak—is missing. If nothing beyond this draft had survived, how might it have been factored into a history of Schubert's last music?

The pleasures of *Der Graf von Gleichen*, even as we imagine how a finished version might have sounded, how it would move on the stage, are often palpable. Much is worth reconstructing. The quality of the music in the draft encourages no argument that the opera had been deliberately abandoned. The cherished repertory of works by Schubert that remained unfinished is itself canonical.[41] Sphinx-like, each fragment conceals its own end. The hieroglyphic mystery of the inscription only enhances its value. *Der Graf von Gleichen*, taken as a whole, remained unfinished primarily in its vertical axis. For while some of the individual numbers in it break off before the end, the opera is drafted straight through to what might well have been conceived as its penultimate structural cadence. The quintet that was the last number for which Schubert composed music closes with an Andante con moto: the Count sings "Nun aber kommt, ihr holden Frauen" in a noble, arching phrase redolent of another Count's "Contessa perdono," another Andante, the penultimate music in *Figaro*.[42]

Why did Schubert trouble to set a book whose censorship stood little chance of exoneration? Its literary merit had been sternly questioned.[43] But the deeper inquiry of recent scholarship sets Bauernfeld's book in a rich historical and literary context.[44] One pokes gingerly into the mean-

41. These matters are explored in some depth in my *Unfinished Music* (Oxford: Oxford University Press, 2008, rev. 2012), chapters 13 ("Toward an Epistemology of Fragment") and 14 ("*Reliquie*").

42. The motionless, subdominant quiet before the final resolution to the tonic and the closing *bruit* in *Figaro* might be taken as a model for how the quintet would be placed in the finale of *Der Graf von Gleichen*. Like the penultimate number in *Figaro*, the quintet recapitulates the key of the opening number (E♭ major), and from this we might presume that the final number, and the overture as well, would have been set in B♭ major.

43. "A lifeless hotch-potch of stock stage situations with, moreover, a bigamous marriage as the central theme," is how Maurice J. E. Brown puts it in *The New Grove Schubert* (New York: W. W. Norton, 1983), 51: "Once again we are faced with the extraordinary inability of the composer to assess the merit of opera texts."

44. See especially Kristina Muxfeldt's remarkably documented "The Matrimonial Anomaly (Schubert's Opera for Posterity)," in her *Vanishing Sensibilities*, 43–82, tracing the source of the legend back to accounts from the thirteenth century, and reading the influence, among others, of Goethe's play *Stella* (1776) and its revision of 1806, now with a tragic ending. "The new ending is attached with surgical precision, leaving the main body of the play intact," writes Muxfeldt; and then: "At the climactic point of crisis—roughly

ing that this text might have held for Schubert and his comrades. The intimacy among them, as has been probed finally with scorching insight, was in no sense innocent.[45] Surely something in the theme of the opera vibrates sympathetically with the intimacies emanating from within the Schubert circle: the *ménage à trois*, which always stipulates a homoerotic aspect; the romance of the moral taboo—bigamy, in this instance, as the socially more tolerable transgression (legitimized in historical incident and stamped with papal license), cloaking the condition of homosexuality; the elevation of love to some Platonic ideal, admittedly only suggested in Bauernfeld's text. Even the "Persian" aspect, no quaint stage prop, extends beyond historical incident for its meaning.[46]

Goethe, who figured prominently in the agenda of Schubert's *Lesegesellschaft*, dwells in the subtext of Bauernfeld's book as well.[47] Suleika will bring to mind the two poems in her name ("Ach, um deine feuchten Schwingen" and "Was bedeutet die Bewegung?") that Schubert set from the *West-östlicher Divan* in 1821 (D 717 and 720).[48] Ottilie, as the Countess is named, will elicit her namesake in Goethe's *Die Wahlverwandtschaften* (*Elective Affinities*, as it is commonly translated), whose shifting triangular relationships are very much felt beneath the surface of Bauernfeld's plot.[49]

---

the same point at which Schubert's opera draft breaks off—a newly crafted hinge negotiates the shift from comedy to tragedy." We are by implication invited to contemplate similar indecision at this point in Schubert's draft, and yet the libretto seems clear enough as to the outcome.

45. The topic of Schubert's sexuality was famously broached in Maynard Solomon's "Franz Schubert and the Peacocks of Benvenuto Cellini," in *19th-Century Music* 12 (1989): 193–206, provoking in response a complete issue of that journal, 17, no. 1 (Summer 1993), with substantial contributions by Rita Steblin (and Solomon's sage response—"Some Consequences of Nostalgia"—to her refusal of his argument), Kristina Muxfeldt, and David Gramit, with additional commentary by Kofi Agawu, Susan McClary, James Webster, and Robert S. Winter. The dialogue continues.

46. Franz von Schober, a brilliantly eccentric, somewhat devious figure in the Schubert circle, "affected the manner of an oriental prince . . . [holding forth] in rooms carpeted and upholstered in Persian style." See Solomon, "Franz Schubert and the Peacocks," 197.

47. Something of the magnetic appeal of Goethe to the circle is conveyed in my *Distant Cycles* (Chicago: University of Chicago Press, 1994), in a chapter titled "A Poetics of the Remote: Goethe's *Entfernte*," esp. 98–99.

48. Both poems were in fact written by Marianne von Willemer, and somewhat revised by Goethe in the manuscript for the *Divan*. This was not commonly known in the 1820s, and Schubert cannot have known it.

49. Suleika, the innocent third member, is rather the Ottilie figure here; the Count and the Countess resemble Eduard and Charlotte, the central couple in Goethe's novel (better, *Novelle*, as it has been called). In Goethe's *Stella*, a *ménage à trois* is conversely inspired by a narrative in act 5 in which precisely the story of the Count von Gleichen (though he is unnamed) is recounted to the assembled principals. But it was *Die Wahlver-*

And then there is *Wonne der Wehmuth*. When the Countess sings these burnished lines—when Bauernfeld makes them her very first lines—the oracular figure of the poet is conjured. Did Bauernfeld wish to hint that Ottilie was about to need the sympathetic protection of Goethe's bold and well-known views on conjugal love?[50]

Robert Winter has proposed that the entire draft of *Der Graf von Gleichen* was the work of the summer of 1827.[51] There is little reason to doubt him. Hilmar's view that the work extended into the spring of 1828 depends upon a discrimination in handwriting that remains unexplained and unproved, and implies an unsettling lack of concentration on the project. It needs to be kept in mind that Schubert had yet to undertake any of the full scoring for the opera. The manuscript that survives suggests two things: that Schubert worked intensely and yet methodically to draft out the opera from beginning to end; and that the preparation of a full score, a more tedious and time-consuming labor, was very likely put off until the prospects, or even the possibility, of a performance were closer to hand.

It is not given to us to know whether the opera was alive in Schubert's mind as he lay dying. If Lachner and Bauernfeld are to be believed, then it is conceivable that *Der Graf von Gleichen* remained one of several unfinished projects that Schubert took with him to the grave. In the face of works left unfinished, it inevitably falls to the survivors to puzzle out what had gone wrong. To claim in this instance that Schubert, recognizing a doomed project, merely came to his senses is to dismiss a work that stands prominently if enigmatically in the midst of Schubert's last thoughts.

Epilogue

Today, nearly two centuries after Schubert's death, we seem better positioned to contend with the contradictory conditions, the mysteries, the lacunae enshrouding the exceptional music inscribed and forever impris-

---

wandtschaften that was influencing thought and behavior in the 1820s; see *"Die Wahlverwandtschaften": Eine Dokumentation der Wirkung von Goethes Roman, 1808–1832*, ed. Heinz Härtl (Weinheim: Akademie Verlag, 1983; repr. Göttingen: Wallstein, 2013).

50. One thinks here of another *ménage à trois*: Truffaut's *Jules et Jim*, and the memorable scene in which Jules (Oscar Werner), isolated on the balcony above Catherine and Jim, intones some lines from Goethe's *Rastlose Liebe*: "Alle das Neigen / Von Herzen zu Herzen, / Ach wie so eigen / Schaffet das Schmerzen," setting loose a sequence in which *Les Affinités électives* is passed among the points of the triangle, the book itself displayed as a symbol for the ideas within it, as though its very presence were an inducement to act. See the film script *Jules et Jim: A Film by François Truffaut*, trans. Nicholas Fry (New York: Simon and Schuster, 1968), 70–72.

51. Winter, "Paper Studies," 245.

oned in this rough draft. "Die Tonkunst begrub hier einen reichen Besitz" (the art of music entombed here a rich possession): Grillparzer's famous lines, inscribed on Schubert's tombstone, seem no less fitting an epigraph for this remarkable fragment.[52] "Aber noch viel schönere Hoffnungen," it concludes: but yet far fairer hopes. Grillparzer's envoi has had its critics— Deutsch writes of "this low estimate of Schubert's creative maturity"[53]— but that is to trivialize its deeper message. Whatever the incommensurate achievements through November 1828, we inevitably allow ourselves to imagine what might have issued from that prodigious mind, a futile exercise that should remind us that the creative adventure, the composer in search of himself, is a private affair, inaccessible to us. This, too, speaks to our draft. The study of such fragments invites similar speculation, as though one could appropriate the internal conversation, the agon of decision-making at the core of Schubert's lonely adventure.

The ensuing fugal lessons with Sechter, the closer study of those last quartets of Beethoven, and much else that would have occupied Schubert in those months not given to him: how might any of this have found its way into his work? Perhaps it would only have driven him more deeply into the solitude of his own world. At the very least, Grillparzer's "yet far fairer hopes" invites us to contemplate these imponderable questions, for which of course there can be no answers.[54]

52. The four alternatives together with the final inscription are given in, for one, Franz Grillparzer, *Sämtliche Werke: Ausgewählte Briefe, Gespräche, Berichte*, I, ed. Peter Frank and Karl Pörnbacher (Munich: Carl Hanser, n.d.), 397; and in Deutsch, *Documents*, 899.

53. *Documents*, 899.

54. Christopher Gibbs suggests that Grillparzer's epitaph should be read "as evidence of how the composer's genuine artistic achievement was not fully appreciated during his own time," but that would attribute to Grillparzer a privileging of the reception of Schubert's music in his lifetime over against the achievement itself and the "far fairer hopes" for a music that Schubert did not live to create. See his introductory essay to *The Cambridge Companion to Schubert*, ed. Gibbs (Cambridge: Cambridge University Press, 1997), 1.

✳ POSTSCRIPT ✳

...and Beyond

Those two figures that gaze out at the horizon in Caspar David Friedrich's landscape return to haunt these closing chapters. In the projects of their final months, circumscribed each in its own idiolect, Schubert and Beethoven take the measure of their own horizons. What they might have envisioned must be left to the imagination and the enterprise of a younger generation who would create a new Romanticism from the echo of these last works, a resonance manifest not in slavish imitation of their music but rather in the more obscure traces of influence hidden in a deeper consciousness of their inestimable achievement.

Among the composers of the so-called generation of the 1830s, Robert Schumann perhaps more than any of his compatriots felt himself responsible to the legacy of Beethoven and Schubert, and yet his music, when it looks back, conveys more the sense of ironic rehearing than of nostalgia. The bold Sonata in F♯ Minor (op. 11, 1833–1835) does not look back in any conventional mode. Its originality is breathtaking, from the opening arpeggios and the hortatory theme of its *Introduzione*—less an introduction than a self-contained character piece—to the closing *accelerando* that drives those arpeggios to self-annihilation, *fortissimo*, leaving in its wreckage only a skeletal *pianissimo* cadence without even the barest harmony. And yet the music seems to extend the ethos of the Beethovenian sense of sonata in its exploitation of technique toward the extremities of expression. *Dichterliebe*, drawn from Heine's *Lyrisches Intermezzo*, if it owes the concept of cycle, but not its idiosyncrasies, to the iconic models of Schubert's Müller cycles and Beethoven's *An die ferne Geliebte*, reconceives the marriage of voice and piano, finding a musical diction to match the sardonic irony and wit of Heine's verse.

But perhaps no work of the 1830s has been more closely identified with Beethoven than Schumann's *Fantasie*, op. 17. Inspired by early plans in 1835 for the dedication of a monument to Beethoven in Bonn, Schumann entered in his diary for early December 1836 a "Sonate für Beethoven." Later that month, the project would be described in a letter to Carl Friedrich Kistner as "Große Sonate: Ruinen, Trophäen, Palmen," which he would entitle "Obolus auf Beethovens Denkmal"—for Beethoven's monument. This ambivalence in the naming of the work, and even the shifting dedications—to the memory of Beethoven, to the intimacy of his relationship to Clara Wieck (in a letter to her), and finally to Franz Liszt on the published title page (1839)—have been amply documented.[1] But two aspects of this naming invite further reflection. On the title page of the autograph score of the first movement—a document that was sold at auction in 1984, and has since disappeared into private hands[2]—Schumann wrote in ink: "Ruines. Fantaisie pour le Pianoforte dediée à [word deleted] par Robert Schumann Op. 16a." Nicholas Marston may have been the first to note that this title "strongly suggests that Schumann originally composed the first movement as an independent 'fantasy' called *Ruines*."[3] Whether or not this single movement was conceived with the Beethoven monument in mind, that epithet must give us pause. Surely it cannot, as has been suggested, have been meant to signify the first stage of Beethoven's career. No reading of Beethoven's early works—those composed before, say, the "Eroica" Symphony—can reasonably be subsumed under the rubric "Ruinen," nor can the events of his early life.[4] In the Romantic imagination, however, the ruin in its literal, pictorial, and metaphoric sense is a familiar trope. Did Schumann wish to conjure precisely that image in the dissonance of its opening bars, suggesting, as they do, that we encounter its striking theme in mid-phrase as if coming upon a fragment, a relic with an unknown past? In its impetuous unfolding of idea, no less evocative of fragment and ruin, heard against the back story of the planning for a Beethoven monument,

---

1. See, in particular, Nicholas Marston, *Schumann: Fantasie, Op. 17* (Cambridge: Cambridge University Press, 1992), 1–10.

2. Sotheby's, *Continental Books, Manuscripts and Music*, London, 22 and 23 November 1984, item 534.

3. Marston, *Schumann: Fantasie, Op. 17*, 7. In another essay, Marston offers a compelling demonstration that *Dichterliebe* owes much of its tonal rhetoric to Beethoven's String Quartet in C♯ Minor. See his "Schumann's Monument to Beethoven," in *19th-Century Music* 14 (1991): 247–64.

4. ". . . the three movements were later called 'Ruins,' 'Triumphal Arch' and 'Starry Crown,' in pictorial allusion to Beethoven's heroic career," writes Alan Walker in "Schumann, Liszt and the C Major Fantasie, Op. 17: A Declining Relationship," in *Music & Letters* 60, no. 2 (1979): 156–65, esp. 156.

the music hints at autobiography, of Schumann engaged at full throttle in the creation of a future from the ruins of the past. It is the adventure of seizing the future after Beethoven that is captured here, not the frozen memorial to a dead hero.

That brings us to the last page of the first movement of the *Fantasie*, its music now commonly taken as an allusion to, if not an outright quotation of, the opening of the sixth song of Beethoven's *An die ferne Geliebte*, necessarily invoking the unspoken poetic text of that music: "Nimm sie hin denn, diese Lieder, die ich dir, Geliebte, sang" (take, then, these songs, beloved, that I sang to you)—which some have regarded as an explicitly coded message to the beloved Clara. Schumann's phrase is, however, incommensurate with the scansion of the poetic line; the accents are all out of place, its Adagio a misreading of Beethoven's innocent Andante con moto, cantabile. The legitimacy of the allusion, however broadly defined, must be subject to question. And then there is the significance of this phrase in the unfolding of the movement. We hear it in a stripped-down gestalt at the outset, at mm. 14–18, as the consequent phrase that brings the first great thematic rush to partial closure; and then again, at mm. 49–52, now in D minor. In a more elegant variant, the phrase is isolated at mm. 156–60 at a poignant moment in the section titled *Im Legendenton*: "Erzählend im Legendenton" (narrated in the manner of legend), as it was originally inscribed by Schumann in the *Stichvorlage*, invoking the diction of narrative, the epochal distance of legend, of myth, of ruin.[5] When the phrase returns at m. 295 in a quiescent envoi to the movement, finally sounding the very first tonic triad in root position, its slight transformation edges a bit closer to Beethoven's tune. Against all arguments to the contrary, we are met with the fraught topic of allusion: fraught, because the claims of allusion carry with it a responsibility to establish the evidentiary grounds, circumstantial as they may be, in support of the plausibility of intent.

It would be deeply affecting to believe that in this auspicious work, conceived at the outset to honor the memory of Beethoven, Schumann would insinuate into its thematic fabric what is in many ways Beethoven's most intimate expression of the absent lover: here is not the heroic Beethoven, neither the *Mensch* of high moral purpose nor the composer pushing the envelope of technique, of formal exploration, but this other Beethoven, the wistful singer of love unconsummated. To hold such a view would, however, impede the complex course of thematic unfolding true to the self-referential narrative of Schumann's music. Must we then put

---

5. Nicholas Marston, "'Im Legendenton': Schumann's 'Unsung Voice,'" in *19th-Century Music* 16, no. 3 (1993): 227–41, esp. 234.

out of mind the allusive scent of Beethoven's cycle? We can't, of course. Even if we adamantly believe it to play no role in the text of the *Fantasie*, we are confronted with the classic conundrum: the purity of the work as autonomous structure defended against this permeable music alive in the shifting contexts of historical discourse. In the end, these two conditions are forever in conflict, the meanings of the work lodged uncomfortably in their midst.

There is a bit more to this story. When the engraver's copy of the *Fantasie*, now at the Széchényi National Library in Budapest, was studied by Alan Walker for an essay published in 1979, he revealed that at this late stage, the closing bars of the third movement displayed a recurrence (with slight but telling differences) of those allusive closing bars of the first movement—a memory of them, now made the capstone of the work.[6] But before publication of the work by Breitkopf & Härtel in 1839, Schumann replaced this ending with the one that everyone knows, the music expiring without thematic incident.[7] Here, once again, is the familiar dilemma: how to acknowledge the authenticity of the two versions, granting to each its own sense of an ending (to paraphrase Frank Kermode); how finally to come to terms with the consequences of their contradictions, without betraying the confidence of a version that Schumann would in the end have preferred to keep to himself.

In a sense, it is this play of the one against the other that drives the plot lines of the topics in earlier chapters: the implicit narrative structure of an original Hölty group against Schubert's later impulse to redistribute a few of its songs into different contexts; the remarkable inquiry of A. B. Marx into the poetic idea of Goethe's *Meeres Stille* and the intrusion of music— Beethoven's music and, by extension, Schubert's—into its meaning; the discomfiting alliance between the extreme magnitude of the *große Fuge* and the blithe Allegro that replaced it as the finale of Beethoven's op. 130. But in the Schumann *Fantasie*, the topic is removed to another sphere, the space narrowed between the musically absolute and the historically allusive: this is the Romantic condition.

Positing the Schumann *Fantasie* here in the final pages of a book on

6. Walker's essay is "Schumann, Liszt and the C Major Fantasie, Op. 17: A Declining Relationship," in *Music & Letters* 60 (1979): 156–65. The original ending was given as a footnote in the Henle edition edited by Wolfgang Boetticher in 1987, and then withdrawn in a more recent Henle edition (as defended at the Henle website) on the grounds that this earlier version, rejected by the composer, is consequently without textual authority!

7. This, however, has not discouraged some pianists from preferring this newly discovered original ending to the published version, only complicating the significance of the putative allusion to Beethoven's cycle.

Schubert and Beethoven may seem quixotic.[8] No other work, I'd like to think, so eloquently establishes the profound and complex program of the composer determined to reset the compass in the few years following the departure from the stage of these two sovereign figures. Schumann's music, issuing its bold Romantic challenge, still resonates with its immediate past. Of the influence, variously construed, flowing from the music of Beethoven and Schubert in the course of the long nineteenth century, there will be no end. The Schumann *Fantasie* invites us to relive that indelible moment when their final music, still new, had yet to be absorbed into the mythologies of a cultural history.

8. No sooner had I written these few lines than I happened upon the closing pages of Charles Rosen's *The Classical Style*, an "epilogue" that takes its gambit from the Schumann Fantasy and the final song in Beethoven's cycle: "clearly quoted at the very end of the first movement," writes Rosen (451). Surely I had read Rosen's chapter soon after its publication in 1971—some fifty years ago!—and its ideas no doubt lodged somewhere in my subconscious. In any case, these pages of mine are in no sense meant as a corrective to Rosen's, unique and inspiring as they remain.

Acknowledgments

The incipient ideas from which this book took shape were cultivated in a casting about toward a topic for a keynote address to be delivered at the meeting of the Biennial Conference on Nineteenth-Century Music at Toronto in 2014. Eventually, focus sharpened on the year 1815 in Vienna, and on two of its citizens at very different stages in their careers, each absorbed in the distant poetry of the Enlightenment: Schubert, exploring the *empfindsame* lyrics of Ludwig Hölty, and Beethoven, probing Johann Gottfried Herder's *Nachdichtungen* of the thirteenth-century Persian poet Sadi and the sixteenth-century Turkish poet Mesihi. My gratitude to the conference committee for tendering the invitation, to Sherry Lee for her guidance, and to Mary Ann Smart for her gracious words of introduction and her penetrating comments at the end. A colloquium in 2017 at the University of Michigan, for its music theorists, provided the opportunity to develop in greater depth the ideas that became chapter 1.

At the invitation of Alan Gosman and Julia Ronge, I delivered a talk on the Largo that precedes the fugal finale of the Sonata in B♭ Major, op. 106, for the conference *Beethoven-Perspektiven* at the Beethoven-Haus in Bonn in celebration of the Beethoven year 2020. In a much-expanded revision, this is now chapter 5. Since Beethoven's lifelong pursuit of fugue would figure as well in chapters 6 and 8, it seemed to me that an earlier essay of mine, "*Gradus ad Parnassum*: Beethoven, Schubert, and the Romance of Counterpoint" (*19th-Century Music* 11, no. 2, 1987), now revised and updated as chapter 4, would serve well to inaugurate that line of inquiry. It was Walter Frisch who invited me to contribute something to that special issue of the journal—*Preparations*, it was called—and then applied his astute editorial judgment in making it a better piece. The officers of the University of California Press graciously endorsed its republication here.

When it became clear that this would be a book about Beethoven and Schubert, more about the ironies of their careers as they evolved from that moment in 1815, it was obvious to me that an earlier essay on Schubert's grand Sonata in G Major, op. 78, with its exploration of a strain of poetic diction lodged in its expansive narrative, would be central to one line of argument. That essay grew from a plenary talk at the conference "Thanatos as Muse? Schubert and Concepts of Late Style" at the National University of Ireland, Maynooth, in 2011. Lorraine Byrne Bodley lent her gracious support and enthusiasm for this project and saw it through its original publication in *Schubert's Late Music: History, Theory, Style* (2016). My thanks to the directors of Cambridge University Press for granting permission to republish that essay, now chapter 7.

The hermeneutics of late style, as it goes in the title of that study, would assume increasing significance in the final chapters. The pursuit, early in chapter 8, of those two riddling bars that initiate the Lento assai of op. 135 was an idea inspired by a symposium in 2019, On Beethoven's String Quartet in F Major, op. 135, sponsored by the Boston University Center for Beethoven Research. Passages in my formal response to a stimulating presentation by Christopher Reynolds found their way into the argument of chapter 8, and I am indebted to Chris for provoking these thoughts, and to Jeremy Yudkin for the invitation to offer them.

It was again Walter Frisch who invited what became the review-essay "Posthumous Schubert" (*19th-Century Music* 14, no. 2, 1990), and again, my thanks go to the University of California Press for permission to run it here, where it has been revised to serve as a chapter in this study—a closing chapter, fittingly, for during those twenty-some months following upon Beethoven's death, his latest music, both in its ghostly echoes from the ruins of Enlightenment and in those wondrous breaches into what must have seemed a new language, continued to play into Schubert's consciousness, entering subliminally into the conception of these final works.

As always in such endeavors, the scholarly adventure profits from exchanges with colleagues and the curators of archives and research centers. Of these many such encounters, I think here of Robin Wallace, who graciously shared with me the texts of his translations of reviews that would ultimately appear in his *The Critical Reception of Beethoven's Compositions by His German Contemporaries, Op. 112 to Op. 122*; of Darwin Scott, who furnished digital images of the Scheide manuscripts at the Princeton University Library before they were promoted to its website; of Walburga Litschauer, who provided prompt and helpful answers to my questions regarding the recent peregrinations of several Schubert manuscripts; of Jens Dufner, at the Beethoven-Archiv at Bonn, and Federica Rovelli, at the Università di Pavia, who lent their expertise in reading Beethoven's often indecipherable sketch hand. Kristina Muxfeldt's thoughtful responses to my frustrations with the proper translation of a few passages in A. B. Marx deserve to be published. Otto Biba welcomed, as always, my scrutiny of the Beethoven and Schubert autographs at the archives of the Gesellschaft der Musikfreunde in Vienna, of which he was then its formidable director. Thanks, too, to the curators of the Stefan Zweig collection at the British Library and the William Scheide Library housed at the Firestone Library at Princeton University for their prompt responses to my inquiries.

Marta Tonegutti, whose bold and innovative list for the University of Chicago Press must be the envy of her peers, once again took on the challenges of these idiosyncratic reflections of mine. For her unwavering support and keen criticism in the course of publication, I shall be forever in her debt. Dylan Montanari, at the press, kept me on track in the complicated preparation of the book, solving all those mysteries of the digital text that are beyond my ken. Chris Kayler and Matthew Cron prepared the complex music examples with consummate artistic skill. Georg Burgstaller prepared the index expertly.

Finally, I must thank the directors of the University of Rochester Press for agreeing to the publication here, as chapter 6, of my contribution to *The New Beethoven: Evolution, Analysis, Interpretation* (2020). Though its title does not say so, that volume, edited by Jeremy Yudkin, was conceived in appreciation of the magisterial scholarly work of Lewis Lockwood, in homage no less to the man himself, whose humane presence hovers everywhere across its pages. It is a presence that I have sensed deeply in the course of my own writing over these many years, inspired at the outset in a now legendary seminar on the Beethoven sketches at Princeton in 1965, its bold agenda coupling a rigorous engagement with the music and its sources together with piercing insights into historical context and biography. For this rich legacy, for an enduring friendship, this book is offered in humble gratitude.

Tables, Examples, and Figures

Tables

Table 1.1 — Schubert autographs of Hölty settings. 5

Table 2.1 — Beethoven's copies from Herder, *Blumenlese.* 46

Examples

Ex. 1.1 — Schubert, *An die Nachtigall* (Hölty, rev. Voss), D 196. 6–7

Ex. 1.2 — Schubert, *Auf den Tod einer Nachtigall* (Hölty, rev. Voss), D 201. Fragment. 9

Ex. 1.3 — Schubert, Sonata in F♯ Minor (July 1817), D 571. Fragment. 11

Ex. 1.4 — Schubert, *An die Apfelbäume, wo ich Julien erblickte* (Hölty), D 197. 13–15

Ex. 1.5 — Schubert, *Seufzer* (Hölty, rev. Voss), D 198. 17–18

Ex. 1.6A — Schubert, *An den Mond* (Hölty), D 193. 20–21

Ex. 1.6B — Schubert, *Die Nonne* (Hölty), D 208. From the autograph of 29 May 1815. 22–23

Ex. 1.7A — Schubert, *Die Nonne,* D 208. From the fragmentary autography of 29 May. 23

Ex. 1.7B — Schubert, *Die Nonne,* D 208. From the autograph of the revision of 16 June. 24

Ex. 1.8 — Schubert, from the final bars of *Der Liebende* (Hölty), D 207; and the opening bars of *Die Nonne* (16 June). 25

Ex. 1.9 — Schubert, the Hölty settings of May/June 1815 in a synoptic sketch. 26

Ex. 2.1 — Beethoven, *Die laute Klage* (Herder), WoO 135. 38–40

Ex. 2.2 — Beethoven, *Die laute Klage,* from the composing draft. 41

Ex. 2.3 — Beethoven, *Der Gesang der Nachtigall* (Herder), WoO 141. 42–43

Ex. 3.1A — Schubert, *Meeres Stille* (Goethe). Earlier version, 20 June 1815, D 215A. 51

228   TABLES, EXAMPLES, AND FIGURES

Ex. 3.1B   Schubert, *Meeres Stille* (Goethe). Published version (op. 3, no. 2), 21 June 1815, D 216.   52

Ex. 3.2   Beethoven, *Meeres Stille [und Glückliche Fahrt]* (Goethe), op. 112, mm. 23–34, in short score, winds and brass omitted.   58

Ex. 4.1   Beethoven, exercise for Albrechtsberger, fourth species, "freie Satz."   80

Ex. 4.2   Beethoven, String Quartet in E♭, op. 74, first movement.   84

Ex. 4.3   Beethoven, String Quartet in E♭, op. 74, first movement.   84

Ex. 4.4   Schubert, *Mirjams Siegesgesang*, D 942, from the final strophe.   87

Ex. 4.5   Beethoven, *Große Fuge*, op. 133, mm. 609–20.   94

Ex. 5.1   Beethoven, sketches for the "alla fuga" in op. 35. Wielhorsky Sketchbook, p. 32; transcription in Fishman, ed. (Moscow, 1962).   99

Ex. 5.2   Beethoven, Piano Sonata in B♭, op. 106, Allegro risoluto. Subject in retrograde, at m. 153.   101

Ex. 5.3A   Beethoven, Piano Sonata in B♭, op. 106. Final bars of the Adagio sostenuto.   103

Ex. 5.3B   Beethoven, Piano Sonata in B♭, op. 106. Largo; and opening bars of the Allegro risoluto and subject of the Fuga.   104–5

Ex. 5.3C   Beethoven, Piano Sonata in B♭, op. 106. From Allegro risoluto, the new episode in G♭ major, at m. 75.   106

Ex. 5.3D   Beethoven, Piano Sonata in B♭, op. 106. From Allegro risoluto, subject in retrograde, at m. 153.   106

Ex. 5.4   Beethoven, sketches for Largo, op. 106, in Scheide ms. 132, fol. 4v → 3r. Princeton University Library.   110

Ex. 5.5   J. S. Bach, *Well-Tempered Clavier* II, from the Fugue in C♯ Minor.   115

Ex. 6.1   Beethoven, Sonata in D Major for Piano and Violoncello, op. 102, no. 2, first movement, mm. 1–7.   122

Ex. 6.2   Beethoven, Sonata in D Major for Piano and Violoncello, op. 102, no. 2, first movement, mm. 88–95.   123

Ex. 6.3   Beethoven, entry in the Scheide Sketchbook, p. 37.   127

Ex. 6.4A   Beethoven, Sonata in D Major for Piano and Violoncello, op. 102, no 2, third movement, mm. 5–10.   131

Ex. 6.4B   Beethoven, Sonata in D Major for Piano and Violoncello, op. 102, no 2, third movement, mm. 143–50.   131

Ex. 6.4C   Handel, *Messiah*, from the chorus "And with His Stripes."   131

Ex. 6.5   Beethoven, Sonata in D Major, op. 102, no. 2, first movement, showing the opening cello arpeggiation and the octave at m. 5, and the transformation of these motives at mm. 92–93.   134

Ex. 7.1   Schubert, String Quintet in C, D 956 (op. post. 163), first movement, beginning of development, mm. 155–72.   138

Ex. 7.2   Schubert, Piano Sonata in G, D 894 (op. 78), first movement, mm. 1–17.   141

Ex. 7.3   Schubert, *Schwestergruß* (Bruchmann), D 762, mm. 1–17.   146–47

Ex. 7.4   Schubert, *Schwestergruß*, D 762, mm. 55–63, 74–79.   148–49

TABLES, EXAMPLES, AND FIGURES 229

Ex. 7.5   Schubert, Piano Sonata in G, D 894 (op. 78), first movement, mm. 65–76. 150

Ex. 7.6   Schubert, Piano Sonata in G, D 894 (op. 78), first movement, mm. 87–96. 151

Ex. 7.7   Schubert, Piano Sonata in G, D 894 (op. 78), third movement, Trio. 153

Ex. 7.8   Schubert, *Am Flusse*, D 766, mm. 1–11. 157

Ex. 8.1   Beethoven, String Quartet in C♯ Minor, op. 131, from the close of the first movement to the opening of the second. 166

Ex. 8.2A   Beethoven, String Quartet in C♯ Minor, op. 131, final bars of the sixth movement and opening of the seventh. 168

Ex. 8.2B   Beethoven, String Quartet in C♯ Minor, op. 131. Entry, ca. 20 June 1826, in *Konversationshefte* 9, p. 315. 169

Ex. 8.3A   Beethoven, String Quartet in F Major, op. 135, third movement, opening theme, mm. 1–14. 172

Ex. 8.3B   Beethoven, String Quartet in F Major, op. 135, third movement: variation in C♯ minor, from m. 26, and return to D♭ major at m. 32. 173

Ex. 8.4   Beethoven, String Quartet in F Major, op. 135, third movement, m. 32, as in the autograph score. 175

Ex. 8.5   Beethoven, String Quartet in F Major, op. 135, first movement, mm. 1–7 and mm. 99–103. 181

Ex. 9.1   Schubert, Sonata in B♭ Major, D 960, first movement. Draft for the coda at its opening bars. 194

Ex. 9.2   Schubert, Sonata in B♭ Major, D 960, first movement. Draft for end of exposition. 194

Ex. 9.3   Schubert, Sonata in B♭ Major, D 960, first movement, mm. 113–18b, final version. 197

Ex. 9.4   Schubert, *Der Graf von Gleichen*, act 1, sc. 2. Draft, fol. 5r. 202

Ex. 9.5   Schubert, *Der Graf von Gleichen*, act 1, sc. 2. 202

Ex. 9.6   Schubert, *Der Graf von Gleichen*, act 2, sc. 2. 203

Ex. 9.7   Schubert, *Der Graf von Gleichen*, act 2, sc. 3. Draft, fol. 24r. 204

Ex. 9.8A   Schubert, *Der Graf von Gleichen*, act 1, sc. 11. Draft, fol. 18r–19v. 204

Ex. 9.8B   Schubert, *Der Graf von Gleichen*, act 1, sc. 11. Draft, fol. 19v. 205

Ex. 9.9   Schubert, *Wonne der Wehmut*, D 260, closing bars, shown against the expansion for the Countess's aria, *Der Graf von Gleichen*, act 2, sc. 1. Draft, fol. 21v. 207

Ex. 9.10   Schubert, *Der Graf von Gleichen*, act 2, sc. 9. Draft, fol. 31r. 209

Ex. 9.11   Schubert, *Der Graf von Gleichen*, act 2, sc. 10. Draft, fol. 34r. 213

Ex. 9.12   Schubert, Sonata in A Major, D 959, first movement. Draft for opening phrase. 213

Figures

Frontispiece Caspar David Friedrich (1774–1840), *Two Men at the Sea*, 1817.   ii

Fig. 2.1   Beethoven's copies from Herder, *Blumen aus morgenländischen Dichtern gesammlet*.   36

Fig. 3.1   Draft in Beethoven's hand of the inscription from the *Odyssey* of Homer in the Voss translation.   64

Fig. 3.2   The inscription from Homer, on the verso of the title page of the first edition of Beethoven, *Meeres Stille und Glückliche Fahrt*, op. 112.   66

Fig. 5.1   Beethoven, sketches for Largo, op. 106.   109

Fig. 5.2   Beethoven, sketches for Largo, op. 106.   112

Fig. 5.3   Beethoven, copy of passages from J. S. Bach, *Well-Tempered Clavier* II, among sketches for op. 106 fugue.   113

Fig. 6.1   Beethoven, sketches for the Sonata in D Major, op. 102, no. 2.   126

Fig. 6.2   Beethoven, Sonata in D Major, op. 102, no. 2, autograph score, p. 16.   128

Fig. 6.3   Beethoven, Sonata in D Major, op. 102, no. 2, autograph score, p. 6.   133

Fig. 8.1   Beethoven, score draft for String Quartet in C♯ Minor, op. 131, finale.   165

Fig. 8.2   Beethoven, score draft for String Quartet in F, op. 135, third movement.   176

Fig. 8.3   Beethoven, score draft for String Quartet in F, op. 135, third movement.   178

Fig. 8.4   Beethoven, score draft for String Quartet in F, op. 135, third movement.   179

Works Cited

Documents and Bibliographies

Anderson, Emily, ed. and trans. *The Letters of Beethoven*. London: Macmillan & Co.; New York: St. Martin's Press, 1961.

Bartlitz, Eveline. *Die Beethoven-Sammlung in der Musikabteilung der Deutschen Staatsbibliothek; Verzeichnis*. Berlin: Deutsche Staatsbibliothek, 1970.

Beethoven, Ludwig van. *Briefwechsel Gesamtausgabe*. 7 vols. Edited by Sieghard Brandenburg. Munich: G. Henle, 1996–1998.

———. *Ludwig van Beethovens Konversationshefte*, 11 vols. Edited by Karl-Heinz Köhler, Grita Herre, Dagmar Beck, and Günter Brosche. Leipzig: Deutscher Verlag für Musik, 1968–2001.

Biba, Otto. *Franz Schubert und seine Zeit*. Catalogue of an exhibition at the Gesellschaft der Musikfreunde in 1978. Vienna: Gesellschaft der Musikfreunde in Wien, 1978.

Braubach, Max. *Die Stammbücher Beethovens und der Babette Koch*. Bonn: Verlag des Beethovenhauses, 1970.

Deutsch, Otto Erich. *Franz Schubert. Die Dokumente seines Lebens*. Kassel: Bärenreiter, 1964; rev. Wiesbaden: Breitkopf & Härtel, 1996.

———. *Franz Schubert: Thematisches Verzeichnis seiner Werke in chronologischer Folge* (= Schubert: *Neue Ausgabe sämtlicher Werke*, VIII/4). Kassel: Bärenreiter, 1978.

———. *Schubert: Die Erinnerungen seiner Freunde*. Leipzig: Breitkopf & Härtel, 1957; 2nd ed., Leipzig: Breitkopf & Härtel, 1966.

———. *Schubert: Memoirs by His Friends*. Translated by Rosamond Ley and John Nowell. New York: Macmillan, 1958.

———. *The Schubert Reader: A Life of Franz Schubert in Letters and Documents*. Translated by Eric Blom. New York: W. W. Norton, 1947.

Dorfmüller, Kurt, Norbert Gertsch, and Julia Ronge. *Ludwig van Beethoven: Thematisch-bibliographisches Werkverzeichnis*. Revidirte und wesentliche erweiterte Neuausgabe des Verzeichnisses von Georg Kinsky und Hans Halm. Munich: G. Henle, 2014.

Haydn, Joseph. *Gesammelte Briefe und Aufzeichnungen*. Edited by Dénes Bartha. Kassel: Bärenreiter, 1965.

WORKS CITED

Hilmar, Ernst. *Verzeichnis der Schubert Handschriften in der Musiksammlung der Wiener Stadt- und Landesbibliothek*. Kassel: Bärenreiter, 1978.

Johnson, Douglas, Alan Tyson, and Robert Winter. *The Beethoven Sketchbooks: History, Reconstruction, Inventory*. Edited by Douglas Johnson. Berkeley: University of California Press, 1985.

Kinsky, Georg. *Manuskripte, Briefe, Dokumente von Scarlatti bis Stravinsky: Katalog der Musikautographen-Sammlung Louis Koch*. Stuttgart: Hoffmannsche Buchdruckerei Felix Krais, 1953.

———. *Das Werk Beethovens: Thematisch-bibliographisches Verzeichnis seiner sämtlichen vollendeten Kompositionen*, completed and edited by Hans Halm. Munich: G. Henle, 1955.

———. "Zur Versteigerung von Beethovens musikalischem Nachlaß." *Neues Beethoven-Jahrbuch* 6 (1935), 66–86.

Klein, Hans-Günter. *Ludwig van Beethoven. Autographe und Abschriften. Katalog*. Staatsbibliothek Preussischer Kulturbesitz, Kataloge der Musikabteilung, edited by Rudolf Elvers; Erste Reihe: Handschriften, vol. 2. Berlin: Merseburger, 1975.

Leitzmann, Albert. *Ludwig van Beethoven: Berichte der Zeitgenossen, Briefe und persönliche Aufzeichnungen*. Leipzig: Insel, 1921.

MacArdle, Donald W., and Ludwig Misch, eds. and trans. *New Beethoven Letters*. Norman: University of Oklahoma Press, 1957.

Mandyczewski, Eusebius, ed. *Zusatz-Band der K. K. Gesellschaft der Musikfreunde in Wien*. Sammlungen und Statuten. Vienna: by the Board of Directors of the K. K. Gesellschaft der Musikfreunde, 1912.

Nohl, Ludwig. *Briefe Beethovens*. Stuttgart: Cotta, 1865.

Schmidt, Hans. "Verzeichnis der Skizzen Beethovens." *Beethoven-Jahrbuch* 6 (1969), 7–128.

Searle, Arthur. *The British Library Stefan Zweig Collection: Catalogue of the Music Manuscripts*. London: British Library, 1999.

Sotheby's. *Continental Books, Manuscripts and Music*. London, 22 and 23 November 1984.

Strunk, Oliver. *Source Readings in Music History*, rev. ed. Edited by Leo Treitler. New York: W. W. Norton, 1998.

Tyson, Alan. *The Authentic English Editions of Beethoven*. London: Faber and Faber, 1963.

Primary Texts and Original Sources

Albrechtsberger, Johann Georg. *Gründliche Anweisung zur Composition*. Leipzig: Johann Gottlob Immanuel Breitkopf, 1790.

Benjamin, Walter. *The Correspondence of Walter Benjamin, 1910–1940*. Edited and annotated by Gershom Scholem and Theodor W. Adorno, translated by Manfred R. Jacobson and Evelyn M. Jacobson. Chicago: University of Chicago Press, 1994.

Breuning, Gerhard von. *Memories of Beethoven: From the House of the Black-Robed Spaniards*. Edited by Maynard Solomon. Translated by Henry Mins and Maynard Solomon. Cambridge: Cambridge University Press, 1992.

Burney, Charles. *A General History of Music*. London: Printed for the author, 1776, 2nd ed. 1789. Newly published with critical and historical notes by Frank Mercer, 2 vols. London, 1935. Reprint, New York: Dover Publications, 1957.

Cramer, Carl Friedrich. *Magazin der Musik*. 2 vols. Hamburg: in der Musicalischen Niederlage, 1783–1786. Reprint, Hildesheim: Georg Olms, 1971.

Chrysander, Friedrich. *Jahrbücher für musikalische Wissenschaft*, I. Leipzig, 1863.

WORKS CITED   233

Forkel, Johann Nikolaus. *Allgemeine Geschichte der Musik*. Leipzig: Schwickert, 1788. Reprint edited by Othmar Wessely, Graz: Akademische Druck- u. Verlagsanstalt, 1967.

Fux, Johann Joseph. *Gradus ad Parnassum*. In Fux, *Sämtliche Werke*, VII/1. Kassel: Bärenreiter, 1967.

———. *Gradus ad Parnassum, oder Anführung zur Regelmäßigen Musikalischen Composition*. Translated from Latin to German by Lorenz Christoph Mizler. Leipzig: Mizlerischen Bücherverlag, 1742. Reprint, Hildesheim: Georg Olms, 1974.

———. *The Study of Counterpoint: From Johann Joseph Fux's* Gradus ad Parnassum. Translated and edited by Alfred Mann. New York: W. W. Norton, rev. ed. 1965.

Goethe, Johann Wolfgang. *Werke. Hamburger Ausgabe in 14 Bänden*. Band 1: Gedichte und Epen 1. Edited by Erich Trunz. Munich: C. H. Beck, 1981.

Grillparzer, Franz. *Sämtliche Werke: Ausgewählte Briefe, Gespräche, Berichte*, I. Edited by Peter Frank and Karl Pörnbacher. Munich: Carl Hanser, 1960.

Heine, Heinrich. *Werke*, I. Edited by Stuart Atkins. Munich: C. H. Beck, 1973.

Herder, Johann Gottfried. *Sämtliche Werke*, edited by Bernhard Suphan, vol. 26, Poetische Werke 2, edited by Carl Redlich. Berlin: Weidmann, 1882. Reprint, Hildesheim: Georg Olms, 1968.

Hoffmann, E. T. A. *Schriften zur Musik. Nachlese*. Edited and annotated by Friedrich Schnapp. Munich: Winkler, 1963.

———. *Die Serapions-Brüder: Gesammelte Erzählung und Märchen* (1819). Reprint, with a *Nachwort* by Walter Müller-Seidel and notes by Wulf Segebrecht. Munich: Winkler, 1963.

Hölty, Ludwig Christoph Heinrich. *Gedichte von Ludewig Heinrich Christoph Hölty. Nebst Briefen des Dichters*. Edited by Karl Halm. Leipzig: F. A. Brockhaus, 1869.

———. *Gesammelte Werke und Briefe*. Kritische Studienausgabe. Edited by Walter Hettche. Göttingen: Wallstein, 2nd ed., 2008.

———. *Werke und Briefe*. Edited by Uwe Berger. Berlin: Aufbau, 1966.

Homer. *Homers Odüßee*. Translated into German by Johann Heinrich Voß. Hamburg: auf Kosten des Verfassers [at the author's expense], 1781.

———. *The Odyssey*. Translated by Robert Fagles, introduction and notes by Bernard Knox. New York: Penguin Books [Viking Penguin], 1996.

———. *The Odyssey*. Translated by A. T. Murray. Loeb Classical Library. Cambridge, MA: Harvard University Press; London: William Heinemann Ltd., 1919.

Kirnberger, Johann Philipp. *Gedanken über die verschiedenen Lehrarten in der Komposition, als Vorbereitung zur Fugenkenntniß*. Berlin: Georg Jacob Decker, 1782. Reprint, Hildesheim: Georg Olms, 1974.

———. *Die Kunst des reinen Satzes in der Musik*. Berlin: Voss, 1771; Berlin: Decker and Hartung, 1774–1776. Reprint, Hildesheim: Georg Olms, 1968. English as *The Art of Strict Musical Composition*, translated by David Beach and Jürgen Thym. New Haven, CT: Yale University Press, 1982.

Koch, Heinrich Christoph. *Musikalisches Lexikon*. Frankfurt am Main: August Hermann, 1802. Reprint, Hildesheim: Georg Olms, 1985.

Kunze, Stefan, ed. *Ludwig van Beethoven: Die Werke im Spiegel seiner Zeit. Gesammelte Konzertberichte und Rezensionen bis 1830*. Laaber: Laaber, 1987.

Mann, Alfred. "Haydn's Elementarbuch: A Document of Classic Counterpoint Instruction." *Music Forum* 3 (1973), 197–237.

Marpurg, Friedrich Wilhelm. *Abhandlung von der Fuge*. 2 vols. Berlin: Haude, Spener, und der Academie der Wissenschaften Buchhändler, 1753–1754. Reprint, Hildesheim: Georg Olms, 1970.

Schenker, Heinrich. *Ein Beitrag zur Ornamentik als Einführung zu Ph. Em. Bachs Klavierwerken.* Vienna: Universal Edition, newly revised and enlarged ed., 1908. English as "A Contribution to the Study of Ornamentation," translated by Hedi Siegel (based on a preliminary draft by Carl Parrish), in *The Music Forum* 4: 1–140. New York: Columbia University Press, 1976.

———. *Counterpoint: A Translation of* Kontrapunkt *by Heinrich Schenker.* Translated by John Rothgeb and Jürgen Thym, edited by John Rothgeb. New York: Schirmer Books, 1987.

———. *Der freie Satz.* Edited by Oswald Jonas. Vienna: Universal-Edition, 1935, rev. 1956. English as *Free Composition (Der freie Satz).* Translated and edited by Ernst Oster. New York: Longman, in cooperation with the American Musicological Society, 1979.

Schumann, Robert. *Gesammelte Schriften über Musik und Musiker.* Edited by Martin Kreisig. Leipzig: Breitkopf & Härtel, 1914. Reprint, Westmead, Hampshire: Gregg International, 1969.

Solomon, Maynard. "Beethoven's Tagebuch of 1812–1818." In *Beethoven Studies 3,* ed. Alan Tyson, 193–288. Cambridge: Cambridge University Press, 1982.

———. *Beethovens Tagebuch.* Edited by Sieghard Brandenburg. Mainz: v. Hase & Koehler, 1990.

Sulzer, Johann Georg. *Allgemeine Theorie der schönen Künste.* Leipzig: M. G. Weidmanns Erben und Reich, 1771–1774. Neue vermehrte zweite Auflage. 4 vols. Leipzig: Weidmann, 1792–1794; reprint, Hildesheim: Georg Olms, 1967–1970.

Truffaut, François. *Jules et Jim: A Film by François Truffaut.* Translated by Nicholas Fry. New York: Simon and Schuster, 1968.

Wackenroder, Wilhelm Heinrich. *Herzensergiessungen eines kunstliebenden Klosterbruders.* Berlin: Johann Friedrich Unger, 1797. Translation in Oliver Strunk, *Source Readings in Music History,* rev. ed. (1998), 1061–72.

Wallace, Robin, ed. and trans. *The Critical Reception of Beethoven's Compositions by His German Contemporaries, Op. 126 to WoO 140* (2018); *The same: Op. 112 to Op. 122* (2020). Online at the Center for Beethoven Research, Boston University.

Weber, Carl Maria von. *Writings on Music.* Edited by John Warrack; translated by Martin Cooper. Cambridge: Cambridge University Press, 1981.

Studies

Abbate, Carolyn. *Unsung Voices.* Princeton, NJ: Princeton University Press, 1991.

Adorno, Theodor W. *Beethoven: Philosophie der Musik.* Edited by Rolf Tiedemann. Frankfurt am Main: Suhrkamp, 1993. English as *Beethoven: The Philosophy of Music. Fragments and Texts.* Edited by Rolf Tiedemann, translated by Edmund Jephcott. Stanford, CA: Stanford University Press, 1998.

———. "Schubert." In *Moments musicaux* (Frankfurt am Main: Suhrkamp, 1964), 18–36. English as "Schubert (1928)," trans. Jonathan Dunsby and Beate Perrey, in *19th-Century Music* 29, no. 1 (2005): 3–14.

Becker, Katrin. *"Die Welt entzwei gerissen": Heinrich Heines Publizistik der 1830er Jahre und der deutsch-französische Kulturtransfer.* Inaugural dissertation, Albert-Ludwigs-Universität Freiburg, 2008.

Beethoven: Interpretationen seiner Werke. Edited by Albrecht Riethmüller, Carl Dahlhaus, and Alexander L. Ringer. Laaber: Laaber, 1994.

Beghin, Tom. "Beethoven's *Hammerklavier* Sonata, Opus 106: Legend, Difficulty, and the Gift of a Broadwood Piano." *Keyboard Perspectives* 7 (2014): 81–121.

Benjamin, Walter. *Illuminations*. Edited by Hannah Arendt. Translated by Harry Zohn. New York: Schocken Books, 1969.

————. "The Ruin." In *The Work of Art in the Age of Its Technological Reproducibility and Other Writings on Media*, edited by Michael W. Jennings, Brigid Doherty, and Thomas Y. Levin; translated by Edmund Jephcott, Rodney Livingstone, Howard Eiland, et al., 180–86. Cambridge, MA: Belknap, 2008.

Bloom, Harold. *The Anxiety of Influence: A Theory of Poetry*, 2nd ed. New York: Oxford University Press, 1997.

Bockholdt, Rudolf. "Der letzte Satz von Beethovens letzter Violoncellosonate, op. 102 Nr. 2." In *Beethovens Werke für Klavier und Violoncello. Bericht über die Internationale Fachkonferenz Bonn, 18–20. Juni 1998*, edited by Sieghard Brandenburg, Ingeborg Maas, and Wolfgang Osthoff, 265–82. Bonn: Verlag Beethoven-Haus Bonn, 2004.

Brendel, Alfred. "Schubert's Last Sonatas." *New York Review of Books*, 2 February 1989, revised and expanded in Brendel, *Music Sounded Out: Essays, Lectures, Interviews, Afterthoughts*, 72–141. New York: Farrar, Straus & Giroux, 1990.

Brenneis, Clemens. "Das Fischhof-Manuskript: Zur Frühgeschichte der Beethoven-Biographik." In *Zu Beethoven: Aufsätze und Annotationen* 1, edited by Harry Goldschmidt, 90–116. Berlin: Verlag Neue Musik, 1979.

Brown, Maurice J. E. *The New Grove Schubert*. Work-List Eric Sams. New York: W. W. Norton, 1983.

————. "Schuberts Fuge in E moll." *Oesterreichische Musikzeitschrift* 23 (1968): 65–70.

Chae, Lana. "Beethoven's Sketches for the Piano Sonata Opus 106, Hammerklavier: The Sketching of a Performance." Unpublished DMA dissertation, University of California, Los Angeles, 2014.

Cohen, Roger. "The Violent World of Elena Ferrante." *New York Review of Books* 63, no. 9 (May 26, 2016): 51.

Cone, Edward T. "Schubert's Beethoven." *Musical Quarterly* 56 (1970): 779–93. Reprint in *The Creative World of Beethoven*, ed. Paul Henry Lang, 277–91. New York: W. W. Norton, 1971.

Cook, Nicholas. "The Other Beethoven: Heroism, the Canon, and the Works of 1813–14." *19th-Century Music* 27 (2003): 3–24.

Cooper, Barry. "The Autograph Score of the Slow Movement of Beethoven's Last Quartet, Opus 135." In *The New Beethoven: Evolution, Analysis, Interpretation*, edited by Jeremy Yudkin, 332–54. Rochester: University of Rochester Press, 2020.

————. *Beethoven's Folksong Settings: Chronology, Sources, Style*. Oxford: Clarendon Press [Oxford University Press], 1994.

Dahlhaus, Carl. "'Von zwei Kulturen der Musik': Die Schlußfuge aus Beethovens Cellosonate opus 102, 2." *Die Musikforschung* 31 (1978): 397–405.

Deutsch, Otto Erich. "Beethovens Goethe-Kompositionen." In *Jahrbuch der Sammlung Kippenberg* 8 (1930): 102–33.

Doflein, Erich. "Historismus in der Musik." In *Die Ausbreitung des Historismus über die Musik*, edited by Walter Wiora, 9–39. Regensburg: Gustav Bosse, 1969.

Dufner, Jens. "Ludwig van Beethoven, Zwei Sonaten für Klavier und Violoncello op. 102,

Überprüfte Abschriften." In *Auf den Spuren Beethovens: Hans Conrad Bodmer und seine Sammlung,* edited by Nicole Kämpken and Michael Ladenburger, 188–92. Bonn: Verlag Beethoven-Haus Bonn, 2006.

Dürr, Walther. "Franz Schuberts Wanderjahre." In *Franz Schubert. Jahre der Krise 1818–1823,* edited by Werner Aderhold, Walther Dürr, and Walburga Litschauer, 11–21. Kassel: Bärenreiter, 1985.

Ehrenbaum, Dominique. Con alcune licenze: *Die Instrumentalfuge in Spätwerk Ludwig van Beethovens.* Bonn: Verlag Beethoven-Haus Bonn, 2013.

Federhofer, Helmut. *Heinrich Schenker: Nach Tagebüchern und Briefen in der Oswald Jonas Memorial Collection.* Hildesheim: Georg Olms, 1985.

Feil, Arnold. *Franz Schubert: Die schöne Müllerin. Die Winterreise.* Stuttgart: Philipp Reclam, 1975. English translation by Ann C. Sherwin. Portland, OR: Amadeus Press, 1988.

Ferrante, Elena. *Frantumaglia: A Writer's Journey,* translated by Ann Goldstein. New York: Europa Editions, 2016.

Feuerzeig, Lisa. "Elusive Intimacy in Schubert's Last Opera, *Der Graf von Gleichen.*" In *Rethinking Schubert,* edited by Lorraine Byrne Bodley and Julian Horton, 333–54. Oxford: Oxford University Press, 2016.

Fischer, Kurt von. "Bemerkungen zu Schuberts As-dur-Messe." In *Franz Schubert: Jahre der Krise. 1818–1823,* edited by Werner Aderhold, Walther Dürr, and Walburga Litschauer, 121–28. Kassel: Bärenreiter, 1985.

Friedlaender, Max. *Das deutsche Lied im 18. Jahrhundert.* Stuttgart: J. G. Cotta, 1902. Reprint, Hildesheim: Georg Olms, 1962.

Frimmel, Theodor von. *Beethoven-Studien II: Bausteine zu einer Lebensgeschichte des Meisters.* Munich: Georg Müller, 1906.

Genette, Gérard. *Narrative Discourse: An Essay in Method,* trans. Jane E. Lewin. Ithaca, NY: Cornell University Press, 1980.

Gertsch, Norbert. "Ludwig van Beethovens 'Hammerklavier'-Sonate op. 106: Bemerkungen zur Datierung und Bewertung der Quellen." *Bonner Beethoven-Studien* 2 (2001): 63–93.

Gibbs, Christopher H. "Introduction: The Elusive Schubert." In *The Cambridge Companion to Schubert,* edited by Christopher Gibbs, 1–11. Cambridge: Cambridge University Press, 1997.

Golz, Jochen, and Michael Ladenburger, eds. *Beethoven und Goethe:* "meine Harmonie mit der Ihrigen verbunden." An exhibition catalogue. Bonn: Beethoven-Haus; Weimar: Stiftung Weimarer Klassik, 1999.

Gülke, Peter. "Neue Beiträge zur Kenntnis des Sinfonikers Schubert: Die Fragmente D 615, D 708A und D 936A." In *Musik-Konzepte. Sonderband Franz Schubert,* 187–220. Edited by Heinz-Klaus Metzger and Rainer Riehn. Munich: Edition Text + kritik, 1979.

———. "Zum Bilde des späten Schubert." In *Musik-Konzepte. Sonderband Franz Schubert,* 107–66.

Härtl, Heinz, ed. *"Die Wahlverwandtschaften": Eine Dokumentation der Wirkung von Goethes Roman, 1808–1832.* Weinheim: Acta humaniora / Berlin (DDR): Akademie-Verlag, 1983. Reprint, Göttingen: Wallstein, 2013.

Hecker, Jutta. *Das Symbol der Blauen Blume im Zusammenhang mit der Blumensymbolik der Romantik.* Jena: Frommann,1931.

Hertzmann, Erich. "The Newly Discovered Autograph of Beethoven's 'Rondo a capriccio,' op. 129." *Musical Quarterly* 32 (1946): 171–95.

Hoorickx, P. Reinhard van. "Two Essays on Schubert." *Revue Belge de Musicologie* 24 (1970), 81–95.

Hyland, Anne, and Walburga Litschauer. "Records of Inspiration: Schubert's Drafts for the Last Three Piano Sonatas Reappraised." In *Rethinking Schubert*, edited by Lorraine Byrne Bodley and Julian Horton, 173–206. Oxford: Oxford University Press, 2016.

Kerman, Joseph. *The Beethoven Quartets.* New York: Alfred A. Knopf, 1967.

Kier, Herfrid. *Raphael Georg Kiesewetter (1773–1850): Wegbereiter des musikalischen Historismus.* Regensburg: Gustav Bosse, 1968.

Kirkendale, Warren. *Fugue and Fugato in Rococo and Classical Chamber Music.* Rev. and expanded 2nd ed. Translated from the German edition by Margaret Bent and the author. Durham, NC: Duke University Press, 1979.

Költzsch, Hans. *Franz Schubert in seinen Klaviersonaten.* Leipzig: Breitkopf & Härtel, 1927. Reprint, Hildesheim: Georg Olms, 1976 and 2002.

Kramer, Lawrence. "Primitive Encounters: Beethoven's 'Tempest' Sonata, Musical Meaning, and Enlightenment Anthropology." *Beethoven Forum* 6 (1998): 31–65.

Kramer, Richard. "Between Cavatina and Ouverture: Opus 130 and the Voices of Narrative." *Beethoven Forum* 1 (1992): 165–89.

———. *Cherubino's Leap: In Search of the Enlightenment Moment.* Chicago: University of Chicago Press, 2016.

———. *Distant Cycles: Schubert and the Conceiving of Song.* Chicago: University of Chicago Press, 1994.

———. "In Search of Palestrina: Beethoven in the Archives." In *Haydn, Mozart, & Beethoven: Studies in the Music of the Classical Period*, 283–300. Edited by Sieghard Brandenburg. Oxford: Oxford University Press, 1998.

———. Review of *Heinrich Schenker: Selected Correspondence*, ed. Ian Bent, David Bretherton, and William Drabkin (Woodbridge, UK: Boydell Press, 2014). In *Music Theory Spectrum* 40, no. 2 (2018): 357–60.

———. *Unfinished Music.* Oxford: Oxford University Press, 2008, rev. 2012.

Kropfinger, Klaus. *Beethoven.* Kassel: Bärenreiter; Stuttgart: Metzler, 2001.

———. "Das gespaltene Werk—Beethovens Streichquartett op. 130/133." In *Beiträge zu Beethovens Kammermusik. Symposion Bonn 1984*, edited by Sieghard Brandenburg and Helmut Loos, 296–335. Munich: G. Henle, 1987.

Küthen, Hans-Werner. "*Quaerendo invenietis*. Die Exegese eines Beethoven-Briefes an Haslinger vom 5. September 1823." In *Musik, Edition, Interpretation: Gedenkschrift Günter Henle*, edited by Martin Bente, 282–313. Munich: G. Henle, 1980.

Lambert, Sterling. *Re-Reading Poetry: Schubert's Multiple Settings of Goethe.* Woodbridge, UK: Boydell Press, 2009.

Landon, Christa. "Neue Schubert-Funde: Unbekannte Manuskripte im Archiv des Wiener Männergesang-Vereines." *Oesterreichische Musikzeitschrift* 24 (1969): 299–323. Reprinted in *Christa Landon zum Gedächtnis* (Private printing by Bärenreiter, 1978), 19–43. In English as "New Schubert Finds," in *Music Review* 31 (1970): 215–31.

Lenz, Wilhelm von. *Beethoven. Eine Kunst-Studie.* Hamburg: Hoffmann & Campe, 1860.

Lockwood, Lewis. *Beethoven: The Music and the Life.* New York: W. W. Norton, 2003.

———. "Beethoven's Emergence from Crisis: The Cello Sonatas of Op. 102 (1815)." *Journal of Musicology* 16 (1998): 301–22.

Mann, Alfred. "Beethoven's Contrapuntal Studies with Haydn." *Musical Quarterly* 56 (1970): 711–26. Reprinted in *The Creative World of Beethoven*, edited by Paul Henry Lang (New York: W. W. Norton, 1971), 209–24.

238 WORKS CITED

———. *The Great Composer as Teacher and Student: Theory and Practice of Composition.* New York: W. W. Norton, 1987. Revised, New York: Dover Publications, 1994.

———. "Haydn as Student and Critic of Fux." *Studies in Eighteenth-Century Music: A Tribute to Karl Geiringer on His Seventieth Birthday*, edited by H. C. Robbins Landon, 323–32. London: George Allen and Unwin, 1970.

———. "Zu Schuberts Studien im strengen Satz." In *Schubert-Kongress Wien 1978: Bericht*, edited by Otto Brusatti, 127–39. Graz: Akademische Druck- u. Verlagsanstalt, 1979. English as "Schubert's Lesson with Sechter," in *19th-Century Music* 6 (1982): 159–65.

Marston, Nicholas. "Approaching the Sketches for Beethoven's 'Hammerklavier' Sonata." *Journal of the American Musicological Society* 44, no. 3 (Fall 1991): 404–50.

———. "From A to B: The History of an Idea in the 'Hammerklavier' Sonata." *Beethoven Forum* 6 (1998): 97–127.

———. *Heinrich Schenker and Beethoven's "Hammerklavier" Sonata.* Royal Musical Association Monographs 23. Farnham, UK: Ashgate, 2013.

———. "'Im Legendenton': Schumann's 'Unsung Voice.'" *19th-Century Music* 16 (1993): 227–41.

———. *Schumann: Fantasie, Op. 17.* Cambridge: Cambridge University Press, 1992.

———. "Schumann's Monument to Beethoven." *19th-Century Music* 14 (Spring 1991): 247–64.

Mathew, Nicholas. "Beethoven and His Others: Criticism, Difference, and the Composer's Many Voices." *Beethoven Forum* 13, no. 2 (Fall 2006): 148–87.

———. *Political Beethoven.* Cambridge: Cambridge University Press, 2013.

Michael, Wilhelm. *Überlieferung und Reihenfolge der Gedichte Höltys.* Halle: Max Niemeyer, 1909.

Mies, Paul. "Die Entwürfe Franz Schuberts zu den letzten drei Klaviersonaten von 1828." *Beiträge zur Musikwissenschaft* 2 (1960): 52–68.

Morante, Basilio Fernández. "A Panoramic Survey of Beethoven's *Hammerklavier* Sonata, Op. 106: Composition and Performance." *Notes: Quarterly Journal of the Music Library Association* 71, no. 2 (December 2014): 237–62.

Moscheles, Ignace, ed. *The Life of Beethoven.* [See below, under Schindler.]

Muxfeldt, Kristina. *Vanishing Sensibilities: Schubert, Beethoven, Schumann.* Oxford: Oxford University Press, 2012.

Nottebohm, Gustav. *Beethoveniana.* Leipzig: C. F. Peters, 1872.

———. *Beethovens Studien.* Leipzig: J. Rieter-Biedermann, 1873. Reprint, Niederwalluf bei Wiesbaden: Sändig, 1971.

———. *Zweite Beethoveniana: Nachgelassene Aufsätze*, edited by E. Mandyczewski. Leipzig: C. F. Peters, 1887.

Ong, Seow-Chin. "Aspects of the Genesis of Beethoven's String Quartet in F Minor, Op. 95." In *The String Quartets of Beethoven*, edited by William Kinderman, 132–67. Urbana: University of Illinois Press, 2006.

Oster, Ernst. "Register and the Large-Scale Connection." *Journal of Music Theory* 5, no. 1 (1961): 54–71. Reprinted in *Readings in Schenker Analysis and Other Approaches*, edited by Maury Yeston, 54–71. New Haven, CT: Yale University Press, 1977.

Perrey, Beate. "Exposed: Adorno and Schubert in 1928." *19th-Century Music* 29 (2005): 15–24.

Reed, John. *Schubert: The Final Years.* London: Faber, 1972.

———. *The Schubert Song Companion.* Manchester: Manchester University Press, 1985.

Rewald, Sabine, ed. *The Romantic Vision of Caspar David Friedrich: Paintings and Draw-*

ings from the U.S.S.R. New York: Metropolitan Museum of Art, New York, [and] Art Institute of Chicago, 1990.

Rosen, Charles. *Beethoven's Piano Sonatas: A Short Companion.* New Haven, CT: Yale University Press, 2002.

———. *The Classical Style: Haydn, Mozart, Beethoven.* New York: W. W. Norton, 1971; expanded ed., 1997.

Rosenthal, Albi. "'Ein Böcklein aus dem Stall': Beethovens Anmerkungen in einem Exemplar der Erstausgabe von op. 102." In *Beethovens Werke für Klavier und Violoncello. Bericht über die Internationale Fachkonferenz Bonn, 18–20. Juni 1998,* edited by Sieghard Brandenburg, Ingeborg Maaß, and Wolfgang Osthoff, 229–38. Bonn: Verlag Beethoven-Haus, 2004.

———. "'A Little Buck Out of Its Stable': Some Corrections by Beethoven in a Copy of the First Edition of Opus 102." In *Pianist, Scholar, Connoisseur: Essays in Honor of Jacob Lateiner,* edited by Bruce Brubaker and Jane Gottlieb, 146–50. Stuyvesant, NY: Pendragon Press, 2000.

Ross, Megan. "The Power of Allusion: Beethoven's *Grosse Fuge* and Opus 130 VI." *Philomusica On-Line,* vol. 18, no. 1 (2019).

Rowland, David. *A History of Pianoforte Pedalling.* Cambridge: Cambridge University Press, 1993.

Rumph, Stephen. *Beethoven and Napoleon: Political Romanticism in the Late Works.* Berkeley: University of California Press, 2004.

Said, Edward W. *On Late Style: Music and Literature Against the Grain.* New York: Pantheon Books, 2006.

Schenker, Heinrich. "Zu Schuberts 'Meeresstille.'" *Der Tonwille 6* (1923): 41; English, in *Der Tonwille 2,* edited by William Drabkin, translated by Ian Bent and William Drabkin, 35–36. Oxford: Oxford University Press, 2005.

Schiff, Stacey. *A Great Improvisation: Franklin, France, and the Birth of America.* New York: Henry Holt and Company, 2005.

Schindler, Anton Felix. *Beethoven as I Knew Him.* Edited by Donald W. MacArdle, translated by Constance S. Jolly. London and Chapel Hill: University of North Carolina Press, 1966.

———. *The Life of Beethoven, Including His Correspondence with His Friends . . .* 2 vols. Edited by Ignace Moscheles. London: Henry Colburn, 1841.

Schmid, Ernst Fritz. "Beethovens Bachkenntnis." *Neues Beethoven-Jahrbuch 5* (1933): 64–83.

Seyfried, Ignaz. *Ludwig van Beethovens Studien im Generalbasse, Contrapuncte und in der Compositions-Lehre.* Vienna: Tobias Haslinger, 1832.

Sichardt, Martina. *Entwurf einer narratologischen Beethoven-Analytik.* Bonn: Verlag Beethoven-Haus Bonn, 2012.

Solomon, Maynard. *Beethoven.* New York: Schirmer Books, 1977; 2nd, rev. ed., 1998.

———. "The Dreams of Beethoven." *American Imago 32* (1975): 113–44. Reprint, in Solomon, *Beethoven Essays,* 56–76. Cambridge, MA: Harvard University Press, 1988.

———. "Franz Schubert and the Peacocks of Benvenuto Cellini." *19th-Century Music 12* (1989): 193–206.

———. "Franz Schubert's 'My Dream.'" *American Imago 38,* no. 2 (1981): 137–54.

———. "Schubert and Beethoven." *19th-Century Music 3* (1979): 114–25.

———. "Schubert: Some Consequences of Nostalgia." *19th-Century Music 17* (Summer 1993): 34–46.

Solvik, Morten. "Schubert's Kosegarten Settings of 1815: A Forgotten *Liederspiel*." In *Franz Schubert and His World*, edited by Christopher H. Gibbs and Morten Solvik, 115–56. Princeton, NJ: Princeton University Press, 2014.

Staehelin, Martin. "Another Approach to Beethoven's Last String Quartet Oeuvre: The Unfinished String Quintet of 1826/27." In *The String Quartets of Haydn, Mozart, and Beethoven: Studies of the Autograph Manuscripts*, edited by Christoph Wolff, 302–23. Cambridge, MA: Harvard University Department of Music, 1980.

———. "Aus der Welt der frühen Beethoven-'Forschung': Aloys Fuchs in Briefen an Anton Schindler." In *Musik, Edition, Interpretation: Gedenkschrift Günter Henle*, edited by Martin Bente, 427–46. Munich: G. Henle, 1980.

Stravinsky, Igor, and Robert Craft. *Dialogues and a Diary*. Garden City, NY: Doubleday, 1963.

Thayer, Alexander Wheelock. *Ludwig van Beethovens Leben*, 2nd ed. Translated by Hermann Deiters, edited and augmented by Hugo Riemann. Leipzig: Breitkopf & Härtel, 1907–15.

———. *Thayer's Life of Beethoven*. Revised and edited by Elliot Forbes. Princeton, NJ: Princeton University Press, 1967.

Tovey, Donald Francis. "Some Aspects of Beethoven's Art Forms." *Music & Letters* 8 (1927): 131–55. Reprinted in *Essays and Lectures on Music* and as *The Main Stream of Music and Other Essays* (London: Oxford University Press, 1949).

Turner, M. Lucy. "'So Here I Am, in the Middle Way': The Autograph of the 'Harp' Quartet and the Expressive Domain of Beethoven's Second Maturity." In *The New Beethoven: Evolution, Analysis, Interpretation*, edited by Jeremy Yudkin, 261–73. Rochester, NY: University of Rochester Press, 2020.

Tusa, Michael C. "Weber's *Große Oper*: A Note on the Origins of *Euryanthe*." *19th-Century Music* 8 (1984): 119–24.

Tyson, Alan. "Beethoven's 'Heroic Phase.'" *Musical Times* 110 (1969): 139–41.

Unger, Max. *Ludwig van Beethoven und seine Verleger S. A. Steiner und Tobias Haslinger in Wien, Ad. Mart. Schlesinger in Berlin*. Berlin: Schlesinger, Robt. Lienau, 1921.

Van der Zanden, Jos. "A Beethoven Sketchleaf in The Hague." *Bonner Beethoven-Studien* 3, 153–67. Bonn: Verlag Beethoven-Haus Bonn, 2003.

Walker, Alan. "Schumann, Liszt and the C Major Fantasie, Op. 17: A Declining Relationship." *Music & Letters* 60, no. 2 (1979): 156–65.

Wilkinson, Elizabeth M. *Goethe, Poet and Thinker*. London: 1962. Cited here in Johann Wolfgang von Goethe, *Werke (Hamburger Ausgabe in 14 Bänden)*1, Gedichte und Epen 1, edited by Erich Trunz, 555–56.

Winter, Robert. "Paper Studies and the Future of Schubert Research." In *Schubert Studies: Problems of Style and Chronology*, edited by Eva Badura-Skoda and Peter Branscombe, 209–75. Cambridge: Cambridge University Press, 1982.

———. "Plans for the Structure of the String Quartet in C Sharp Minor, Op. 131." In *Beethoven Studies* 2, edited by Alan Tyson, 106–37. London: Oxford University Press, 1977.

———. "Recomposing the Grosse Fuge: Beethoven and Opus 134." In *Variations on the Canon: Essays on Music from Bach to Boulez in Honor of Charles Rosen on His Eightieth Birthday*, edited by Robert Curry, David Gable, and Robert L. Marshall, 130–60. Rochester, NY: University of Rochester Press, 2008.

Youens, Susan. "The 'Problem of Solitude' and Critique in Song: Schubert's Loneliness." In *Schubert's Late Music: History, Theory, Style*, edited by Lorraine Byrne Bodley and Julian Horton, 309–30. Cambridge: Cambridge University Press, 2016.

WORKS CITED 241

Zenck, Martin. *Die Bach-Rezeption des späten Beethoven: Zum Verhältnis von Musikhistoriographie und Rezeptionsgeschichtsschreibung der "Klassik."* Stuttgart: Franz Steiner, 1986.

Music Editions and Facsimiles

Bach, Johann Sebastian. *The Well-Tempered Clavichord* [sic], I. Edited by Ferruccio Busoni. New York: G. Schirmer, [1894].

Beethoven, Ludwig van. *Gott, welch Dunkel hier; In des Lebens Frühlingstagen* aus der Oper "Fidelio." Faksimile nach dem Autograph aus dem Nachlaß des Komponisten in der Deutschen Staatsbibliothek Berlin. Edited by Karl-Heinz Köhler. Leipzig: Deutscher Verlag für Musik, 1976.

———. *Beethovens sämtliche Kanons. Notentext mit Kommentar.* Edited by Rudolf Klein. Vienna: Doblinger, 1970.

———. *Klaviersonate A-dur Opus 101: Faksimile nach dem Autograph im Besitz des Beethoven-Hauses Bonn.* Commentary by Sieghard Brandenburg. Munich: G. Henle, 1998.

———. *Sechs Bagatellen für Klavier Op. 126. Faksimile der Handschriften und der Originalausgabe.* Edited by Sieghard Brandenburg. Bonn: Beethoven-Haus Bonn, 1984.

———. *Sechste Symphonie F-dur Opus 68, Sinfonia pastorale. Faksimile nach dem Autograph* ... Bonn: Verlag Beethoven-Haus Bonn, 2000.

———. *Ein Skizzenbuch aus dem Jahre 1809 (Landsberg 5).* Edited by Clemens Brenneis. Bonn: Beethoven-Haus Bonn, 1992–1993.

———. *Ein Skizzenbuch zur Pastoralsymphonie Op. 68 und zu den Trios Op. 70, 1 und 2.* Transcribed by Dagmar Weise. Bonn: Beethovenhaus Bonn, 1961.

———. *Kniga eskizov Beethoven za 1802–1803 gody* (The Wielhorsky Sketchbook in facsimile and transcription, with commentary). Transcribed and edited by N. L. Fishman. 3 vols. Moscow: Gos. Muzykal'noe izd-vo, 1962.

———. *Sonaten für Klavier und Violoncello/Sonatas for Pianoforte and Violoncello,* ed. Jonathan Del Mar. Kassel: Bärenreiter, 2004.

———. *Werke: Gesamtausgabe, X/2. Werke für Chor und Orchester.* Edited by Armin Raab. Munich: G. Henle, 1998.

———. *Werke: Gesamtausgabe, XII/1. Lieder und Gesänge mit Klavierbegleitung,* Kritischer Bericht. Edited by Helga Lühning. Munich: G. Henle, 1990.

———. *Werke: Gesamtausgabe, XIII/1. Kompositionsstudien bei Joseph Haydn, Johann Georg Albrechtsberger und Antonio Salieri.* 3 vols. Edited by Julia Ronge. Munich: G. Henle, 2014.

Mozart, Wolfgang Amadeus. *Neue Ausgabe sämtliche Werke, X/30, vol. 1. Thomas Attwoods Theorie- und Kompositionsstudien by Mozart.* Submitted by Erich Hertzmann and Cecil Oldman, completed by Daniel Heartz and Alfred Mann. Kassel: Bärenreiter, 1965.

Schubert, Franz. *Bühnenwerke. Kritische Gesamtausgabe der Texte.* Edited by Christian Pollack. Tutzing: Hans Schneider, 1988.

———. *Drei große Sonaten für das Pianoforte, D 958, D 959, und D 960 (Frühe Fassungen).* Facsimile from the Autographs in the Wiener Stadt- und Landesbibliothek. (Publications of the International Franz Schubert Institut, vol. 1). Text and commentary by Ernst Hilmar. Tutzing: Hans Schneider, 1987.

———. *Der Graf von Gleichen. Oper in zwei Akten (D 918).* Text von Eduard von Bauernfeld. Erstveröffentlichung der Handschrift. Edited with commentary by Ernst Hilmar, and a contribution by Erich W. Partsch. Tutzing: Hans Schneider, 1988.

———. *Fantasie in f-Moll D 940 für Klavier zu vier Händen.* Faksimile-Ausgabe. Edited by Hans-Joachim Hinrichsen. Tutzing: Hans Schneider, 1991.

———. *Franz Schubert's Werke. Kritisch durchgesehene Gesammtausgabe.* Revisionsbericht, Series 10, Sonaten für Pianoforte. Leipzig: Breitkopf & Härtel, 1897. Reprint, New York: Dover Publications, 1969.

———. *Neue Ausgabe sämtlicher Werke.* II/17. *Der Graf von Gleichen.* Edited by Manuela Jahrmärker. Kassel: Bärenreiter, 2006.

———. *Neue Ausgabe sämtlicher Werke.* IV/1 a and b. *Lieder.* Edited by Walther Dürr. Kassel: Bärenreiter, 1970.

———. *Piano sonata in G major, op. 78 (D. 894). Facsimile of the autograph manuscript in the British Library, Add. MS 36738.* Introduction by Howard Ferguson and a note on the paper of the manuscript by Alan Tyson. British Library Music Facsimiles II. London: British Library, 1980.

———. *Sechzehn Goethe-Lieder: Faksimile-Ausgabe nach dem im Besitz der Deutschen Staatsbibliothek Berlin befindlichen Autograph,* together with Peter Hauschild, "Die Goethe-Lieder des jungen Schubert: Beiheft zur Faksimile Ausgabe." Leipzig: Edition Peters, 1978.

———. *Winterreise: The Autograph Score.* With an introduction by Susan Youens. New York: Pierpont Morgan Library and Dover Publications, 1989.

Index

Page numbers in italic refer to figures or musical examples.

Adorno, Theodor W.: on Beethoven and Schubert, xv, 137; *Hohlräume*, concept of, 139–40, 143, 145, 152; on lateness, 33, 156–58, 161; *Moments musicaux*, xv, 137n2, 158n20

Albrechtsberger, Johann Georg: death of, 82; *Gründliche Anweisung*, 75, 93n59, 113; teaching of Beethoven, xiii, 78, 79–80, *80*, 96–98, 100, 115

Artaria, Matthias, 185

Bach, Carl Philipp Emanuel, x, 80, 82, 161

Bach, Johann Sebastian: *Chromatische Fantasie*, 107; *Das Wohltemperierte Klavier*, 88, 98, 100, *113*, 113–14, *115*, 116; influence on Beethoven, 93; transcriptions by Beethoven, 82

Bauernfeld, Eduard von, *Der Graf von Gleichen* libretto, 198–99, 201, 204–5, 208, 210n35, 211, 214–16

Beethoven, Ludwig van
–*Akademie* of 22 December 1808, 82–83
–*An die ferne Geliebte*, xiv, 48, 85, 124, 167, 218, 220
–Bagatelles, op. 119, reviewed by Marx, 67–68
–*Christus am Oelberge*, 98
–death of, 88–89

–*Der Gesang der Nachtigall*, 37, 41–46, *43*
–*Die laute Klage*, 35–40, *38–40*
–*Fidelio*, 33, 62, 161; influence on Schubert's *Der Graf von Gleichen*, 200–203, *202*, *204*, *205*; and Schubert, xvi–xvii
–final composition, 186–88
–folk song settings, 43–44
–and Handel, 90
–and Haydn, 162
–on hexameter, 34, 43, 48
–*Große Fuge*, op. 133, *93*, *94*; as finale of op. 130, xvi, 93, 126–27, 163, 180, 184, 221
–late style vs. lateness, 161–63
–Mass in C Major, 98
–*Meeres Stille und glückliche Fahrt*, reviewed by A. B. Marx, xiii, 50, 55–61, *58*, 66, 66–69
–Piano Sonata in A major, op. 101: autograph, 102; and late works, 161; sketches, xiv, 124
–Piano Sonata in B♭, op. 106: third movement, 69, 101–3, *103*, *105*; Largo and Fuga, xiv, 100–115, *104*, *105*, *106*, *107*, *109*, *112*, 113
–Piano Concerto in D Major, unfinished, 123

244 INDEX

Beethoven, Ludwig van (*continued*)
–Piano Sonata in G Major, op. 31, no. 1, and Schubert Sonata in A Major, 191–92
–Piano Sonata "quasi una Fantasia," op. 27, no. 2, 170
–Piano Trio in F Minor, unfinished, 123
–Preludes through the Twelve Major Keys, op. 39, no. 1, 170
–Sonata for Piano and Cello in C Major, op. 102, no. 1, 33, 123, 161
–Sonata for Piano and Cello in D Major, op. 102, no. 2: performance aspects, xi, xiv–xv, 121–23, *122, 123, 124;* and Schenker, 132; sketches, xi, xiv–xv, 124–29, *126, 128, 131, 133, 134,* 161
–String Quartet in B♭, op. 130: first performance of, 180; and *Große Fuge,* op. 133, xvi, 93, 126–27, 163, 180, 184, 221; new finale of, 180–86, *182,* 187–88, 221; relation to String Quartet in F Major, op. 135, 163, *164*
–String Quartet in C♯ minor, op. 131: and D♭ major postscript, 163–71, *168, 169;* relation to String Quartet in F major, op. 135, xvi, 163–64, 171, 177
–String Quartet in E♭ Major, op. 74, xiii, 83, *84,* 93
–String Quartet in F Major, op. 135, Lento assai, 171–80, *172, 173, 175, 176, 178, 179, 181*
–String Quartet in F Minor, op. 95, xiii, 99–100
–Symphony no. 3, xii, 219
–Symphony no. 6, 41, 43n6
–Variations, op. 35, 99, *99*
–Wielhorsky Sketchbook, 99, *99*
Beghin, Tom, 101, 102n19
Benjamin, Walter: on art history, 155; ruin, concept of, ix–x
Berke, Dietrich, 26
Berlinger, Joseph, 73
Bloom, Harold, *Anxiety of Influence,* 154–55
Brandenburg, Sieghard, xiv
Breitkopf & Härtel, 3, 82, 190, 192, 221
Brendel, Alfred, 54n6, 191n6, 195n18
Breuning, Gerhard von, 90

Brown, Maurice J. E., 88, 214n43
Bruchmann, Franz, *Schwestergruß,* xv,10, 143–45, *146,* 152, 154
Burney, Charles, *A General History of Music,* 161–62

Casals, Pablo, 132
Cone, Edward T., "Schubert's Beethoven," 191
Congress of Vienna, x–xi, 49
Cooper, Barry, 43n7, 104n22, 171n21, 174n24
Cramer, Carl Friedrich, *Magazin der Musik,* 98

Dahlhaus, Carl, 100, 131n22
Deutsch, Otto Erich, 27, 89, 91–92, 137n1, 198, 208, 212, 217
Diabelli, Anton, xvi, 186, 188, 189–90, 192
Dufner, Jens, 128n15, 178n27
Dürr, Walther, 10, 155

Empfindsamkeit, xvii, 223
Enlightenment: and Beethoven, x, xvii; drama of, 184; poetry of, 223; as ruin, ix, 224

Fagles, Robert, 63
Ferrante, Elena, 26
Fischer, Kurt von, 86
Fischhof, Joseph, 91n52
Forkel, Johann Nikolaus, 75
Friedrich, Caspar David: *Der Mönch am Meer,* 59n17; Two Men at the Sea, ii, xi, xvii–xviii, 218
Fröhlich, Katerina, 90
Fuchs, Aloys, 64n27, 91n53
Fuxian counterpoint: and Beethoven, xiii, 77–80, 82, 96–97; *Gradus ad Parnassum,* 74, 76n10, 78, 81n21; influence on Classical composers, 76; and Schenker, 74–76

Goethe, Johann Wolfgang von: *Am Flusse,* 156; *Claudine von Villa Bella,* xii; dedication of Beethoven's *Meeres Stille und glückliche Fahrt,* 33, 64–68; Marx on, 56, 58–59, 66, 221; *Meeres Stille* and *Glückliche Fahrt,* xii, xiin9, 49–50, 221;

Nähe des Geliebten, 3; *Rastlose Liebe*, 3; Schubert's engagement with, xiii, xvi, 3–4, 27, 48, 68–69; Schubert's setting of *Meeres Stille*, 3–4, 50, *51–52*, 53–55, 68–69; *Wer kauft Liebesgötter?*, 3; *Wonne der Wehmuth*, xvi, 3, 205

Grillparzer, Franz, 86, 210, 217

Gülke, Peter, 95n62, 138–40, 142, 149

Handel, George Frideric, 82, 89–92, 130, *131*

Haslinger, Tobias, 77–79, 80n17, 91–92, 140, 185, 189

Hauer, Josef, 89

Haydn, Joseph: on Fux's *Gradus ad Parnassum*, 76; teaching of Beethoven, xiii, 78–81, 96

Heine, Heinrich: *Der Atlas*, 16, 19; *Die Bäder von Lucca*, 139 *Lyrisches Intermezzo*, 218; Schubert *Schwanengesang* settings, 88, 189; *Weltriß*, concept of, 137–39, 149

Herder, Johann Gottfried: Beethoven's engagement with, xii–xiii, 34–36, 46–48; Beethoven's settings of, 35–40, *40*, 46; *Blumen aus Morgenländischen Dichtern gesammlet*, Beethoven's copies from, xii, 34–36, *36*; *Der Gesang der Nachtigall*, 37, *41–43*, *43*, *45–46*; *Die laute Klage*, 35; *Morgengesang der Nachtigall*, 47

hexameter: Beethoven and, 34, 43, 48; Herder and, 37, 43, 45–46, 48; Voss and, 33–34

Hilmar, Ernst, 193, 210–11, 216

Hoffmann, E. T. A., 77n11, 85, 184

Hoffmeister & Kühnel, 113–14

Hölty, Ludwig: *An den Mond*, 12, 20; *An die Apfelbäume, wo ich Julien erblickte*, 12–14, *14*, 31–32; *An eine Nachtigall, die vor meinem Kammerfenster sang*, 4–8, 12–14, 28–29; *Auf den Tod einer Nachtigall*, 8–10, 29–31; *Die Mainacht*, 12; *Die Nachtigall*, 16–18, 32; *Die Nonne*, 19–20; and Schubert, xii, xv, xvii; *Seufzer*, 16, 26, 32

Holz, Karl, 77n11, 89, 94, 129n16, 162, 165–67, 167n16, 180

Homer: *Iliad*, 34; *Odyssey*, Beethoven's epigraph from, xiii, 33, 63–66, *64*, *66*, 68

Jeitteles, Alois, 48

Kerman, Joseph, 170

Kermode, Frank, 221

Kiesewetter, Rafael, 89–90

Kirnberger, Johann Philipp, 75, 76, 80

Kistner, Carl Friedrich, 219

Klein, Hans-Günter, 164

Klopstock, Friedrich Gottlieb, xiii, 3, 27–28

Koch, Heinrich Christoph, 127n14

Költzsch, Hans, 192

Körner, Theodor, xii, 3

Kosegarten, Ludwig, 3, 27

Kramer, Lawrence, 154n12

Kreissle von Hellborn, Heinrich, 89

Kropfinger, Klaus, 183–84

Kullak, Franz, "Kullak" sketchbook, 163, 187

Kunstgrammatik, 73–74, 83

Küthen, Hans-Werner, 93n58, 101

Lachner, Franz, 87, 210, 216

Landon, Christa, 88

lateness, late style, xvi–xvii, 158, 161–62, 180, 197

Lichnowsky, Karl Alois, 91

Liszt, Franz, 219

Litwin, Stefan, 142n2, 152n11, 154

Lockwood, Lewis, v, 123n3, 127n12, 188, 225

Lühning, Helga, 46

Mandyczewski, Eusebius, 3

Marpurg, Friedrich Wilhelm, 80, 86, 113

Marston, Nicholas, 169n18, 219

Marx, Adolph Bernhard: on Beethoven's Bagatelles, op. 119, 67–68; on Beethoven's *Meeres Stille und glückliche Fahrt*, xiii, 50, 55–61, *58*, 66–69; *dichterische Pausen*, concept of, 140

Mendelssohn, Felix, 95

Messchaert, Johannes, 54–55, 60

Meyerbeer, Giacomo, 92

Mies, Paul, *Beethovens Skizzen*, 193,195, 211

Mosel, Ignaz von, 89

Mozart, Wolfgang Amadeus: *Don Giovanni*, 203–4; on Fux's *Gradus ad Parnassum*, 76; *Le nozze di Figaro*, 205, 214; *Requiem*, 82

Müller, Wilhelm, xvi, 208, 218

Muxfeldt, Kristina, 208n31, 214n44

Nägeli, Hans Georg, 113

Neefe, Christian Gottlob, 98, 114

Nohl, Ludwig, 81

Nottebohm, Gustav: *Beethoveniana*, 80; *Beethoven's Studien*, 79n16, 80-81, 83, 96–99

Oster, Ernst, 121–23, 125, 134

Palestrina, Giovanni Pierluigi da 74

Partsch, Erich, 206, 212n40

Rampl, Wenzel, 127

Reed, John, 91–92, 208n31

Rellstab, Ludwig, 88, 189

Richter, Sviatoslav, 140n8

Ries, Ferdinand, 103–4, 184

Ronge, Julia, 97–98, 223

Rosen, Charles: on Beethoven's Piano Sonata in B♭, op. 106, xiv, 101, 107; *The Classical Style*, 101, 191–92, 222n8

Rosenthal, Albi, 135

Rudolph, Archduke of Austria, 80–81

Said, Edward, 156, 161n1

Scheide, William, collection at Princeton University library, Beethoven manuscripts at, xiv, 107–8, *109, 110, 111, 112, 113*, 114n30, 116, 124n4, 125, *126*, 126n11, 127, *128*, 224–25

Schenker, Heinrich: on Beethoven's Sonata in D Major for Piano and Violoncello, op. 102, no. 2, 132; on counterpoint, 74–76; on Schubert's *Meeres Stille*, 54–55

Schiller, Friedrich: Schubert's engagement with, 3–4, 27; *Musenalmanach*, 49

Schindler, Anton, xvi–xvii, 64n27, 91n50, 91, 114, 168, 187, 200–201

Schlesinger, Adolf Martin, 66,

Schlesinger, Maurice, 171n21, 174

Schmid, Ernst Fritz, 114

Schmid, Hans, 116

Schubert, Ferdinand, 5, 8, 189, 190

Schubert, Franz
–*Am Flusse*, D 766, 156, 157

–*An den Mond*, D 193, 12, 20, 26

–*An die Apfelbäume, wo ich Julien erblickte*, D 197, 12–14, 26

–*An die Nachtigall*, D 196, 4–8, 13–14, 26

–*Auf den Tod einer Nachtigall*, D 201, 8–10

–choice of poets, 3–4

–*Dem Unendlichen*, D 291, 3, 27–28

–*Der Graf von Gleichen*: and Beethoven's *Fidelio*, 200–203, *202, 204, 205*; censorship of libretto, 198–99, 214–15; creative process, 210–12; and *Die Nebensonnen*, 208–9; *209*, 213; and Mozart's *Don Giovanni*, 203–4; and Mozart's *Le nozze di Figaro*, 205, 214; and *Wonne der Wehmuth*, D 260, 206, 207, 216

–*Der Liebende*, D 207, 24, 25, 26

–*Der Tod und das Mädchen*, D 531, use of pedal, 143

–*Die Mainacht*, D 194, 12, 26

–*Die Nonne*, D 208, 5, 19–21, 22, 23, 24, 25

–and Enlightenment composers, ix

–Fantasy in C Major, D 760, "Wanderer," 143

–Fantasy in F Minor, D 940, 86

–Fugue in E Minor for Organ or Piano, Four Hands, D 952, 87

–late style vs. lateness, 156–58

–Mass in A♭ Major, D 678, 86

–Mass in E♭ Major, D 950, 86

–*Meeres Stille*, settings of, 3–4, 50, *51–52*, *53–55*, 68–69

–*Mein Gebet* (poem), 155–56

–"Mein Traum" (prose), 155

–*Mirjams Siegesgesang*, D 942, 86, 87

–*Nähe des Geliebten*, D 162, 3

–Piano Sonata in A major, D 959: and Beethoven's Piano Sonata in G Major, op. 31, no 1, 191–92; drafts of, 193, 196

–Piano Sonata in A Minor, D 784, use of moderator pedal, 142

–Piano Sonata in A Minor, D 845, use of pedal, 142

–Piano Sonata in B♭ Major D 960, 193–97, *194, 197*

INDEX 247

–Piano Sonata in D Major, D 850, use of pedal, 142
–Piano Sonata in F♯ Minor, D 571, 10–11, *11*
–Piano Sonata in G Major, D 894: and concept of late style, 137–54, *141, 150, 151, 153*; and *Schwestergruß*, D 762, 143–54
–*Sängers Morgenlied*, D 163, 3
–*Schwanengesang*, D 957, 16, 87–88, 189
–*Schwestergruß*, D 762: and Piano Sonata in G, D 894, 143–54, *146–47*; setting of, xv, 10
–*Seufzer*, D 198, 16, *26*
–String Quintet in C Major, D 956, 137, *138*
–Symphony in B Minor, D 759, 143
–*Winterreise*, D 911, *Die Nebensonnen*, xvi, 208–9, *209, 213*
–*Wonne der Wehmuth*, D 260, as revised in *Der Graf von Gleichen*, xvi, 205–6, *207, 216*
Schumann, Clara, 219–20
Schumann, Robert: "Aus Franz Schubert's Nachlaß," 190–92, 197; *Dichterliebe*, 169–70, 218; *Fantasie*, op. 17, 219–22; fugues, 95; on Schubert's last three piano sonatas, xvi, 140n7, 189–90; Sonata in F♯ Minor, op. 11, 218
Schulz, Johann Abraham Peter, 44
Schuppanzigh, Ignaz, 89, 165, 180
Schober, Franz von, 143, 215n46
Schwind, Moritz von, 143
Sechter, Simon, xiii, 88–89, 91–92, 95, 191, 217
Seyfried, Ignaz, 80n17, 81n20, 96n1
Shakespeare, William, *The Tempest*, 170–71
Sichardt, Martina, 125n10, 129–31

Simrock, Nikolaus, 113, 135
Solomon, Maynard, 34, 94, 155n16, 205n28, 215n45
Sonnleithner, Leopold von, 90–91
Spaun, Josef von, x, 27, 50
Spina, Carl Anton, 186
Staehelin, Martin, 188
Steiner, S. A., xii, 33, 62, 64–65, *66*, 68
Stumpff, Johann Andreas, 90, 116
Sulzer, Georg, *Allgemeine Theorie der schönen Künste*, 75

Thomson, George, 43–44, 104
Toscanini, Arturo, 130n20
Treitschke, Georg, 33
Türk, Daniel Gottlob, 80

Voss, Johann Heinrich: edition of Hölty poems, 5–9, 12, 16, 28–32 and hexameter, 33–34; translation of *Odyssey*, 33–34, *63, 64*

Waldstein, Ferdinand Ernst Joseph Gabriel von, 82
Walker, Alan, 221
Wagner, Richard, *Tristan und Isolde*, 145
Weber, Carl Maria von: death of, 168; *Euryanthe*, 199
Wegeler, Franz, 185
Wieck, Clara. *See* Schumann, Clara
Winter, Robert, 27n15, 86–88, 99n9, 111n27, 124n4, 162, 163n7, 163n9, 164, 174, 186n40, 187n42, 188, 216
Wolff, Christoph, 188

Youens, Susan, on solitude, xviiin17

Zenck, Martin, 101, 107